Lab Manual for
A+ Guide to Hardware:

Managing, Maintaining, and Troubleshooting

Jean Andrews, Ph.D.

THOMSON

COURSE TECHNOLOGY

Australia • Canada • Mexico • Singapore • Spain • United Kingdom • United States

THOMSON
COURSE TECHNOLOGY

**Lab Manual for A+ Guide to Hardware:
Managing, Maintaining, and Troubleshooting**
is published by Course Technology.

Senior Editor:
Lisa Egan

Managing Editor:
Jennifer Locke

Senior Vice President, Publisher:
Kristen Duerr

Senior Production Editor:
Catherine G. DiMassa

Developmental Editor:
Ann Shaffer

Associate Product Manager:
Tim Gleeson

Editorial Assistant:
Nick Lombardi

Manuscript Quality Engineers:
Nicole Ashton, Chris Scriver

Manufacturing:
Denise Sandler

Marketing Manager:
Jason Sakos

Text Designer:
GEX Publishing Services

Cover Designer:
Julie Malone

TABLE OF CONTENTS

CHAPTER ONE

HOW COMPUTERS WORK 1

    Lab 1.1 Use Device Manager 2

    Lab 1.2 Gather and Record System Information 5

    Lab 1.3 Convert Numbers 7

    Lab 1.4 Compare Costs 11

    Lab 1.5 Plan an Ideal System 14

CHAPTER TWO

HOW HARDWARE AND SOFTWARE WORK TOGETHER 17

    Lab 2.1 Observe the Boot Process 18

    Lab 2.2 Load Drivers in Real Mode 19

    Lab 2.3 Create and Examine a Windows 98 Startup Disk 22

    Lab 2.4 Use Microsoft Diagnostics with Windows 25

    Lab 2.5 Use Shareware to Examine a Computer 28

CHAPTER THREE

ELECTRICITY AND POWER SUPPLIES 33

    Lab 3.1 Take a Computer Apart and Put it Back Together 34

    Lab 3.2 Find Documentation on the Internet 40

    Lab 3.3 Learn PC Power Supply Facts 43

    Lab 3.4 Measure the Output of Your Power Supply 45

    Lab 3.5 Replace a Power Supply 48

CHAPTER FOUR

THE MOTHERBOARD 51

    Lab 4.1 Examine and Adjust CMOS Settings 52

    Lab 4.2 Use a Motherboard Diagnostic Utility 56

    Lab 4.3 Identify a Motherboard and Find Documentation on the Internet 59

    Lab 4.4 Remove and Replace the Motherboard 63

    Lab 4.5 Identify Motherboard Components and Form Factors 66

CHAPTER FIVE

SUPPORTING I/O DEVICES 69

    Lab 5.1 Gather Information on Your System 70

    Lab 5.2 Identify Hardware Conflicts Using Device Manager 73

    Lab 5.3 Diagnose Simple Hardware Problems 76

Lab 5.4 Plan and Design a Null Modem Cable 78

Lab 5.5 Use a Multimeter to Inspect Cables 81

Lab 5.6 Critical Thinking: Sabotage and Repair a System 84

CHAPTER SIX

MEMORY AND FLOPPY DRIVES 87

Lab 6.1 Research RAM on the Internet 88

Lab 6.2 Install and Troubleshoot a Floppy Drive 91

Lab 6.3 Use TestDrive to Test a Floppy Drive 94

Lab 6.4 Format a Floppy Disk 98

Lab 6.5 Use the Diskcopy and Xcopy Commands 101

CHAPTER SEVEN

UNDERSTANDING AND SUPPORTING HARD DRIVES 105

Lab 7.1 Install and Partition a Hard Drive 106

Lab 7.2 Format a Drive and Test it with ScanDisk 112

Lab 7.3 Test Hard Drive Performance Using SANDRA 115

Lab 7.4 Research Data Recovery Options on the Internet 118

Lab 7.5 Troubleshoot Hard Drives 122

Lab 7.6 Critical Thinking: Sabotage and Repair a Hard Drive Subsystem 125

CHAPTER EIGHT

ALL ABOUT SCSI 129

Lab 8.1 Compare SCSI to Competing Technologies 130

Lab 8.2 Compare SCSI Standards 132

Lab 8.3 Install a Host Adapter and Hard Drive 134

Lab 8.4 Install an External Drive 137

Lab 8.5 Critical Thinking: Plan a SCSI System 139

CHAPTER NINE

MASS STORAGE AND MULTIMEDIA DEVICES 143

Lab 9.1 Install a Sound Card 144

Lab 9.2 Install a PC Camera 148

Lab 9.3 Compare CD and DVD Technologies 153

Lab 9.4 Install Dual Monitors in Windows 9x 158

Lab 9.5 Research Digital Cameras 162

Lab 9.6 Explore Windows 98 Audio Features 166

CHAPTER TEN

SUPPORTING MODEMS 171

Lab 10.1 Simulate Serial Port Communication 172

Lab 10.2 Install and Test a Modem 176

Lab 10.3 Use AT Commands to Control a Modem 178

Lab 10.4 Simulate Modem Problems 182

Lab 10.5 Critical Thinking: Use Two Modems to Create a Multilink Connection 185

CHAPTER ELEVEN
CONNECTING A PC TO A NETWORK **191**
    Lab 11.1 Install and Test an Ethernet NIC 192
    Lab 11.2 Inspect Cables 196
    Lab 11.3 Compare Options for a Home LAN 199
    Lab 11.4 Troubleshoot with TCP/IP Utilities 204
    Lab 11.5 Practice Solving Network Connectivity Problems 209

CHAPTER TWELVE
NOTEBOOKS, PDAS, AND PRINTERS **213**
    Lab 12.1 Examine Notebook Documentation 214
    Lab 12.2 Compare Notebooks and Desktops 218
    Lab 12.3 Replace a Notebook Hard Drive 221
    Lab 12.4 Research Software Available for PDAs 226
    Lab 12.5 Install and Share a Printer 231
    Lab 12.6 Critical Thinking: Sabotage and Repair a Network Printer 235

CHAPTER THIRTEEN
TROUBLESHOOTING AND MAINTENANCE FUNDAMENTALS **239**
    Lab 13.1 Produce Help-Desk Procedures 240
    Lab 13.2 Flash BIOS 244
    Lab 13.3 Troubleshoot General Computer Problems 248
    Lab 13.4 Troubleshoot Hypothetical Situations 251
    Lab 13.5 Critical Thinking: Update Motherboard Drivers 255

CHAPTER FOURTEEN
PURCHASING A PC OR BUILDING YOUR OWN **259**
    Lab 14.1 Choose a System 260
    Lab 14.2 Determine System Requirements 263
    Lab 14.3 Compare What You Need with What You Can Afford 266
    Lab 14.4 Check System Compatibility 273
    Lab 14.5 Evaluate an Upgrade 276

GLOSSARY **281**

PREFACE

This Lab Manual is designed to be the very best tool to help you get the hands-on practical experience you need to learn to troubleshoot and repair personal computers. It is designed to be used along with *A+ Guide to Hardware: Managing, Maintaining, and Troubleshooting* by Jean Andrews, also published by Course Technology. It has more than 70 labs, each of which target a very practical problem you are likely to face in the real world of troubleshooting PCs. We have made every attempt to write labs that allow you to use generic hardware devices. A specific hardware configuration is not necessary to complete these labs. Each chapter contains labs designed to provide the structure needed by novices, as well as labs that challenge the experienced and inquisitive student.

This book helps prepare you for the revised A+ Core Certification examination offered through the Computer Technology Industry Association (CompTIA). Because the popularity of this certification credential is quickly growing among employers, obtaining certification increases your ability to gain employment, improve your salary, and enhance your career. To find more information about A+ Certification and its sponsoring organization, CompTIA, go to CompTIA's Web site at www.comptia.org.

Whether your goal is to become an A+ certified technician, or a PC hardware technician, the *Lab Manual for A+ Guide to Hardware,* combined with the *A+ Guide to Hardware: Managing, Maintaining, and Troubleshooting* textbook, will take you there!

FEATURES

To ensure a successful experience for both instructors and students, this book includes the following pedagogical features:

- **Objectives**—Every lab opens with a list of learning objectives that sets the stage for students to absorb the lessons of the lab.
- **Materials Required**—This feature outlines all the materials students need to complete the lab successfully.
- **Activity Background**—A brief discussion at the beginning of each lab provides important background information.

- **Estimated Completion Time**—To help students plan their work, each lab includes an estimate of the total amount of time required to complete the activity.

 Activity—Detailed, numbered steps walk students through the lab. These steps are divided into manageable sections, with explanatory material between each section.

- **Review Questions**—Exercises at the end of each lab let students test their understanding of the lab material.

- **Web Site**—For updates to this book and information about other A+ and PC Repair products, go to *www.course.com/pcrepair*.

Acknowledgments

I would like to give special thanks to Ann Shaffer for her patience, support and encouragement throughout this entire project.

I would also like to extend my sincere appreciation to Catherine DiMassa, Chris Scriver, Lisa Egan, and all the Course Technology staff for their instrumental roles in the development of this Lab Manual.

Many thanks also to the reviewers for their insights and valuable input. A sincere thank you to:

Ken Quamme	Williston State College
Al Souder	Seneca College
Martin Levy	Montgomery College

Thank you to Scott Johns, Jennifer Dark, and Sarah Sambol, who were with me all the way as this book was written. Scott, drawing on his experience as a PC repair technician in the military, is credited with the ideas for many of these labs. This book is dedicated to the covenant of God with man on earth.

CLASSROOM SETUP

Lab activities have been designed to explore many different hardware setup and troubleshooting problems while attempting to keep the requirements for specific hardware to a minimum.

Most labs take 30 to 45 minutes; a few may take a little longer. Most schools teaching Windows 98 or Windows 2000 should have computers that meet or exceed the minimum requirements.

For several of the labs, your classroom should be networked and provide access to the Internet. The minimum hardware requirements are:

- 90 MHz or better Pentium-compatible computer
- 24 MB of RAM
- 540-MB hard drive
- Windows 98 or Windows 2000 operating system (In several labs, students will also need access to the Windows installation CD or setup files stored at another location.)
- A PC toolkit with ground bracelet (ESD strap)

A few of the labs focus on special equipment. For example, one lab requires a sound card and speakers. Two labs require a multimeter, and another lab uses a PC camera. Also, one lab requires a modem and a working phone line.

LAB SETUP INSTRUCTIONS

Configuration Type and Operating Systems

Each lab begins with a list of required materials. Before beginning a lab activity, verify that each student group or individual has access to the needed materials. Then, make sure that the proper operating system is installed and in good health. In some labs, device drivers are needed. Students will be able to work more efficiently if these drivers are available on floppy disk or on a network drive prior to beginning the lab. When needed, the Windows setup files can be provided on the Windows CD, on a network drive, or, in some cases, on the local hard drive.

Access to the Internet

Several labs require access to the Internet. In these labs, if necessary, you can use one computer to search the Internet to download software or documentation and another computer for performing the lab procedures. If the lab does not have Internet access, you can download the needed software or documentation prior to lab and bring the files to lab stored on floppy disk.

THE TECHNICIAN'S WORK AREA

When opening a computer case, it is important to have the proper tools and be properly grounded to ensure that you don't cause more damage than you repair. Now, let's take a look at the components of an ideal technician's work area:

- Grounding mat (with grounding wire properly grounded)
- Grounding wrist strap (attached to the grounding mat)

- Non–carpet flooring
- A clean work area (no clutter)
- A set of screwdrivers
- ¼" Torx bit screwdriver
- ⅛" Torx bit screwdriver
- Needle–nose pliers
- A PLCC (Plastic Leadless Chip Carrier)
- Pen light (flashlight)
- Several new antistatic bags (for transporting and storing hardware)

At minimum, you must have at least two key items. The first is a ground strap. If a grounding mat isn't available, you can attach the ground strap to the computer's chassis, and in most cases, provide sufficient grounding for handling hardware components inside the computer case. The second key item is, of course, a screwdriver. You won't be able to open most chassis without some type of screwdriver.

PROTECT YOURSELF, YOUR HARDWARE, AND YOUR SOFTWARE

When you work on a computer, it is possible to harm both the computer and yourself. The most common accident that happens when attempting to fix a computer problem is erasing software or data. Experimenting without knowing what you are doing can cause damage. To prevent these sorts of accidents, as well as the physically dangerous ones, take a few safety precautions. The text below describes the potential sources of damage to computers and how to protect against them.

Power to the Computer

To protect both yourself and the equipment when working inside a computer, turn off the power, unplug the computer, and always use a grounding bracelet. Consider the monitor and the power supply to be "black boxes." Never remove the cover or put your hands inside this equipment unless you know about the hazards of charged capacitors. Both the power supply and the monitor can hold a dangerous level of electricity even after they are turned off and disconnected from a power source.

STATIC ELECTRICITY, OR ESD

Electrostatic discharge (ESD), commonly known as static electricity, is an electrical charge at rest. A static charge can build up on the surface of a nongrounded conductor and on nonconductive surfaces such as clothing or plastic. When two objects with dissimilar electrical charges touch, static electricity passes between them until the dissimilar charges are made equal. To see how this works, turn off the lights in a room, scuff your feet on the carpet, and touch another person. Occasionally you may see and feel the charge in your fingers. If you can feel the charge, then you discharged at least 3,000 volts of static electricity. If you hear the discharge, then you released at least 6,000 volts. If you see the discharge, then you released at least 8,000 volts of ESD. A charge of less than 3,000 volts can damage most electronic components. You can touch a chip on an expansion card or system board and damage the chip with ESD and never feel, hear, or see the discharge.

There are two types of damage that ESD can cause in an electronic component: catastrophic failures and upset failures. A catastrophic failure destroys the component beyond use. An upset failure damages the component so that it does not perform well, even though it may still function to some degree. Upset failures are the most difficult to detect because they are not easily observed.

Protect Against ESD

To protect the computer against ESD, always ground yourself before touching electronic components, including the hard drive, system board, expansion cards, processors, and memory modules. Ground yourself and the computer parts, using one or more of the following static control devices or methods:

- *Ground bracelet or static strap:* A ground bracelet is a strap you wear around your wrist. The other end is attached to a grounded conductor such as the computer case or a ground mat, or it can plug into a wall outlet (only the ground prong makes a connection!).

- *Grounding mats:* Ground mats can come equipped with a cord to plug into a wall outlet to provide a grounded surface on which to work. Remember, if you lift the component off the mat, it is no longer grounded and is susceptible to ESD.

- *Static shielding bags:* New components come shipped in static shielding bags. Save the bags to store other devices that are not currently installed in a PC.

The best way to protect against ESD is to use a ground bracelet together with a ground mat. Consider a ground bracelet to be essential equipment when working on a computer. However, if you find yourself in a situation where you must work without one, touch the computer case before you touch a component. When passing a chip to another person, ground yourself. Leave components inside their protective bags until ready to use. Work on hard floors, not carpet, or use antistatic spray on the carpets.

Besides using a grounding mat, you can also create a ground for the computer case by leaving the power cord to the case plugged into the wall outlet. This is safe enough because the power is turned off when you work inside the case. However, if you happen to touch an exposed area of the power switch inside the case, it is possible to get a shock. Because of this risk, in this book, you are directed to unplug the power cord to the PC before you work inside the case.

There is an exception to the ground-yourself rule. Inside a monitor case, the electricity stored in capacitors poses a substantial danger. When working inside a monitor, you *don't* want to be grounded, as you would provide a conduit for the voltage to discharge through your body. In this situation, be careful *not* to ground yourself.

When handling system boards and expansion cards, don't touch the chips on the boards. Don't stack boards on top of each other, which could accidentally dislodge a chip. Hold cards by the edges, but don't touch the edge connections on the card.

After you unpack a new device or software that has been wrapped in cellophane, remove the cellophane from the work area quickly. Don't allow anyone who is not properly grounded to touch components. Do not store expansion cards within one foot of a monitor, because the monitor can discharge as much as 29,000 volts of ESD onto the screen.

Hold an expansion card by the edges. Don't touch any of the soldered components on a card. If you need to put an electronic device down, place it on a grounded mat or on a static shielding bag. Keep components away from your hair and clothing.

Protect Hard Drives and Disks

Always turn off a computer before moving it to protect the hard drive, which is always spinning when the computer is turned on (unless the drive has a sleep mode). Never jar a computer while the hard disk is running. Avoid placing a PC on the floor, where the user can accidentally kick it.

Follow the usual precautions to protect disks. Keep them away from magnetic fields, heat, and extreme cold. Don't open the floppy shuttle window or touch the surface of the disk inside the housing. Treat disks with care and they'll generally last for years.

CHAPTER ONE

HOW COMPUTERS WORK

Labs included in this chapter

➤ Lab 1.1 Use Device Manager

➤ Lab 1.2 Gather and Record System Information

➤ Lab 1.3 Convert Numbers

➤ Lab 1.4 Compare Costs

➤ Lab 1.5 Plan an Ideal System

LAB 1.1 USE DEVICE MANAGER

Objectives

The goal of this lab is to help you become familiar with Device Manager, a powerful Windows tool used to manage hardware devices. After completing this lab, you will be able to:

➤ Open Device Manager

➤ Explain which components are installed on a system

➤ Examine component configurations

Materials Required

This lab will require the following:

➤ Windows 9x, Windows 2000, or Windows XP operating system

➤ Workgroup of 2–4 students

Activity Background

Any time you open a computer case in order to inspect, remove or replace parts, you risk introducing problems. Therefore, it is important to be able to find out as much information as possible about a system without having to open the case. In this activity you will examine a system the easy way using Device Manager, a configuration utility included with Windows 95, Windows 98, Windows Me, Windows 2000, and Windows XP (but not with Windows NT). From within Device Manager, you can view and print information about your computer's hardware configuration.

Estimated completion time: **45 minutes**

ACTIVITY

To access Device Manager in Windows 9x, follow these steps:

1. Click the **Start** button on the taskbar, click **Settings**, and then click **Control Panel**.

2. In the Control Panel window, double-click the **System** icon.

3. In the System Properties dialog box, click the **Device Manager** tab.

Follow these steps in Windows 2000:

1. Click the **Start** button on the taskbar, click **Settings**, and then click **Control Panel**. (To open Control Panel in Windows XP, click **Start** on the taskbar and then click **Control Panel**.)

2. In the Control Panel window, double-click the **System** icon.

1

3. In the System Properties dialog box, click the **Hardware** tab.

4. Click the **Device Manager** button.

The opening menu of Device Manager appears as shown in Figure 1-1. You can select an item from the list and then click Properties to view information about that item, or you can view the item's Properties by double-clicking the item. When you click the + sign to the left of an item, a list of the installed devices for that item appears beneath the item.

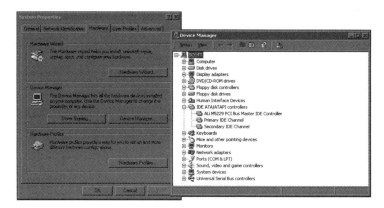

Figure 1-1   Device Manager can be accessed from the System Properties window

With Device Manager open, answer these questions about your computer:

1. Does your computer have a network card installed? If so, what is the name of the card? _____

_____

2. What are three settings that can be changed under Device Manager?

_____

_____

_____

3. What are the devices listed under the headings "Display adapters" and "Network adapters?" _____

_____

4. In what two ways can you view devices in Device Manager? _____

_____

5. What are two ways to view the properties of a device? _____

_____

_____

6. What devices are listed under Floppy disk controllers? _____

_____

_____

7. What resources does the keyboard currently use? _____

_____

8. What is another way to access Device Manager other than the method given in this lab? _____

_____

_____

9. List the steps required to uninstall a device in Device Manager.

_____

_____

_____

Review Questions

1. Name the Windows operating systems that include Device Manager.

_____

_____

2. What type of file can Device Manager provide information about?

_____

_____

3. In what version(s) of Windows is Device Manager *not* included?

_____

_____

4. Is Device Manager a tool used to find information about file structure?

_____

5. What is the symbol used in Device Manager for a USB controller or device?

_____

6. What does the + sign mean beside an entry in Device Manager?

_____

LAB 1.2 GATHER AND RECORD SYSTEM INFORMATION

Objectives

The goal of this lab is to use a system's physical characteristics and other sources to determine how the system is configured. After completing this lab, you will be able to:

➤ Gather system information by observing a system

➤ Use available tools to access specific system information

Materials Required

This lab will require the following:

➤ Windows 9x

➤ Workgroup of 2-4 students

Activity Background

When working with a computer system, it is a good idea to know what components are installed on the system. This lab will help you identify some of these components as you gather information by observing the system and by using system tools.

Estimated completion time: **15 minutes**

ACTIVITY

Observe the physical characteristics of your system and answer the following questions:

1. Does the system have any identification on it indicating manufacturer, model or component information? If so, list them. _____

_____

_____

2. How many floppy drives does your system have? _____

_____

_____

3. Describe the shape of the connection used by your mouse. How many pins does the connection have? _____

_____

_____

4. Does your system have CD-ROM or DVD-ROM drives? If so, how many?

_____

5. How many internal hard drives does your system have? Explain how you got your answer. _____

_____

_____

After booting your system, open the System applet from the Control Panel. With the General tab visible, record the following:

1. What OS is installed? _____

_____

2. What is the version number of your operating system? _____

_____

3. Who is the system registered to? _____

_____

4. What type of CPU is your system built around? _____

_____

5. How much RAM is installed in your system? _____

_____

Close the system applet.

Open My Computer and locate the following information:

1. How many floppy disk drives appear and which drive letters are assigned to them?

_____

2. How many local disk drives appear and which drive letters are assigned to them?

_____

3. How many other disk drives appear and which drive letters are assigned to them?

_____

Review Questions

1. What is another tool in Windows, other than My Computer, that you can use to examine your system? _____

_____

2. What is one other place, not within Windows or any documentation, where you would be able to determine what CPU, CPU speed, and amount of RAM are installed on your system? _____

_____

3. What differences, if any, are there between a list of components derived from a physical inspection versus a list of components derived from My Computer and System Properties? _____

_____

_____

LAB 1.3 CONVERT NUMBERS

Objectives

The objective of this lab is to practice converting numbers between decimal, binary and hexadecimal forms. After completing this lab, you will be able to:

➤ Convert decimal numbers to hexadecimal and binary form

➤ Convert hexadecimal numbers to binary and decimal form

➤ Convert binary numbers to decimal and hexadecimal form

Materials Required

This lab will require the following:

➤ Pencil and paper and/or Windows Calculator

➤ Appendix C of *A+ Guide to Hardware*

➤ Windows 98 or Windows 2000

Activity Background

You will sometimes want to know what resources are being reserved for a device. This information is often displayed on a computer in hexadecimal (or, hex) numbers, which is shorthand for the binary numbers that computers actually use. Often, you will want to convert these into the more familiar decimal numbers. This will give you a better picture about which resources are reserved for a device.

Estimated completion time: **45 minutes**

ACTIVITY

1. Convert the following decimal numbers to hexidecimal notation using either a calculator or the instructions provided in Appendix C of *A+ Guide to Hardware*. (To access the Windows Calculator, click **Start** on the taskbar, point to **Programs**, point to **Accessories**, and then click **Calculator**.)

   ■ 13 = _____

   ■ 240 = _____

   ■ 255 = _____

   ■ 58880 = _____

   ■ 65535 = _____

2. Convert the following binary numbers to hexadecimal notation:

   ■ 100 = _____

   ■ 1011 = _____

   ■ 111101 = _____

   ■ 11111000 = _____

- 10110011 = _____

- 00000001 = _____

3. Convert the following decimal numbers to binary numbers:

- 14 = _____

- 77 = _____

- 128 = _____

- 223 = _____

- 255 = _____

4. Hexadecimal numbers are often preceded with "0x." Convert the following hex numbers to binary numbers:

- 0x0016 = _____

- 0x00F8 = _____

- 0x00B2B = _____

- 0x005A = _____

- 0x1234 = _____

5. For Windows 98, click the **Start** button on the taskbar, click **Run**, type **winipcfg** and click **OK**. In the IP Configuration window, click the **More Info** button. (For Windows 2000, to open a Command window, click **Start** on the taskbar, point to **Programs**, point to **Accessories**, and then click **Command Prompt**. At the command prompt, type **ipconfig /all**.) A network card is assigned an address that identifies the card on the network. For Windows 98, the address is called the Adapter Address, and for Windows 2000, the address is called the Physical Address. Either way, the address assigned to the network card is expressed in a series of paired hexadecimal numbers separated by dashes. Convert each pair to a binary number.

- Adapter address in hexadecimal form: _____

_____

- Adapter address in binary pairs: _____

_____

6. Convert the following hexadecimal numbers to decimal:

- 0x0013 = _____

- 0x00AB = _____

- 0x01CE = _____

- 0x812A = _____

7. Referring to Figure 1-2, convert the numbers in the memory range and determine how many bytes, expressed in a decimal number, are in its memory address range. _____

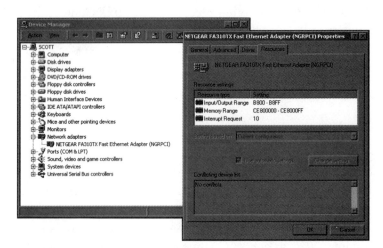

Figure 1-2   Memory Range and Input/Output Range expressed as hex numbers

8. Convert the following binary numbers to decimal:

- 1011 = _____

- 11011 = _____

- 10101010 = _____

- 111110100 = _____

- 10111011101 = _____

- 11111000001111 = _____

Review Questions

1. Computers actually work with _____ numbers.

2. Computers often express numbers in _____ format, which is a base-sixteen number system.

3. Most people are more comfortable when working within a _____, or base-ten number system.

4. In hex, what decimal value does the letter A represent? _____

   _____

5. Hexadecimal numbers are often preceded by _____ so that a value containing only numerals is not mistaken for a decimal number.

Lab 1.4 Compare Costs

Objectives

The objective of this lab is to compare a pre-assembled system and the components that could be assembled to build a comparable system. After completing this lab, you will be able to:

➤ Identify the key components of a pre-assembled system

➤ Locate prices for components needed to assemble a comparable system

➤ Compare the cost of a pre-assembled system versus a self-assembled system

Materials Required

This lab will require the following:

➤ Internet access and/or access to a computer publication such as *Computer Shopper*

Activity Background

In this Lab you will compare the cost of a "Brand Name" system with the cost of a system with the same specifications assembled from individual components. If you can't find an exact match for components, find the closest possible substitute. Use the Internet and available computer-related publications as your source for information.

Estimated completion time: **45 minutes**

Activity

1. Find an advertisement for a complete, pre-assembled system similar to the one shown in Figure 1-3.

Figure 1-3 Complete, pre-assembled system

2. Study the advertisement and list the following specifications:

- Processor/MHz:_____

- RAM:_____

- OS:_____

- HDD capacity:_____

- Monitor:_____

- Sound/Speakers:_____

- Other Drives:_____

- Bonus Items:_____

- Bundled Software:_____

- Total Price:_____

3. Find advertisements similar to those shown in Figure 1-4. Notice that the items are grouped by component type.

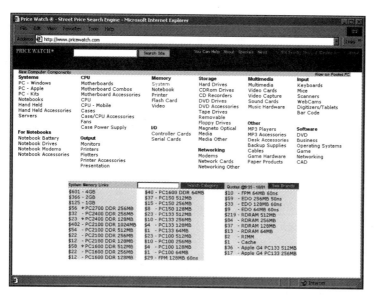

Figure 1-4   Components for sale

4. Using the following table, list and describe the comparable components, their individual prices, and the source of your information. You may wish to check several sources to find the best price. Remember, most mail order or on-line purchases have shipping costs associated with them. If you can determine an exact price for each particular component, include this as part of the component's price. If you cannot find the exact shipping price, include a ten percent fee as part of the price for each shipped component.

Component	Description	Source	Price
Processor/MHz			
RAM			
OS			
HDD capacity			
Monitor			
Sound/speakers			
Other drives			
Bonus items			
Bundled software			
TOTAL SYSTEM PRICE			

Review Questions

1. What approach to acquiring a system seems to be less expensive?

_____

2. What is the single most expensive component of a system built from individual components? _____

_____

3. What was the estimated cost of shipping (if any) associated with the component-built system? _____

_____

LAB 1.5 PLAN AN IDEAL SYSTEM

Objectives

The objective of this lab is to plan and price your own ideal system within a budget. After completing this lab, you will be able to:

➤ Describe what you want your system to be able to do

➤ Pick components that best meet your goal

➤ Stay within a budget

Materials Required

This lab will require the following:

➤ Internet access and/or access to a computer publication such as *Computer Shopper*

Activity Background

In the future you may be in a position to build a system to your specifications from individual components. Within a budget of $1200, what system would you put together? In this activity, you'll find out.

Estimated completion time: **30 minutes**

ACTIVITY

1. On a separate piece of paper, make a table similar to the one used in Lab 1.4. Use the table to list the components that you would like to include in your system, the cost of each component, and the source for each component. To begin, list everything you want and do not worry about price.

2. Once you have determined the total price of all the components you want to include in your ideal system, add up the prices and see if you are within your $1200 budget.

3. If you are under budget, consider including additional components in your system or better versions of components you are already including. If you are overbudget, determine what components you need to exclude or whether you need to use less expensive versions of some components. Either way, record what components you choose. Also, note how you altered your ideal system to meet your budget.

Review Questions

1. What is the goal of your system? In other words, how do you plan to use your system? Explain your choices for components. _____

_____

_____

_____

2. How would you change your choices if you were to use this computer at a corporate office as a business workstation? _____

_____

_____

3. What single change would you make if you had an extra $200 in the budget?

_____

4. How might you change your design if your budget was only $1000?

_____

_____

HOW HARDWARE AND SOFTWARE WORK TOGETHER

Labs included in this chapter

➤ Lab 2.1 Observe the Boot Process

➤ Lab 2.2 Load Drivers in Real Mode

➤ Lab 2.3 Create and Examine a Windows 98 Startup Disk

➤ Lab 2.4 Use Microsoft Diagnostics with Windows

➤ Lab 2.5 Use Shareware to Examine a Computer

LAB 2.1 OBSERVE THE BOOT PROCESS

Objectives

In this lab you will observe the sequence of events in a PC's boot process. After completing this lab, you will be able to:

➤ Describe the boot process in detail

➤ Halt the boot process

➤ Diagnose problems in the boot process

Materials Required

This lab will require the following:

➤ Lab PC designated for disassembly

➤ PC toolkit including screw drivers and ground strap

➤ Windows 9x or Windows 2000 operating system

➤ Blank floppy disk

➤ Workgroup of 2-4 students

Activity Background

This lab will familiarize you with the boot process and give you some practice recognizing when the boot process halts and observing the resulting information displayed on the monitor. Working in teams, you will begin by observing a PC booting up and noting every step, from turning on the power to the appearance of the Windows desktop. Once you are familiar with all the steps in the boot process, your workgroup will intentionally introduce a problem that will cause the boot process to fail on your PC. At that point, your workgroup will switch PCs with another workgroup's PC, and attempt to figure out why that workgroup's PC failed to boot. The teams will then switch PCs and repeat the process.

Estimated completion time: **45 minutes**

ACTIVITY

1. Boot your team's PC and then, using the information displayed on the monitor as a guide, record every step in the process. (List this information on a separate piece of paper.) You may have to boot the PC several times in order to record all of the steps.

2. Do one of the following to introduce a problem in the boot process of your team's PC:

   ▪ Insert a blank floppy disk into the floppy drive

- Unplug the keyboard
- Unplug the mouse
- Unplug the monitor or adjust a setting on the monitor   *size changed*

2

3. Switch places with another team. Do not tell the other team what problem you caused in Step 2.

4. Detect, diagnose, and remedy the problem on the other team's PC. On a separate piece of paper, describe the problem as a user unfamiliar with PC technology might describe it. List any error messages that you see.

5. After you have repaired the problem and ensured that the PC boots properly, repeat Steps 2 through 5. Continue until each workgroup has diagnosed and corrected all the problems listed in Step 2.

Review Questions

1. What is the first message displayed on the monitor after you turn on the power?

   observed : Bios Id , and
   Devias ID

2. What happens after Plug and Play Devices are initialized? _____

   Windows Sreen

3. Of all the problems you studied during the activity, which halts the boot process earliest in the process? _____

   Keyboard problem. , not deTecTed

4. Which two problems result in messages about the operating system not being present? _____

   Blank Floppy , invalid boot
   Mouse noT detected.

LAB 2.2 LOAD DRIVERS IN REAL MODE

Objectives

The objective of this lab is to learn to use configuration files that affect the MS–DOS command line environment. Specifically, you will load drivers that make it possible to use a mouse in the command line environment. You will also learn to use utilities executed at the command line. After completing this lab, you will be able to:

➤ Create a bootable floppy disk

➤ Copy files to a floppy disk

➤ Modify configuration files

Materials Required

This lab will require the following:

➤ Windows 9x operating system

➤ Files needed to load a 16-bit generic mouse driver (for example, Autoexec.bat, Config.sys, and Mouse.com)

➤ Blank floppy disk

➤ Workgroup of 2-4 students

Activity Background

In this lab you will boot to a command prompt by using a bootable floppy disk. As you will see, normally a command prompt environment does not allow you to use the mouse. Once the PC is booted, you will use Microsoft Diagnostics Utility (MSD), a program that displays information about the hardware environment, to verify that the PC does not provide mouse support. Then you will add mouse support by adding configuration files to your system. These files normally come on a floppy disk bundled with a mouse. Finally, you will reboot the PC, run MSD again, and verify that mouse support has indeed been enabled.

Estimated completion time: **45 minutes**

ACTIVITY

Follow these steps on a Windows 9x PC to create a bootable floppy disk and to copy a file to the disk.

1. Click **Start** on the task bar, point to **Programs**, and then click **MS-DOS Prompt**.

2. Insert a blank floppy disk.

3. Type **FORMAT A: /S** and press **Enter**.

4. The following prompt appears: "Insert new diskette for drive A: and press Enter when ready." Press **Enter** to start formatting the disk.

5. Watch as the floppy disk is formatted and the system files are transferred to the floppy disk.

6. When prompted, type a volume name if you wish and press **Enter** (or simply press **Enter** to bypass this step entirely).

7. When asked if you want to format another disk, type **N** and then press **Enter**. (Note that if your disk was already formatted, you could have used the SYS A: command to copy system files to the disk.)

Now that you have created a boot disk, follow these steps to copy some configuration files to the boot disk.

1. Insert the Windows 9x CD into the CD drive, type **Copy D:\tools\ oldmsdos\msd.exe A:** and then press **Enter**. (If you don't have access to the Windows 9x CD, your instructor might give you an alternate location for the file. If your CD has a drive letter other than D, substitute the appropriate drive letter.)

2. Repeat Step 1 for the following files in the location specified by your instructor:

   ▪ AUTOEXEC.BAT

   ▪ CONFIG.SYS

   ▪ MOUSE.COM

3. Remove the floppy disk and close the Command Prompt window.

At this stage, the boot disk contains the necessary configuration files. Next, you will boot the PC using the boot disk and verify that the mouse is not available.

1. Place the boot disk in the floppy drive and boot the system.

2. To use the Microsoft Diagnostic Utility, at the command prompt, type **MSD.EXE** and then press **Enter**.

3. Move the mouse around. Does the mouse work as you would expect?

   _____

4. Press **F3** to exit MSD.

5. Remove the boot disk from the floppy drive and reboot.

6. When Windows has finished loading, insert the boot disk into the floppy drive and use My Computer or Explorer to view the files on the disk.

7. Right-click the **Autoexec.bat** file and then click **Edit** in the shortcut menu.

8 Click at the bottom of the list of commands in the Autoexec.bat file and type **MOUSE.COM** as a new line.

9. Following directions on the screen, save and then close the file.

10. Shutdown the system, reboot from the floppy disk and run the MSD program. What difference do you see in MSD? _____

    _____

11. Close MSD, remove the floppy disk, and reboot the PC.

Review Questions

1. When formatting a disk, what command can you use to make the floppy disk a boot disk? _____

   _____

2. Suppose you are creating a bootable floppy disk but do not plan to format the disk first. What command can you use to transfer the system files to the floppy disk?

   _____

3. Which configuration file did you modify to cause the mouse to be automatically supported? _____

   _____

4. Did you notice a difference in the boot process after you changed a configuration file? _____

   _____

   _____

5. How could you determine if CONFIG.SYS was used during the boot process?

   _____

   _____

LAB 2.3 CREATE AND EXAMINE A WINDOWS 98 STARTUP DISK

Objectives

The objective of this lab is to learn how a Windows 98 Startup Disk is made and used. After completing this lab, you will be able to:

➤ Create a Windows 98 Startup Disk

➤ Describe the steps in booting from a Startup Disk

Materials Required

This lab will require the following:

➤ Windows 98 operating system

➤ Blank floppy disk

➤ Workgroup of 2-4 students

Activity Background

From within Windows 98, you can create a Startup Disk, which is a great tool for troubleshooting and set up. A Startup disk is a bootable disk that also contains several helpful utilities and drivers. In this activity you will create and experiment with a Startup Disk.

Estimated completion time: **30 minutes**

ACTIVITY

1. Open the Control Panel and double-click the **Add/Remove Programs** icon.

2. In the Add/Remove Programs applet, click the **Startup Disk** tab.

3. In the Startup Disk tab, click the **Create Disk** button and follow the prompts to create the Startup Disk.

4. When the process is complete, close the Add/Remove Programs applet.

Answer the following questions about the Startup Disk:

1. What two files on the Startup disk end in the ".bat" extension?

   _____

2. What are the purposes of these files? _____

   _____

   _____

3. What kind of information is provided in the README.TXT file?

   _____

   _____

With the Startup Disk in the drive, reboot your computer and answer these questions:

1. What prompt do you see while the system boots? _____

   _____

2. What type of drive is set up during the boot process? _____

   _____

3. Why do you think this drive is set up? _____

   _____

To continue exploring the Startup Disk, follow these steps:

1. Using the command prompt provided by the Startup Disk, access the hard drive by using the C: command.

2. Use the DIR command to view the contents of the root directory of the hard drive.

3. Keeping in mind that file names usually describe the file's function, record the names of the files listed as a result of the DIR command. Explain what you think the purpose of each file is. _____

_____

_____

_____

_____

_____

_____

Keep your Startup Disk to use in later labs.

Review Questions

1. Why might you want to use a Startup Disk? _____

_____

_____

2. What icon in Control Panel do you use to create a Startup Disk?

_____

3. Why would you need CD-ROM support when using the Startup Disk?

_____

4. If you wanted to examine the files on the CD-ROM drive, what command(s) would you execute at the command prompt? _____

_____

_____

5. What three files must be on the Startup Disk to make the disk bootable?

_____

LAB 2.4 USE MICROSOFT DIAGNOSTICS WITH WINDOWS

Objectives

The goal of this lab is to observe the boot process. After completing this lab, you will be able to:

➤ Describe each step of the boot process

➤ Describe the symptoms of problems that can interfere with the boot process

➤ Examine a system that will not boot and remedy the problem

Materials Required

This lab will require the following:

➤ Windows 98

➤ Bootable floppy disk from Lab 2.2 or Startup Disk from Lab 2.3

➤ Workgroup of 2-4 students

Activity Background

The Microsoft Diagnostics Utility (MSD), which is provided with both DOS and Windows, examines a system and displays useful information about ports, devices, memory, and the like. To run MSD, you need the file MSD.EXE, which can be found in the Tools/OldMSDOS directory on your Windows 9x installation CD. In this lab you will use MSD to examine your system.

> Estimated completion time: **30 minutes**

ACTIVITY

1. Copy the file **MSD.EXE** from the **Tools/OldMSDOS** directory on your Windows 9x installation CD to your hard drive. Store it in a folder named **\Tools**.

2. To open a command prompt window, click **Start** on the task bar, point to **Programs**, and then click **MS–DOS Prompt**.

3. At the command prompt, type **C:\tools\oldmsdos\msd.exe** and then press **Enter**. Note that, by including the path to the file in the command line, you can execute a program file located in a different directory from the one you are working in. In this command, you told the computer the exact path (C:\tools\oldmsdos) to the file you wanted to execute. (An exact path like this is referred to as an absolute path.)

4. When you receive a message indicating that MSD is best run in DOS Mode, select **OK** and then press **Enter** to continue. You should see a window like the Microsoft Diagnostics window, shown in Figure 2-1.

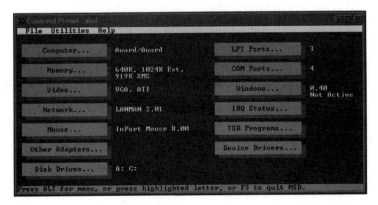

Figure 2-1 The MSD utility

Use the menu options of MSD to answer the following questions about your system:

1. What categories of information are available in MSD? _____

_____

_____

_____

2. What version of the OS are you running? _____

_____

3. What COM ports are available on the system? _____

_____

4. What IRQ and Port Address are associated with COM1? _____

_____

5. How far does the MEMORY map extend? _____

_____

6. What is the Address Range at 1024K? _____

_____

7. Exit MSD.

8. Type **EXIT** to close the Command window.

Now you will work with MSD in real mode. Follow these steps:

1. Reboot using the bootable floppy disk from Lab 2.2 or the Win 98 Startup Disk from Lab 2.3.

2. Start MSD again.

Use the menu options of MSD to answer the following questions about your system:

1. Are the same categories of information available in MSD when run from a command window? _____

_____

_____

2. What version of the operating system does MSD report now?

_____

_____

3. What COM ports are available on the system? _____

_____

_____

4. What IRQ and Port Address are associated with COM1? _____

_____

5. How far does the MEMORY map extend? _____

_____

6. What is the Address Range at 1024K? _____

_____

Compare the information obtained the first time you opened MSD with the information obtained this time, and answer the following questions:

1. What differences do you note? _____

_____

_____

2. What explains those differences? _____

_____

_____

Review Questions

1. What Windows tool is similar to MSD? _____

_____

2. What is an advantage of saving MSD.EXE to the hard drive?

_____

_____

3. What is the absolute path to MSD.EXE on the CD-ROM drive?

_____

4. What category in MSD gives information on the type of network installed?

_____

5. What command did you use to exit MSD? _____

_____

LAB 2.5 USE SHAREWARE TO EXAMINE A COMPUTER

Objectives

The objective of this lab is to use Sisoft's SANDRA to examine your system. After completing this lab, you will be able to:

➤ Download a file from the Internet

➤ Install SANDRA

➤ Use SANDRA to examine your system

Materials Required

This lab will require the following:

➤ Windows 98 operating system

➤ Access to the Internet

➤ Workgroup of 2–4 students

Activity Background

Good PC support people are always good investigators. The Internet offers a wealth of resources to those who take the time to search, download, and investigate the possible uses of software available there. This activity is designed to help you learn to be such an investigator. You will begin by downloading a shareware utility called SANDRA that provides information about the hardware and software on a computer. (The name "SANDRA" stands for System Analyzer Diagnostic and Reporting Assistant.) You will use SANDRA to diagnose PC problems and to print a report about the hardware and software on your computer.

Estimated completion time: **45 minutes**

2

ACTIVITY

1. Open your browser and go to **www.zdnet.com**.

2. Search for **SAN811.ZIP** in the search field on the ZDNet main page, and follow the link for downloading the file.

3. Follow the steps on the screen to download the file **SAN811.ZIP** to your PC. You can then disconnect from the Internet.

Note that if you cannot find SANDRA on the ZDNet Web site, you can use a search engine to locate the shareware. Also, note that later versions of SANDRA might have different file names for the zip file. Next, you can decompress the SANDRA files and install the utility on your PC. Follow these steps:

1. Using Explorer, uncompress Sandra.zip by double-clicking the filename and then extracting all the files including Setup.exe with its components.

2. Run the setup program, **Setup.exe**, which creates a new program in your Program Group.

3. Run the program SiSoft Sandra. You should see a screen similar to the one shown in Figure 2-2.

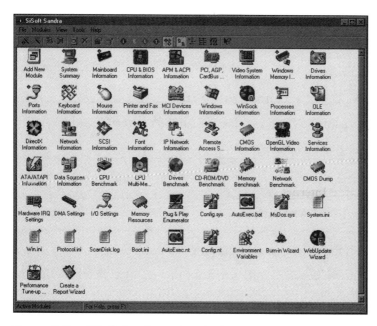

Figure 2-2   SiSoft Sandra main window

You can execute each of the utilities in turn by double-clicking the icons, or you can create a composite report of the results of each selection. To learn more, follow these steps:

1. From the SiSoft Sandra menu bar, click **File** and then click **Create a Report Wizard...**

2. In the wizard introduction window, click **Next**.

3. In the Step 1 of 8 window, click the **Clear All** button and then select the **System Summary** checkbox. Click **Next** to continue.

4. In the Step 2 of 8 window, click the **Clear All** button and then click **Next** to continue.

5. In the Step 3 of 8 window, click the **Clear All** button and then click **Next** to continue.

6. In the Step 4 of 8 window, click the **Clear All** button and then click **Next** to continue.

7. In the Step 5 of 8 window, add any comments that you desire and click **Next** to continue.

8. In the Step 6 of 8 window, click the **Print it or Fax it** option button and then click **Next** to continue.

9. In the print dialog box, click **OK**.

10. Click **Finish** and then collect your report from the printer.

Note that you can add or remove any additional modules in Steps 4–6, depending on how you want to customize the report. Next, use SANDRA to answer these questions:

1. What is the model and speed of your CPU? _____448 MHZ_____

    _____intel (R) , penhum (R) III_____

2. Which version of Windows does SANDRA report you are using?

    Microsoft windows Help 5. 1. 2600. 0 , copyright – 2000 (1990)

3. Which icons are not available to you because your copy of SANDRA is not registered? _not available on this window version_

    _____

You will use SANDRA again in later chapters, so don't erase it,

In this case you downloaded SANDRA from the ZDNet Web site. But many popular utilities are available from multiple sources on the Internet. To see for yourself, follow these steps:

1. Attempt to find SANDRA at **www.shareware.com**.

2. Attempt to find SANDRA at **www.sisoft.com**.

3. Is the program available through these avenues as well? _____

_____ only www. shareware. com _____

Review Questions

1. What does "SANDRA" stand for? _____

_____

2. Which source of information is more complete: Microsoft Diagnostics
   or SANDRA? _____ SANDRA _____

_____

3. In what two ways can SANDRA be used to generate system information?

_____

_____

4. Why would SANDRA provide different information than Microsoft
   Diagnostics? _____

_____

_____

_____

5. What type of software is SANDRA considered? _____

_____

ELECTRICITY AND POWER SUPPLIES

Labs included in this chapter

➤ Lab 3.1 Take a Computer Apart and Put it Back Together

➤ Lab 3.2 Find Documentation on the Internet

➤ Lab 3.3 Learn PC Power Supply Facts

➤ Lab 3.4 Measure the Output of Your Power Supply

➤ Lab 3.5 Replace a Power Supply

LAB 3.1 TAKE A COMPUTER APART AND PUT IT BACK TOGETHER

Objectives

The goal of this lab is to help you get comfortable working inside a computer case. After completing this lab, you will be able to:

➤ Take a computer apart

➤ Recognize components

➤ Reassemble the computer

Materials Required

This lab will require the following:

➤ Computer designated for disassembly

➤ PC toolkit

Activity Background

If you follow directions and take your time, there is no reason to be intimidated by working inside a computer case. This lab will take you step by step through the process of disassembling and reassembling a PC. Follow your computer lab's posted safety procedures when disassembling and reassembling a PC and remember to always wear your ground strap. Also, never force a component to fit into its slot.

You will begin this lab by removing the cover of your PC so that you can access and remove the components inside. Then you will reassemble the components and replace the cover. This lab includes steps for working with a desktop PC and a tower PC. Follow the steps that apply to your situation.

Estimated completion time: **45 minutes**

ACTIVITY

To remove the cover from a desktop PC, follow these steps:

1. Power down the PC and unplug it. Next, unplug the monitor, mouse, keyboard, and any other cables, and move them out of your way.

2. Locate and remove the screws on the back of the case. Look for the screws in each corner and one in the top, as shown in Figure 3-1. Be careful that you don't unscrew any other screws besides these. (These other screws probably are holding the power supply in place, as illustrated in Figure 3-2.)

3

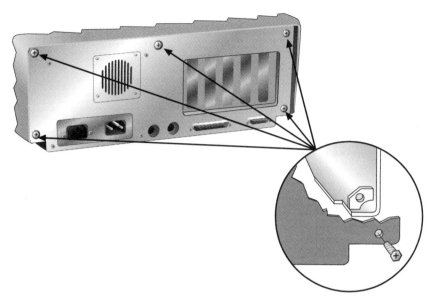

Figure 3-1   Locate the screws that hold the desktop cover in place

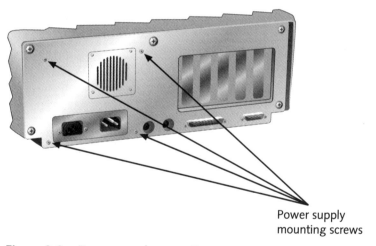

Power supply
mounting screws

Figure 3-2   Power supply mounting screws

3. After you remove the cover screws, slide the cover forward and up to remove it from the case, as shown in Figure 3-3.

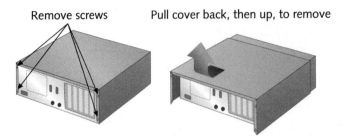

Figure 3-3   Removing a desktop cover

To remove the cover from a tower PC, follow these steps:

1. Power down the PC and unplug it. Next, unplug the monitor, mouse, key-board, and any other cables, and move them out of your way.

2. Look for screws in all four corners and down the sides. Remove the screws and then slide the cover back slightly before lifting it up to remove it. See Figure 3-4. Some tower cases have panels on either side of the case held in place with screws on the back of the case. Remove the screws and slide each panel toward the rear and then lift it off the case.

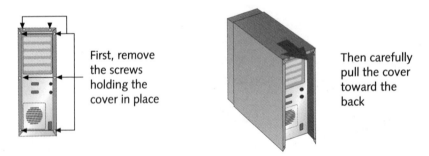

Figure 3-4   Removing a tower cover

With the case removed, you are ready to look for some components. As you complete the following, refer to drawings in Chapters 3 and 4 of *A+ Guide to Hardware* as necessary.

1. Identify the following major components:
   - Power supply
   - Floppy disk drive
   - Hard drive
   - Motherboard

2. Are there other drives, such as a CD-ROM drive? List them here:

Next, you will remove the expansion boards, following the procedure outlined below. (If you are working with a tower case, lay it on its side so that the motherboard is on the bottom.)

1. To make reassembly easier, take notes or make a sketch of the current placement of boards and cables and identify each board and each cable. You can mark the location of a cable on an expansion card with a marker if you like. Note the orientation of the cable on the card. Each cable for the floppy disk drive, hard drive, or CD-ROM drive has a colored marking on one side of the cable called the edge color. This color marks pin 1 of the cable. On the board, pin 1 is marked either with the number 1 or 2 beside the pin or with a square soldering pad on the back side of the board. (See Figure 3-5.) You might not be able to see this soldering pad now.

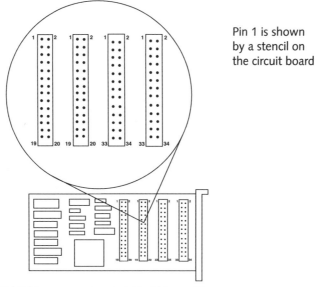

Pin 1 is shown
by a stencil on
the circuit board

Pin 1 is shown by square solder
pads on the reverse side of the circuit board.

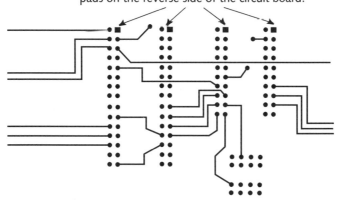

Figure 3-5   How to find pin 1 on an expansion card

2. Remove the cables from the expansion cards. There is no need to remove the other end of the cable from its component (floppy disk drive, hard drive, or CD-ROM drive). Lay the cable over the top of the component or case.

3. Remove the screw holding the card to the case. If for some reason you aren't wearing a ground strap, touch the case before you touch the card.

4. Grasp the card with both hands and remove it by lifting straight up and rocking the card from end to end (not side to side). Rocking the card from side to side might spread the slot opening and weaken the connection.

5. If the card had a cable attached, examine the card connector for the cable. Can you identify pin 1? Lay the card aside on a flat surface.

6. Remove any other expansion cards in the same way.

7. In some proprietary systems, an expansion card assembly attaches to the motherboard, with each card attached to the assembly. If your system has this arrangement, remove it now. It is probably held in place by screws or clips and may or may not have a rail guide that you can use to locate the assembly within the case.

8. To remove the power supply, first remove the cables to the motherboard, case fans, other remaining components and the power switch if necessary. Make notes about which cable attaches to what. Once the cables are removed, support the power supply with one hand and remove the screws attaching it to the case.

9. Remove any case fans.

10. Begin removing the motherboard by removing any power cables connected to any case or component fans. Be sure to make notes or label the cables so that you can reinstall them correctly.

11. Finish removing the motherboard by removing the screws holding the board to the stand-off's. Usually six to nine screws attach the motherboard to the case. Be careful not to gouge the board or otherwise damage components with the screwdriver. Because the screws on the motherboard are often located between components, they are often hard to reach. Be very careful not to damage the motherboard.

12. To remove drives, remove the ribbon cable if it is still attached. Many cases have a removable drive bay. The drives are attached to this bay and the bay may be removed with all the drives attached. This allows easier access to drive mounting screws than from inside the case. If your case has a removable drive bay this is the preferred method of removal. Otherwise remove each drive separately. Be careful not to jar the drive as you remove it from the case.

13. If your system has a removable drive bay, it is likely that the floppy drive came out with the removable bay. If the floppy drive is still in the system, remove the screws holding the drive in place and slide the drive out of the case.

14. Remove any CD-ROM, DVD, or tape drives from the case. These drives are usually in the 5" drive bays and are held in place by four to eight screws. Once the screws are removed, the drive will slide out the front of the case.

15. Remove any other components.

Now that you have removed all the components, you are ready to reassemble the PC. The following steps outline the necessary procedure, which is essentially the reverse of the disassembly procedure:

1. Replace each component carefully. Take care to install each component firmly without over-tightening the screws. Do not force components to fit. If a component will not easily fit the way it should, look for some obstruction preventing it from falling into place. Look carefully for the reason the component will not fit correctly and make any small adjustments as necessary.

2. Place each card in its slot (it doesn't have to be the same slot, just the same bus) and replace the screw. Don't place a PCI or ISA video card near the power supply; otherwise, EMI from the power supply might affect the video picture.

3. Replace the cables, being sure to align the colored edge with pin 1. (In some cases it might work better to connect the cable to the card before you put the card in the expansion slot.)

4. Check to make sure that no cables are interfering with any fan's ability to turn. A common cause for an overheated system is a fan that can't move air because a cable is preventing it from spinning.

5. When all components are installed you should have re-fitted all of the screws that you removed earlier. If some screws are missing, it is particularly important to turn the case upside down and *gently* shake the case to dislodge any wayward screws. Any screw lying on a board has the potential to short that board out when power is applied. Do not use a magnet to try and find missing screws in the case or you might damage the data on hard drives and floppy disks left in the floppy disk drives.

6. Plug in the keyboard, monitor, and mouse.

7. In a classroom environment, have the instructor check your work before you power up.

8. Turn on the power and check that the PC is working properly before you replace the cover. Don't touch the inside of the case while the power is on.

9. If all is well, turn off the PC and replace the cover and its screws. If the PC does not work, don't panic. Turn off the power and then go back and check each cable connection and each expansion card. You probably have not solidly seated a card in the slot. After you have double-checked everything, try again.

Review Questions

1. When removing the case, why should you take care only to remove the screws that hold the cover on?

   Because these other screws are holding the power supply.

2. How should you rock a card to remove it from its slot? Why is it important to know how to properly rock a card?

   End to end, not side to side.
   Because might spread slots / loosen grips and on pins

3. What should you do to help you remember which components connect to which cables?

   Take notes or sketch them

4. What marking on a ribbon cable identifies pin 1?

   By edge color

5. What component(s) defines the system's form factor?

   Power supply plug to MB, case, and Motherboard

6. What form factor does your PC use?

   ATX

LAB 3.2 FIND DOCUMENTATION ON THE INTERNET

Objectives

The goal of this lab is to show you how to locate documentation on the Internet in order to determine how much power a component uses. After completing this lab, you will be able to:

➤ Find the manufacturer and model of a component

➤ Search for a product's documentation or manual

➤ Download and view a product manual

Materials Required

This lab will require the following:

➤ Computer designated for disassembly

➤ Internet access

➤ Adobe Acrobat Reader

➤ PC toolkit

Activity Background

Often the power specifications for a component are not labeled on the component itself but are included in the documentation. When working with PCs, it is very common to encounter a component for which you have no documentation on hand. In this exercise you will learn to find the make and model of a component and, if possible, find online documentation for it.

Estimated completion time: **30 minutes**

ACTIVITY

1. Open the PC's case and locate the component assigned to you by your instructor (or randomly select a component). Each person on your team should be assigned a different component.

2. Examine the component until you find a sticker or stenciled label identifying its manufacturer and model number.

The manufacturer and model are not clearly marked on every component. If you're having trouble finding this information on a component, such as a video card, try researching according to the component's chipset. The information identifying the chip is usually stenciled on the chip. If you need to find out how much power an unlabeled component will use, it's sometimes helpful to consult the documentation for similar components.

3. Take your notes to a computer that has Internet access.

4. If you already know the manufacturer's URL, go to that site and try to find documentation in these locations:

- The Support section of the site, as shown in Figure 3-6
- The Downloads section
- The Customer Service section

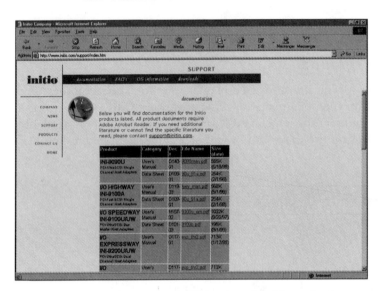

Figure 3-6   Manuals are available for download from the Support section of a manufacturer's Web site

If you are not sure of the manufacturer's URL, try searching for the manufacturer or model number using a good search engine. In fact, searching by model number will often get you to the information in the fewest steps. Keep in mind that most documentation is provided in PDF format, which means you may need Adobe Acrobat Reader or a browser plug-in to view the documentation.

5. Print out or save the documentation and file it as a reference for when you need information about that component.

6. What CPU does your system use?

_____

7. Go to the manufacturer's Web site, find and print the Web page showing the power consumption of your CPU expressed in watts.

Review Questions

1. How is a component commonly marked for identification?

   _____

   _____

2. In what sections of a Web site are manuals commonly found?

   _____

3. What format are manuals commonly provided in?

   _____

4. What software do you need to view a PDF document?

   _____

3

LAB 3.3 LEARN PC POWER SUPPLY FACTS

Objectives

The goal of this lab is to determine if a PC's power supply is adequate for the PC's components. After completing this lab, you will be able to:

➤ Examine documentation and estimate the peak power consumption (in watts) required by the system components

➤ Examine a power supply to determine if it meets the system's needs

Materials Required

This lab will require the following:

➤ Lab computer designated for disassembly

➤ Documentation for system components that includes information about electrical requirements

➤ PC toolkit

➤ Workgroup of 2-4 students

Activity Background

A power supply must be able to provide adequate power for all devices in a system at peak consumption. If the power supply's maximum rated wattage (peak wattage) is not greater than the sum of the peak consumption of all components, the system may crash or spontaneously re-boot (or worse) during heavy use. Furthermore, an inadequate power supply might run well during light use, but then fail when the system is stressed. You can prevent such problems by using documentation to determine whether a power supply is adequate for the demands of a particular system. In this activity you'll learn more about your system's power supply.

Estimated completion time: **30 minutes**

ACTIVITY

Remove the cover from your PC and answer the following questions:

1. How many watts are supplied by your power supply? (This information is usually printed on the label on the top of the power supply.)

   _____

2. How many cables are supplied by your power supply?

   _____

3. Where does each cable lead?

   _____

   _____

   _____

4. Use the documentation for each component you listed in step 3 to determine the total peak power consumption of your system.

   _____

5. Does the power supply provide adequate power for the estimated peak consumption of the system? Fill in the following table:

Component	Wattage
Hard drive	
Floppy drive	
CD-ROM drive	
DVD drive	
Zip drive	
Other drive	
Motherboard	
CPU	

6. Determining the power consumption of the motherboard and CPU can be difficult without adequate documentation. If you were able to locate that documentation in the previous lab, calculate the total wattage requirements for the system. Otherwise, this might not be possible. Total wattage requirements for all components:

_____

Review Questions

1. Where can you usually find electrical information about your power supply?

_____

2. What can happen if the power supply does not meet the electrical demands of the system?

_____

_____

3. When would a system approach its peak power consumption?

_____

_____

4. How can you estimate a system's peak consumption?

_____

_____

5. Will a system with an inadequate power supply always fail immediately when it is powered up? Why or why not?

_____

_____

LAB 3.4 MEASURE THE OUTPUT OF YOUR POWER SUPPLY

Objectives

The goal of this lab is to use a multimeter to measure the various voltages supplied by a power supply. After completing this lab, you will be able to:

➤ Use a multimeter

➤ Measure voltage supplied by a power supply

Materials Required

This lab will require the following:

➤ Lab computer designated for this exercise

➤ PC toolkit

➤ Multimeter

➤ Workgroup of 2-4 students

Activity Background

A multimeter is an electrical tool that performs multiple tests. It can typically measure continuity, resistance, amperage and voltage. It may have a digital or analog meter that displays output. It will also have two leads used to contact the component you are testing. The various models of multimeters work slightly differently. Follow the appropriate procedure for your specific multimeter. In this lab you will measure the electrical voltage supplied to the motherboard and floppy drive. Follow your computer lab's posted safety procedures when completing this activity.

Estimated completion time: **30 minutes**

ACTIVITY

Using your multimeter, measure the power output to your system's motherboard and to the floppy drive, and then fill in the three tables below. Note that the column headings "Red Lead" and "Black Lead" refer to the color of the probes.

Detailed directions for using a multimeter can be found in Chapter 3 of *A+ Guide to Hardware*. Be very careful as you work inside the computer case with the power on. Don't touch any components other than those described below. The following steps outline the basic procedure for using a multimeter:

1. Remove the cover from the computer case.

2. Set the multimeter to measure voltage in a range of 20 volts and set the AC/DC switch to DC. Insert the black probe into the meter's – jack and the red probe into the meter's + jack.

3. Turn on the multimeter and turn on the computer.

4. Measure each circuit by placing a red probe on the lead and a black probe on ground as described in the following table. Write the voltage measurement for each connection in the "Voltage Measure" column.

5. Turn off the PC and replace the cover.

Complete the following table for the AT motherboard:

Red Lead	Black Lead	Voltage Measure
3	5	
3	6	
3	7	
3	8	
4	Ground	
9	Ground	
10	Ground	
11	Ground	
12	Ground	

Complete the following table for the ATX motherboard:

Red Lead	Black Lead	Voltage Measure
1	4	
1	6	
1	8	
1	14	
1	15	
1	16	
1	18	
2	Ground	
5	Ground	
7	Ground	
9	Ground	
10	Ground	
11	Ground	
12	Ground	
13	Ground	
19	Ground	
20	Ground	

Complete the following table for the floppy drive:

Red Lead	Black Lead	Voltage Measure
1	3	
4	2	

Review Questions

1. What is the electrical voltage from the house outlet to the power supply?

   _____

2. What voltages are supplied by the power supply on your system?

   _____

3. What are three things that a multimeter can test?

   _____

   _____

4. What model of multimeter are you using?

   _____

5. List the steps to set this multimeter to measure resistance.

   _____

   _____

   _____

6. Besides voltage and resistance, what else can this multimeter measure?

   _____

LAB 3.5 REPLACE A POWER SUPPLY

Objectives

The goal of this lab is to give you experience replacing a power supply. After completing this lab, you will be able to:

➤ Identify the power supply

➤ Remove the power supply from the case

➤ Install a new power supply and new cabling

Materials Required

This lab will require the following:

➤ Lab PC designated for this exercise

➤ PC toolkit

➤ Workgroup of 2–4 students

Activity Background

This exercise will test your ability to remove and replace a power supply. Power supplies, as a rule, are considered Field Replaceable Units (FRU). This means that because of the danger of working inside a power supply and as a time saver, a PC technician does not repair them. If you find that a power supply is faulty, replace it with a compatible power supply, then send the original off to be reconditioned or recycled.

Estimated completion time: **30 minutes**

ACTIVITY

1. Disconnect the power and all peripherals and remove the case cover.

2. Examine the power supply and record the number and type of connectors needed, and estimate the peak power requirements for the system (which you learned how to do in an earlier lab). If the components required more power than the power supply could provide, this could have contributed to its failure.

_____

3. What type of power connector to the motherboard does the power supply provide?

_____

4. What is the form factor of the power supply?

_____

5. What are the estimated peak power requirements for this system?

_____

6. Remove the cabling and the power supply. Usually the power supply is held in place by four screws in the back of the case. Some proprietary systems may use other methods of securing the power supply.

7. Examine the power supply designated by your instructor, or swap your power supply with your neighbor's.

8. What is the form factor of this new power supply?

_____

9. What is the power rating of this new power supply?

_____

10. Will this new power supply satisfy the needs of your system?

_____

11. Install the new power supply.

12. Close the case, reattach the peripherals, and test the system.

Review Questions

1. How many connectors linked your original power supply to the motherboard?

_____

2. How many watts of peak supply could the original power supply provide?

_____

3. Why should you calculate the peak power required for all components?

_____

_____

4. What are two reasons that PC technicians do not usually repair a power supply?

_____

_____

5. What term is used to refer to components that are commonly replaced but not repaired?

_____

THE MOTHERBOARD

Labs included in this chapter

➤ Lab 4.1 Examine and Adjust CMOS Settings

➤ Lab 4.2 Use a Motherboard Diagnostic Utility

➤ Lab 4.3 Identify a Motherboard and Find Documentation on the Internet

➤ Lab 4.4 Remove and Replace the Motherboard

➤ Lab 4.5 Identify Motherboard Components and Form Factors

LAB 4.1 EXAMINE AND ADJUST CMOS SETTINGS

Objectives

The goal of this lab is to explore and modify CMOS settings. After completing this lab, you will be able to:

➤ Enter the CMOS setup utility

➤ Navigate the CMOS setup utility

➤ Examine some setup options

➤ Save changes to setup options

Materials Required

This lab will require the following:

➤ Windows 9x or Windows 2000 operating system

➤ Workgroup of 2–4 students

Activity Background

When a system is powered up, the startup process is managed by a set of instructions called the BIOS. The BIOS, in turn, relies on a set of configuration information stored in CMOS that is continuously refreshed by battery power even when the system is off. You can access and modify the CMOS setup information via the CMOS setup utility included in the BIOS. In this lab, you will examine the CMOS setup utility, make some changes, and observe the effects of your changes.

Setup utilities vary slightly in appearance and function, depending on manufacturer and version. The steps in this activity are based on the common Award Modular design. You might have to perform different steps to access and use the CMOS utility on your computer.

Estimated completion time: **30 minutes**

ACTIVITY

Before you access the BIOS on your computer, you will record the exact date and time as indicated by your computer's internal clock. (You will use this information later, to confirm that you have indeed changed some CMOS settings.) After you record the date and time, you will determine which version of the BIOS is installed on your computer. To do this, you can use the SANDRA utility, which you installed in Lab 2.5. Follow these steps:

1. Using Windows 9x or Windows 2000, double-click the clock on the taskbar and record the time and date.

2. Close the Time/Date Properties window.

3. Start **SANDRA**, and then double click the **CPU & BIOS Information** icon.

4. Select **System BIOS** in the **Device** field.

5. Record the manufacturer and version information for your BIOS:

4

_____

6. Close SANDRA.

Now that you know what BIOS your computer runs, you can determine how to enter the the setup utility. In general, to start the Setup utility, you need to press a key or key combination as the computer is booting up.

Using the information recorded in step 5, above, consult Table 4-1 to find out how to enter your system's setup utility. (Alternately, you can look for a message on your screen when you first turn on the PC, which might read something like **Press F2 to access setup**.)

Table 4-1   Methods for entering CMOS setup utilities, by BIOS

BIOS	Method for entering CMOS setup
AMI BIOS	Boot the computer, and then press the Delete key
Award BIOS	Boot the computer, and then press the Delete key
Older Phoenix BIOS	Boot the computer, and then press the Ctrl+Alt+Esc or Ctrl + Alt + S key combination
Newer Phoenix BIOS	Boot the computer, and then press the F2 or F1 key
Dell Computers with Phoenix BIOS	Boot the computer, and then press the Ctrl + Alt + Enter key combination
Older Compaq computers like the Deskpro 286 or 386	Place the diagnostics disk in the drive, reboot your system, and choose Computer Setup from the menu
Newer Compaq computers like the Prolinea, Deskpro, DeskproXL, Deskpro LE, or Presario	Boot the computer, wait for two beeps, then, when the cursor is in the upper-right corner of the screen, press the F10 key
All other older computers	Use the setup program on the floppy disk that came with the PC. If the floppy disk is lost, contact the motherboard manufacturer to obtain a replacement

For Compaq computers, the CMOS setup program is stored on the hard drive in a small, non-DOS partition of about 3 MB. If this partition becomes corrupted or the computer is an older model, you must run setup from a diagnostic disk. If you cannot run setup by pressing F10 at startup, it's likely that a damaged partition or a virus is taking up space in conventional memory.

Now you are ready to enter the CMOS setup utility included in your BIOS. Follow these steps:

1. If a floppy disk is necessary to enter the CMOS setup utility, insert it now.

2. Restart the computer.

3. When the system restarts, enter the setup utility using the correct method for your computer.

4. Notice that the CMOS utility groups settings by effect or function. For example, all the power management features will be grouped together in a Power Management window.

5. The main screen usually has a Help section describing how to make selections and exit the utility. Typically, you can use the Arrow Keys or Tab key to move a highlight box. Once you have highlighted your selection, you usually need to press Enter key or the Spacebar. The main screen may or may not display a short summary of the highlighted category. Look for and select a category called something like **Standard CMOS Setup**.

6. In the Standard CMOS setup screen, you should see some or all of the following settings. List the current setting for each of the following:

   - Date: _____

   - Time: _____

   - For IDE drives, a table listing drive size and mode of operation, cylinder, head and sector information:

   _____

   _____

   _____

   - Floppy drive setup information, including drive letter and type:

   _____

   - Halt on error setup (the type of error that will halt the boot process):

   _____

   - Memory summary (summary of system memory divisions):

   _____

7. Exit the Standard CMOS setup screen and return to the main page. Look for and select a section called something like **Chipset Features Setup**.

4

8. Record settings for the following, as well as any other settings in this section:

- RAM setup options:

- AGP setup options:

- CPU-specific setup options:

- Settings for serial and parallel ports:

- Provisions for enabling/disabling onboard drive controllers and other embedded devices:

Most of the CMOS settings never need changing, so it isn't necessary to understand every setting.

9. Exit to the CMOS setup main screen. Notice that there may be options that allow you to load CMOS defaults. Restoring default settings restores everything to factory settings and can be helpful in troubleshooting. You may also see options for exiting with or without saving changes. There probably will be an option to set user and supervisor passwords as well as a utility to automatically detect IDE hard disk drives.

Now that you are familiar with the way the CMOS setup utility works, you will change the date and time settings. Then you will reboot the computer, confirm that the changes are reflected in the operating system, and then return the CMOS date and time to the correct settings.

1. Return to the Standard CMOS setup screen.

2. Highlight the time field(s) and set the time ahead one hour.

3. Move to the date field(s) and set the date ahead one year.

4. Return to the main CMOS setup screen and select an option named something like **Save Settings and Exit**. If prompted, verify that you do wish to save the settings.

5. Wait while the system reboots. Allow Windows to load.

6. At the desktop, check the time and date. Are your CMOS setup changes reflected in Windows?

_____

7. Reboot the computer, return to CMOS setup and change to the correct time and date.

8. Verify that the changes are again reflected in Windows.

CRITICAL THINKING (additional 30 minutes)

Have your instructor make several changes to CMOS setup that result in the system failing to boot. Without restoring CMOS settings to factory default, troubleshoot the system.

Review Questions

1. Do all systems use the same method to enter CMOS setup? Can you enter CMOS setup after the system has booted?

_____

2. How are settings usually grouped in the CMOS setup utility?

_____

3. In what section will you usually find time and date settings in the CMOS setup utility?

_____

4. What type of options are shown on the CMOS setup main screen?

_____

5. What tool in SANDRA can you use to find information on the BIOS version?

_____

LAB 4.2 USE A MOTHERBOARD DIAGNOSTIC UTILITY

Objectives

The goal of this lab is to help you learn how to use a motherboard diagnostic utility. After completing this lab, you will be able to:

➤ Download and install the AMIDiag utility

➤ Use the AMIDiag utility to examine your motherboard

Materials Required

This lab will require the following:

➤ Windows 9x or Windows 2000 operating system

➤ Internet access

Activity Background

AMIDiag, distributed by American Megatrends, Inc., is a well-known diagnostic utility that you can use to solve a variety of computer problems. The utility is DOS-based and works under both DOS and Windows 9x. In this activity, you will download a demonstration version of AMIDiag from the Internet and then learn how to use it.

> Estimated completion time: **30 minutes**

ACTIVITY

1. Use your favorite search engine such as *www.google.com* to search for Diagdemo.zip, which is an archive (a collection of compressed files) containing the files necessary to install the demo version of AMIDiag 4.5.

2. Download Diagdemo.zip to your PC. This file is a shareware version of AMIDiag for PC diagnostics.

3. Close your browser, open Explorer, and then expand the file **amidiag.zip** by double-clicking it.

4. Open a command prompt window, and then switch to the directory where the demo software files are stored.

5. At the command prompt, type **amidiag** and then press **Enter**. The screen shown in Figure 4-1 appears.

Figure 4-1   AMIDiag opening menu

Many times a support technician is not given step-by-step directions when using utility software, but must discover how to use the software by exploring menus and using the software's help functions. The following exercise gives you practice in doing that. Use the AMIDiag software to answer these questions:

1. Perform the test of processor speed. What is the detected speed?

   _____

2. On the Memory menu, perform all the tests that this demonstration version of the software allows. Record any errors detected.

   _____

   _____

   _____

3. On the Misc menu, perform the serial port test. Write down any error messages that appear. If you get an unexpected error, perform the test more than once. Do you get the same results each time?

   _____

4. On the Options menu, select **System Information**. If you received errors in Step 3, this program might lock up, and you might need to reboot. If you completed the information check successfully, record the results here:

   _____

5. On the System board menu, select **DMA Controller Test**. Why doesn't this test work?

   _____

6. Exit the program, and then close the command prompt window.

Review Questions

1. Does the AMIDiag utility run with a GUI interface?

   _____

2. What menu in AMIDiag contains the serial port test?

   _____

3. What are some tests included in the shareware version of AMIDiag?

   _____

4. What menu in AMIDiag contains the System Information program?

_____

5. At what points in the test process did you receive error messages? What do these error messages tell you about your computer?

_____

6. In the following table, list at least three situations where you think it would be appropriate to use AMIDiag for troubleshooting. Describe the problem as the user would describe it to you. For example, "My serial mouse does not work." Then write the suspected source of the problem and the appropriate AMIDiag test. The table includes one example to help you get started.

Description of problem as the user sees it	Suspected source of the problem	AMIDiag test
"My serial mouse does not work."	Serial port does not work	Serial port test

LAB 4.3 IDENTIFY A MOTHERBOARD AND FIND DOCUMENTATION ON THE INTERNET

Objectives

The goal of this lab is to learn to identify a motherboard and find online documentation for it. After completing this lab, you will be able to:

➤ Physically examine a motherboard

➤ Determine a motherboard's manufacturer and model

➤ Search the Internet for motherboard documentation

Materials Required

This lab will require the following:

➤ PC designated for disassembly

➤ Internet access

➤ Adobe Acrobat

➤ PC toolkit

Activity Background

You may often be asked to repair a PC for which the documentation is lost or not available. Fortunately, you can almost always find documentation for a device online as long as you have the manufacturer name and model number for the device. In this lab, you will learn to find the manufacturer name and model number on a motherboard. Then you will locate documentation for that device on the Internet.

Estimated completion time: **30 minutes**

ACTIVITY

1. Boot the PC and use SANDRA, which you installed in Lab 2.5, to learn the type of CPU installed on your computer. Record that information here:

   _____

2. Following safety precautions including using a ground strap, remove the PC's case cover and then remove any components obscuring your view of the motherboard. In some cases you may have to remove the motherboard itself, but this is usually unnecessary.

3. Look for a stenciled or silk-screened label printed on the circuit board itself that indicates the manufacturer and model. Note that other components sometimes have labels printed on a sticker affixed to the component. But on a motherboard, the label is generally printed directly on the circuit board itself. Common motherboard manufacturers include: Abit, Asus, and Intel.

   Also, note that the manufacturer name is often printed in much larger type than the model number. Model numbers often include both letters and numbers and many contain a version number as well. Figure 4-2 contains an example of a motherboard label.

4. Record the information on the motherboard label.

   _____

5. Take your information to a PC with Internet access and open a browser.

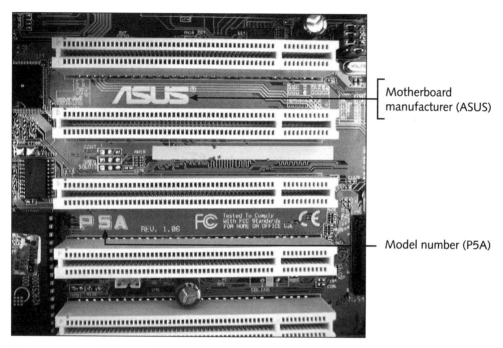

Figure 4-2   Label printed directly on motherboard

6. If you know the URL of the manufacturer, go directly to the Web site. (Table 4-2 shows the URLs for some motherboard manufacturers.) If you do not know the URL of the manufacturer's site, search for the manufacturer or model with your favorite search engine, as shown in Figure 4-3. In the search results, click a link that is associated with the manufacturer. If this link does not take you directly to the documentation, it will usually get you within two or three links away. Continue until you find the manufacturer's Web site.

7. When you have found the site of your motherboard's manufacturer, look for a link for service or support. Click this link, and, if necessary, select the appropriate product category and model number. Sometimes knowing the type of CPU the board supports can be useful in finding the right board.

8. Continue working your way through the site until you find the motherboard documentation. The documentation may include a variety of documents covering technical specification, and installation instructions. The documentation will probably also include a basic manual, which is usually a combination of technical and installation specifications.

Table 4-2   URLs for major motherboard manufacturers

Manufacturer	URL
motherboards.com	www.motherboards.com
American Megatrends, Inc.	www.megatrends.com
ASUS	www.asus.com
Diamond Multimedia	www.diamondmm.com
First International Computer, Inc.	www.fica.com
Giga-Byte Technology Co., Ltd.	www.giga-byte.com
Intel Corporation	www.intel.com
Supermicro Computer, Inc.	www.supermicro.com
Tyan Computer Corporation	www.tyan.com

Figure 4-3   Search results using manufacturer name and model number

9. When you find the documentation, you might also find a link to updated drivers. If you see such a link, click it and make a note on the release date of these drivers. If they are newer than the current drivers, it is often advisable to update these as well. If possible, record the release dates for the updated drivers here.

---

10. Return to the main documentation page, and, if it is available, choose the manual. If it is not, choose the installation instructions.

11. The manual is probably in PDF format, so you will need to have a copy of Adobe Acrobat Reader installed. If you have the browser plug-in, you can choose to open the document from the source location, or you can choose to download the manual to your computer and then open it. Using your preferred method, open the document and print the motherboard documentation. Save this documentation for use in Lab 4.4.

Review Questions

1. How is the label usually applied to a motherboard? How is it most often applied to other components?

_____

2. On the label on a motherboard or other component, how can the manufacturer often be differentiated from the model number?

_____

3. What type of link on a manufacturer's Web site will usually lead you to manuals and other documentation?

_____

4. What other information about your motherboard might you want to examine on the manufacturer's Web site?

_____

5. In what format is documentation most often available for download?

_____

LAB 4.4 REMOVE AND REPLACE THE MOTHERBOARD

Objectives

The goal of this lab is to familiarize you with the process of replacing an old or faulty motherboard. After completing this lab, you will be able to:

➤ Use SANDRA to determine the specifications of your CPU

➤ Remove a motherboard

➤ Configure a new motherboard according to its documentation

➤ Install a replacement motherboard

Materials Required

This lab will require the following:

- ➤ A computer designated for this lab
- ➤ Windows 9x or Windows 2000 operating system
- ➤ SANDRA
- ➤ Workgroup of 2–4 students

Activity Background

In this lab you will exchange a motherboard with another workgroup to simulate the process of replacing a faulty motherboard. When you install the new motherboard, you must configure it for your system by adjusting jumper and CMOS settings according to the documentation printed in Lab 4.3. Then you will install the replacement motherboard.

Estimated completion time: **45 minutes**

ACTIVITY

In this activity, follow safety precautions as you work to remove the motherboard. Be sure to use a ground strap.

1. Launch SANDRA (which you installed in Lab 2.5) and use the CPU & BIOS information utility to examine the CPU in your system. Record the information listed in the Processor section.

_____

_____

_____

2. Power the system down, unplug everything, and remove the case cover. Then remove the cabling and expansion cards from the motherboard. Take all necessary precautions (including using a ground strap) and make a sketch of cabling and component placement.

3. Usually, six screws attach the motherboard to the case via spacers. The spacers prevent the printed circuitry from shorting out on the metal case and provide space for air circulation. Remove the screws attaching the motherboard and set them aside in a cup, bag or bowl so that you don't lose them.

4. Carefully lift the motherboard out of the case. You may have to tilt the board to clear the drive bays and power supply. In some cases you may have to remove the drives to get the motherboard out.

5. Exchange the motherboard and the motherboard documentation with that of another team. You might or might not also exchange the CPU and memory depending on whether your current CPU and memory modules are compatible with the new motherboard. Follow directions given by your instructor as to what to exchange. Be sure you have the new motherboard's documentation.

CRITICAL THINKING

Your instructor might ask you to remove jumpers and reset DIP switches on your motherboard before passing it to the other team. This will make the other team's configuration more challenging.

6. With the new motherboard in front of you, consult the new board's documentation and find any jumpers that must be configured in order to match your system. Older boards use jumpers to adjust clock multipliers and memory speeds as well as to clear the CMOS settings. Unless otherwise instructed *do not* remove the jumper to clear CMOS settings. Note that newer boards are often "jumperless," with all configuration settings done within CMOS setup. The only jumper these boards will have is the one to clear CMOS settings. Remove and replace the jumpers in the configuration specified to match your processor information.

7. Install the motherboard, cabling and expansion cards, and any other components you removed.

8. Boot the system and enter the CMOS setup utility. For jumperless motherboards, make any adjustments specified in the motherboard's documentation.

9. Save settings and exit CMOS setup.

10. Reboot the system and verify that the system is functioning correctly. Describe any error messages here:

_____

11. What are the steps you plan to take to troubleshoot this error?

_____

CRITICAL THINKING (additional 30 minutes)

To learn more about motherboards, do the following:

1. Once the PC is working, ask your instructor to configure a startup password on your computer.

2. Without knowing the password, boot the computer.

3. List the steps required to accomplish this.

_____

_____

_____

Review Questions

1. How many screws usually attach the motherboard to the computer case?

_____

2. What is the purpose of spacers?

_____

3. What one jumper is a jumperless motherboard likely to have?

_____

4. Where can you access the configuration settings for a jumperless motherboard?

_____

LAB 4.5 IDENTIFY MOTHERBOARD COMPONENTS AND FORM FACTORS

Objectives

The goal of this lab is to help you learn to identify motherboard form factors and components. You should be able to:

➤ Identify a motherboard's CPU type

➤ Identify connectors

➤ Identify the form factor based on component type and placement

Materials Required

Instructors are encouraged to supply a variety of motherboards, some common and others not so common. At the very least, this lab will require the following:

➤ Three different motherboards

Activity Background

As a PC technician you should be able to look at a motherboard and determine what type of CPU, RAM and form factor you are working with. You should also be able to recognize any unusual components the board might have. In this lab, you will examine various motherboards and note some important information about them.

Estimated completion time: **30 minutes**

4

ACTIVITY

Fill in the following table for your assigned motherboards. If you have more than three motherboards, use additional paper. When the entry in the Item column includes a question mark (such as "PCI Bus?") write a yes or no answer.

Item	Motherboard 1	Motherboard 2	Motherboard 3
Manufacturer/Model			
BIOS manufacturer			
CPU type			
Chipset			
RAM type/pins			
PCI bus?			
ISA bus?			
AGP bus?			
SCSI controller?			
IDE controller?			
Embedded Audio, Video, etc.			
Jumper-less?			
Form factor			
Describe any unusual components			

1. Of the motherboards you examined, which do you think is the oldest? Why?

   _____

   _____

   _____

2. Which motherboard best supports old and new technology? Why?

   _____

   _____

   _____

3. Which motherboard appears to provide the best possibility for expansion? Why?

   _____

   _____

   _____

4. Which motherboard is most likely the easiest to configure? Why?

   _____

5. Which motherboard is the most expensive? Why?

   _____

CHAPTER FIVE

SUPPORTING I/O DEVICES

Labs included in this chapter

➤ Lab 5.1 Gather Information on Your System

➤ Lab 5.2 Identify Hardware Conflicts Using Device Manager

➤ Lab 5.3 Diagnose Simple Hardware Problems

➤ Lab 5.4 Plan and Design a Null Modem Cable

➤ Lab 5.5 Use a Multimeter to Inspect Cables

 ➤ Lab 5.6 Critical Thinking: Sabotage and Repair a System

LAB 5.1 GATHER INFORMATION ON YOUR SYSTEM

Objectives

The goal of this lab is to teach you how to use SANDRA, the Control Panel, and other sources to compile information on your system specifications. After completing this lab, you will be able to:

➤ Use various SANDRA modules to get information about your system

➤ Use Control Panel applets to get information about your system

➤ Compile a documentation notebook

Materials Required

This lab will require the following:

➤ Windows 98 or Windows 2000 operating system

➤ Documentation that you collected about your computer in Lab 4.3

➤ SANDRA

Activity Background

As you continue to work with different kinds of computers, you will find it extremely useful to maintain a report listing the components installed on each computer. This is especially important if you are responsible for a large number of computers. In this lab you will create such a document. (Note that you will need to refer to this document in future labs.) You will use SANDRA in this lab, which you installed earlier in Lab 2.5.

> Estimated completion time: **45 minutes**

ACTIVITY

Fill in the following charts, which will become part of the total documentation that you will keep about your PC. When necessary, refer to the documentation about your computer that you collected in Lab 4.3 or use the SANDRA software. After you have finished the charts, make copies of them and place them in your computer's documentation notebook. If you are not sure which menus and applets to use in SANDRA, experiment to find the necessary information. Some information can be found in more than one place.

Table 5-1   Computer Fact Sheet

Location of computer	
Owner	
Date purchased	
Date warranty expires	
Size and speed of CPU	
Type of motherboard	
Amount of RAM	
Type of monitor	
Type of video card	
Hard drive type and size	
Size of disk drive A	
Size of disk drive B	

Table 5-2   Software Installed

Software Name	Version	Installed By	Date

Table 5-3   Other Devices

Name of Device	IRQ	I/O Address	DMA Channel	Device Driver Filename
Serial Port 1				
Serial Port 2				
Parallel Port				
Mouse				
Modem				
CD-ROM Drive				
Display Adapter				
Network Card				

Create a documentation notebook or binder for your computer that includes copies of these charts, as well as any other documentation that you have collected about your computer. Save space for troubleshooting steps that you will learn in future labs. You will need this notebook in future labs.

Review Questions

1. How did you determine the CPU type?

_____

_____

2. How did you determine the driver used by your display adapter?

_____

_____

3. List two ways to determine the amount of RAM installed on a system.

_____

_____

LAB 5.2 IDENTIFY HARDWARE CONFLICTS USING DEVICE MANAGER

Objectives

The goal of this lab is to help you learn to use Device Manager to identify hardware conflicts. After completing this lab, you will be able to:

➤ Use Device Manager to investigate your system specifications

➤ Detect hardware conflicts using Device Manager

➤ Use Device Properties to determine which resources are causing a conflict

Materials Required

This lab will require the following:

➤ Windows 98 or Windows 2000 operating system

➤ Workstation with no hardware resource conflicts

➤ Hardware device that you can install in order to create a hardware resource conflict

Activity Background

Device Manager is an excellent tool for finding information about your hardware specifications. You can also use it to diagnose problems with hardware devices, including those caused by two or more devices attempting to use the same system resources (a situation called a hardware resource conflict). Among other things, Device Manager can identify faulty or disabled devices, conflicting devices, and resources currently in use. This lab will teach you how to use Device Manager to discover this information. You will start by examining your system and verifying that no hardware resource conflicts currently exist on your system. Then you will install a device that will create a resource conflict and observe the effects.

Estimated completion time: **30 minutes**

ACTIVITY

You can use Device Manager to print a report about your system. It's a good idea to print such a report when your system is working correctly. You can then use that report later, as a baseline comparison when troubleshooting conflicts or other problems.

1. Open Device Manager and print a report that provides information on all devices and also provides a system summary. Answer the following:

   ■ What were the steps you used to print the report?

   _____

   _____

- How many pages are included in the report?

  _____

- In one or two sentences, describe the type of information included on the report.

  _____

  _____

  _____

- List two items in the report that are not displayed in the Device Manager windows.

  _____

2. Put the Device Manager report in your documentation notebook (which you created in Lab 5.1).

Now you will use Device Manager to verify that there are no hardware conflicts.

1. Using Device Manager, check for any conflicts among devices. If any conflicts exist, they will be identified by a yellow triangle with an exclamation point. (Note that if a device has been disabled and is not working at all, a red circle with a slash through it will appear over the yellow triangle and exclamation point.)

2. Shut down the system and install the component provided by your instructor which should conflict with another component already installed on the system. If you don't have a device that will cause a conflict, remove a nonessential device such as a modem card or sound card, which will at least cause Device Manager to report an error.

3. Reboot and install drivers if prompted. Did you see a message indicating a conflict? If so, record the message here:

   _____

   _____

4. Open Device Manager. Does Device Manager report any conflicting devices? Describe the problem as Device Manager reports it, listing all problematic devices:

   _____

   _____

5. For each device reporting a conflict, access the device's Properties window by right clicking on the device and selecting Properties from the shortcut menu. What messages do you see in the Device Status field?

_____

_____

6. Still using the device's Properties window in Device Manager, click the **Resource** tab. What message do you see in the Conflicting Device field?

_____

7. Examine the Resource Type and Settings field. What resources is the device using? _____

_____

_____

8. Does it appear that you may be able to change the settings for this device?

_____

9. Close the device Properties window.

CRITICAL THINKING (additional 15 minutes)

While the two devices are in conflict, use Device Manager to print a report on your system. Compare the report created when the system was working properly to the report when conflicts existed. Note the differences in the two reports.

Now that you have observed two devices in conflict, you'll remove one of the conflicting devices. When you remove a device, you should first uninstall it in Device Manager. Follow these steps:

1. For Windows 98 highlight the problem device in Device Manager and click **Remove**. For Windows 2000, right click the device and then click **Uninstall** in the shortcut menu. If prompted to restart the computer, click **No**.

2. Close Device Manager and shut down the system.

3. Remove the device you installed earlier.

4. Restart the computer, open Device Manager and verify that no conflicts exist.

Review Questions

1. What symbol in Device Manager indicates a component is not working properly?

_____

2. What two devices in your system were in conflict?

_____

3. What resource(s) was causing a conflict?

_____

_____

4. Before physically removing a device from a system, what should you do first?

_____

LAB 5.3 DIAGNOSE SIMPLE HARDWARE PROBLEMS

Objectives

The goal of this lab is to give you practice diagnosing and repairing simple hardware problems. After completing this lab, you will be able to:

➤ Start with a functioning PC, introduce a problem, and remedy the problem

➤ Diagnose a problem caused by someone else

➤ Record the troubleshooting process

Materials Required

This lab will require the following:

➤ Windows 9x operating system

➤ PC toolkit including screw drivers and ground strap

➤ Pen and paper

➤ Documentation notebook that you began creating in Lab 5.1

➤ Workgroup of 2-4 students

Activity Background

If you ever work in a shop dealing with the general public, about half of the problems you see will be the result of an inexperienced person making a slight mistake when configuring a system and lacking the knowledge to diagnose and remedy the problem. Unless you are very good and very lucky, you yourself will make many of the same mistakes from time to time. Your advantage is that you will have the experience to narrow down and identify the problem and then to fix it. This lab provides experience troubleshooting and repairing simple problems. Before you begin this lab, team up with another workgroup in your class. Your team will work with this other group throughout the lab.

Estimated completion time: **60 minutes**

ACTIVITY

1. Verify that your team's system is working correctly. Also, verify that you have the completed charts for your system from Lab 5.1.

2. Make one of the following changes to your team's system:
   - Remove the power cable from the primary master hard drive
   - Reverse the data cable for the floppy drive
   - Remove the RAM and place it safely inside the case so the other team cannot see it
   - Disable IDE controllers in CMOS
   - Partially remove the data cable from the hard drive
   - Swap master/slave drive assignments

3. Switch places with the other team, and then diagnose, and remedy the problem on that team's PC. Record the troubleshooting process on a separate sheet of paper.

4. Repeat Steps 1 through 3, choosing items at random from the list in Step 2. Continue until your team has made all the changes listed in Step 2.

CRITICAL THINKING (additional 30 minutes)

If time permits, try introducing two changes at a time. This can prove to be a much more difficult situation.

Review Questions

1. What problems resulted in a "non-system disk" error?

   _____

   _____

2. What's typically the first indication that RAM had been removed?

   _____

   _____

3. What is the first symptom of a problem with the primary slave drive?

   _____

   _____

5

4. Name three problems resulting in symptoms similar to those related to a problem with the primary slave drive.

_____

_____

_____

5. What was the first indication of a floppy drive problem?

_____

_____

LAB 5.4 PLAN AND DESIGN A NULL MODEM CABLE

Objectives

The goal of this lab is to help you practice visualizing cable and pin-out arrangements by planning a null modem cable. After completing this lab, you will be able to:

➤ Plan a 25-pin null modem cable

➤ Use the Internet to find information on a 9-pin null modem cable

➤ Plan a 9-pin null modem cable

Materials Required

This lab will require the following:

➤ Internet access

Activity Background

A null modem cable can be used for file transfers between PCs. Such a cable is slow compared to the cables used on a modern network, but it will do in a pinch. This lab explains how to plan the pin-outs for a null modem cable.

Estimated completion time: **30 minutes**

ACTIVITY

1. Complete the drawing in Figure 5-1 to illustrate how pins on a 25-pin null modem cable connect. Draw lines between a pin on the left and its corresponding pin on the right. Use the information in Table 5-4 to complete the drawing.

Table 5-4 Connections on a 25-pin null modem cable

Pin number on the left connector	Pin number on the right connector	How the wire connecting the two pins is used
2	3	Data sent by one computer is received by the other
3	2	Data received by one computer is sent by the other
6	20	One end says to the other end, "I'm able to talk"
20	6	One end hears the other end say, "I'm able to talk"
4	5	One end says to the other, "I'm ready to talk"
5	4	One end hears the other say, "I'm ready to talk"
7	7	Both ends are grounded

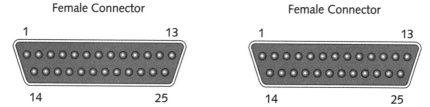

Figure 5-1 Complete the drawing by connecting each pin on the left to a pin on the right that is used by a 25-pin null modem cable

2. Search the Internet for the pinout specification for a 9-pin null modem cable and complete Table 5-5.

3. Use the information entered in Table 5-5 to complete Figure 5-2, which shows how pins on a 9-pin null modem cable connect.

Table 5-5   Connections on a 9-pin null modem cable

Pin number on one connector	Pin number of the other connector	How the wire connecting the two pins is used

Figure 5-2   Complete the drawing by connecting each pin on the left to a pin on the right that is used by a 9-pin null modem cable

CRITICAL THINKING (additional 30 minutes)

If you have access to a null modem cable, use it to network two PCs and pass files between them in both directions. On a separate paper, list the steps you used to do this. If necessary, open Windows Help and search on **Direct Cable Connection**.

Review Questions

1. Should a null modem cable be used in place of a modern network connection, if a network connection is available? Why or why not?

_____

_____

2. How many pins are normally found on a serial connector on the PC itself? Is it male or female?

_____

_____

5

3. With what industry standard should serial cables comply?

_____

_____

4. Describe a situation in which it is appropriate to use a null modem cable that has a 9-pin connector on one end and a 25-pin connector on the other?

_____

_____

CRITICAL THINKING (additional 15 minutes)

Draw a diagram showing the pinouts for a 9-pin to 25-pin null modem cable.

LAB 5.5 USE A MULTIMETER TO INSPECT CABLES

Objectives

The goal of this lab is to teach you how to use a multimeter to test cables. After completing this lab, you will be able to:

➤ Set up a multimeter to measure resistance

➤ Test cables for resistance in order to determine pin arrangements

➤ Test cables for broken connections

➤ Measure resistance in a resistor

Materials Required

This lab will require the following:

➤ A multimeter

➤ Three assorted cables

> ➤ Assorted resistors

> ➤ Pinout specifications for cables from Lab 5.4

> ➤ Workgroup of 2-4 students

Activity Background

One of the multimeter's many uses is to determine if a cable is good or bad. You can also use a multimeter to determine the cable's pin arrangement. All this is done by measuring resistance in the cable. Resistance is measured in Ohms, with infinite resistance indicating that no electricity can flow. A measure of zero Ohms or zero resistance means that electricity can flow (a state referred to as continuity). A resistor is a device that resists or controls the flow of electricity in a circuit, and a multimeter can be used to measure a resistor. You will begin the lab by setting up and testing your multimeter. Then you will measure resistance in cables and resistors.

Estimated completion time: **45 minutes**

ACTIVITY

To set up and test your multimeter:

1. Set the multimeter to measure resistance.

2. With the probes not in contact with anything, observe the reading on the meter. The reading should be infinity, or 99999.99999, or similar.

3. With the probes touching each other, observe the reading on the meter. The reading should be 0 or similar.

Now that you have verified that your multimeter is working properly, you can use it to measure the resistance or continuity in a cable. Examine cables provided by your instructor. In the following steps you will use your multimeter to discover the pinouts for each cable:

1. On a separate piece of paper, create a table (similar to Table 5-4) for each cable indicating the cable's pinouts. Can you identify the cable from your table and your knowledge of cables?

2. For Cable 1, complete the following:

   ■ Description of cable connectors: _____

   ■ Number of pins on each end of the cable: _____

   ■ Number of pins on each end of the cable that are used: _____

   ■ Type of cable: _____

3. For Cable 2, complete the following:

   ■ Description of cable connectors: _____

   ■ Number of pins on each end of the cable: _____

- Number of pins on each end of the cable that are used: _____
- Type of cable: _____

4. For Cable 3, complete the following:
  - Description of cable connectors: _____
  - Number of pins on each end of the cable: _____
  - Number of pins on each end of the cable that are used: _____
  - Type of cable: _____

Suppose a user comes to you with a problem. He has a cable that connects his computer's serial port to a serial printer. He needs to order more of the same cables, but he does not know if this cable is a regular serial cable or a specialized cable made specifically for this printer. One connector on the cable is 9-pin and the other connector is 25-pin. Using this information, answer the following:

1. Describe how to determine what kind of cable he needs to order.

_____

_____

_____

_____

2. Suppose the cable is not a regular serial cable, but a specialized cable. How might you give the user the pin-outs necessary to order new custom-made cables?

_____

_____

_____

_____

_____

So far you have used a multimeter to discover cable specifications. Next, you will use the multimeter to measure the resistances of several resistors.

1. Measure each resistor and record the results in Table 5-6. Note that resistors have colored bands indicating their intended resistance.

Table 5-6   Resistor measurements

Resistor	Resistance Reading

Review Questions

1. When a multimeter is set to measure resistance, what reading would you expect when the probes are touching?

   _____

2. When a multimeter is set to measure resistance, what reading would you expect when the probes are not touching anything?

   _____

3. Suppose all pins match pin-outs except one at each end. Suppose these non-matching pins have no continuity with any other pin. What is the likely condition of the cable?

   _____

   _____

   _____

4. What do the colors on resistors indicate?

   _____

Lab 5.6 Critical Thinking: Sabotage and Repair a System

Objectives

The goal of this lab is to learn to troubleshoot a system by recovering from a sabotaged system.

Materials Required

This lab will require the following:

➤ A PC (containing no important data) that has been designated for sabotage

➤ Workgroup of 2-4 students

Activity Background

You have learned about several tools and methods that you can use to troubleshoot and repair a failed system or failed hardware devices. This lab gives you the opportunity to use these skills in a simulated troubleshooting situation. Your group will work with another group to first sabotage a system and then repair another failed system.

Estimated completion time: **45 minutes**

5

ACTIVITY

1. If the hard drive contains important data, back up that data to another media. Is there anything else you would like to back up before the system is sabotaged by another group?

   _____

2. Trade systems with another group and sabotage the other group's system while they sabotage your system. Do one thing that will cause the system to fail to work or give errors after booting. Use any of the problems introduced in Lab 5.3 or introduce a new problem. (Do *not* alter the operating system files.) What did you do to sabotage the other team's system?

   _____

   _____

3. Return to your system and troubleshoot it.

4. Describe the problem as the user would describe it to you if you were working at a help desk.

   _____

   _____

5. What is your first guess as to the source of the problem?

   _____

6. List the steps you took in the troubleshooting process.

   _____

   _____

   _____

_____

_____

_____

7. What did you do that finally solved the problem and returned the system to good working order?

_____

_____

Review Questions

1. Thinking back on this troubleshooting experience, what would you do differently the next time the same symptoms present themselves? _____

_____

2. What software utilities did you use or could have used to solve the problem?

_____

3. What third-party software utility or hardware device might have been useful in solving this problem?

_____

4. In a real-life situation, what might cause this problem to occur? List three possible causes.

_____

_____

_____

MEMORY AND FLOPPY DRIVES

Labs included in this chapter

➤ Lab 6.1 Research RAM on the Internet

➤ Lab 6.2 Install and Troubleshoot a Floppy Drive

➤ Lab 6.3 Use TestDrive to Test a Floppy Drive

➤ Lab 6.4 Format a Floppy Disk

➤ Lab 6.5 Use the Diskcopy and Xcopy Commands

LAB 6.1 RESEARCH RAM ON THE INTERNET

Objectives

The goal of this lab is to help you learn how to find important information about RAM that you will need when upgrading memory. After completing this lab, you will be able to:

➤ Find documentation on your system's motherboard

➤ Read documentation for your system's RAM specifications

➤ Search the Internet for RAM prices and availability

Materials Required

This lab will require the following:

➤ Windows 98 or Windows 2000 operating system

➤ Internet access

Activity Background

At one time, RAM was literally worth more than its weight in gold. When building a system back then, most people made do with the minimum amount of RAM required for adequate performance. These days RAM is much cheaper, which means you can probably buy all the RAM you need to make your system perform at top speed. Graphics editing software, in particular, benefits from additional RAM. In this lab, you will research how to optimize RAM on a graphics workstation with a memory upgrade budget of $150.

Estimated completion time: **30 minutes**

ACTIVITY

1. Use My Computer to determine the amount of RAM currently installed. Record the amount of RAM here: *Disk compression = None , No PC card socket are installed.*
   127.0MB of RAM , File system 32bit , virtually 32bit

2. Using skills learned in Lab 4.3, determine the manufacturer and model of your motherboard. (If you don't have the motherboard documentation available, search for it on the Web and print it.)

Use the documentation for your motherboard to answer these questions:

1. What type (or types) of memory does your motherboard support? Be as specific as the motherboard documentation is.

   Compaq PC - X86 - based PC. Pentium (r) III
   processor GenuineIntel ~ 930 Mhz.

2. How many slots for memory modules are included on your motherboard?

4 slots for memory modules

3. How many memory slots on your motherboard are used and how much RAM is installed in each slot?

11 memory slots and 2 RAM is installed.

4. What is the maximum amount of memory that your motherboard supports?

_126 MB._

5. What size and how many memory modules will be needed to upgrade your system to the maximum amount of supported memory?

2 modules needed, SDRAM DIMMS.

Now that you have the necessary information about your system's memory, complete the following:

1. Go to a local computer store that sells memory or, using the Internet, go to *Pricewatch.com* or a similar site.

2. What is the price of the memory modules required to configure your system for maximum memory?

_1 $_

3. Will your budget enable you to install the maximum supported amount of RAM?

yes, I doesn't cost much

4. Can you use the existing memory modules to upgrade to the maximum amount of supported memory?

No, I need to add more.

5. What is the most additional memory that you could install and still stay within your budget? (Assume you will use the existing memory modules.)

increasing the amount of RAM

Explore other types of memory on *Pricewatch.com* or a similar site and answer the following questions:

1. On average, what is the least expensive type of memory per MB that you can find? What is its price?

SDRAM DIMM $1

2. On average, what is the most expensive type of memory per MB that you can find? What is its price?

price = 18⁸

OEM 128 MB PC 133 SDRAM 168 Pin Dimm module

3. Is SO-DIMM memory for a notebook computer more or less expensive than the equivalent amount of Rambus memory for a desktop PC? Give specific information to support your answer.

Rambus mem is more expensive than DIMM.
Rambus 128MB/800Mhz = 50.²⁹ . The same
size DIMM = 28

Review Questions

1. Why might you want to upgrade RAM on a system?

Generally, use the faster memory which motherboard can support.

2. How many pins are found on a DIMM? How many on a RIMM?

164 pin DIMM
184 pin RIMM

3. Which is more expensive, DIMM or RIMM?

DIMM is cheaper

4. What is a disadvantage of using two 64MB modules instead of one single 128MB module in a system with three slots for memory modules?

You use 2 memory slot for 64MB rather than 1 memory slot if it's 128MB module.

5. What are two disadvantages of using only one single 256MB module rather than two 128MB modules?

256 MB 32 × 64 (or 72). So
128 M 16 × 64 (72)

LAB 6.2 INSTALL AND TROUBLESHOOT A FLOPPY DRIVE

Objectives

The goal of this lab is to give you practice installing a second floppy drive. After completing this lab, you will be able to:

➤ Install a floppy drive

➤ Verify that a floppy drive is working correctly

➤ Troubleshoot problems related to installing a floppy drive

Materials Required

This lab will require the following:

➤ Windows 98 or Windows 2000 operating system

➤ System with one floppy drive installed and an empty 3.5-inch drive bay or empty 5-inch drive bay with mounting adapter for a second floppy drive

➤ PC toolkit

➤ A second floppy drive ready for installation

➤ Bootable disk

Activity Background

If you are in a position where you need to duplicate several floppy disks, having a second floppy drive will speed the process significantly. In this lab you will install and test a second floppy drive. But first, you will experiment with an installed floppy drive in order to become familiar with the correct orientation of the data cable. This will also give you an opportunity to verify that the installed floppy drive is working correctly, something that you should always do before installing a new drive so that you know your starting point. After the installation, if the first drive does not work, you will know that the problem did not previously exist and was introduced during the installation process. When making changes to a system, always know your starting point.

Estimated completion time: **45 minutes**

ACTIVITY

To experiment with cable orientation on an installed floppy drive:

1. Verify that you can boot from drive A with a bootable disk.

2. Turn off the computer, open the case and examine the data cable to drive A. Look for the twist in the cable. Verify that the cable is connected to the drive so that the twist is in line.

3. Adjust the cable to remove the twist between the drive and the controller. Turn on the PC and try to boot from drive A again. Describe what happens.

_____

_____

_____

4. Turn off the computer and restore the cable to its original position.

5. Verify that you can again boot from drive A with a bootable disk.

6. Reverse the orientation of the connection between the floppy drive cable and the floppy drive controller so that the edge connector is not aligned with pin 1.

7. Boot the PC. What problem occurs? Describe the problem as a user would describe it.

_____

_____

8. Turn off the computer and restore the cable to its correct orientation.

9. Verify that you can again boot from drive A with a bootable disk.

In the following steps you will install and test a second floppy drive:

1. Turn off the computer.

2. Install a second floppy drive in your PC. Install the cable so that the connector without the twist is attached to the new drive. (Your instructor might tell you to remove a floppy drive from another PC to install as a second drive in this PC.)

3. Boot the system and enter the CMOS setup utility. What keys do you press at startup to enter CMOS setup?

_____

4. Use the **Standard CMOS Setup** option (or a similar option) to find the fields on the CMOS setup screen that are used to configure floppy drives. Find the field to enable the B drive. This is the default drive letter assigned to a second floppy drive, the drive that does not require a twist in the floppy drive cable.

5. According to your setup utility, does the ROM BIOS for your computer support an extra-high density 3.5-inch floppy disk drive? List the drive types it does support.

_____

_____

_____

_____

6. Select the option for **1.44MB** (or extra-high density 3.5-inch drive) as the drive type for the new drive B just installed.

7. Save CMOS settings and exit the CMOS setup utility. List the steps required to save your settings and exit the utility.

_____

_____

6

8. Allow the system to reboot from the floppy in drive A while watching the new drive to see if the activity LED comes on. This will be the first indication that the drive has been installed properly.

9. When the system has reached the A:\ prompt, remove the floppy disk from drive A and insert it in drive B.

10. Type **DIR B:** and press **Enter**. Did the drive read the floppy disk as expected?

_____

11. Verify that you can change the default drive to drive B by typing **B:** and pressing **Enter**. What is the new command prompt?

_____

12. Shut down the system.

13. Reverse the drive cabling so that drive A is B and drive B is the new A. Then test by booting from the new drive A.

14. Return the drives to their original assignments and verify that both function as expected.

15. Change the floppy drive type in CMOS setup to an incorrect setting. (Make sure you don't change the hard drive type accidentally.)

16. Reboot. What error did you see?

_____

17. Now correct the setting and reboot to make sure all components work again.

18. Remove the second floppy drive from your system and change CMOS setup to disable drive B so that the BIOS expects to see only a single drive A.

19. Verify that the original drive is functioning correctly. How did you go about verifying that the drive is working properly?

_____

_____

Review Questions

1. Why is it important to verify that original drives already installed in a system are functioning correctly before installing a new drive?

_____

_____

2. Which drive should be attached to the connector that has a twist in the cable?

_____

3. What letter is assigned to any second floppy drive that does not have a twisted cable?

_____

4. What is the capacity of an extra-high density floppy disk?

_____

5. What is one advantage of having two floppy drives on a system?

_____

_____

LAB 6.3 USE TESTDRIVE TO TEST A FLOPPY DRIVE

Objectives

The goal of this lab is to familiarize you with floppy drive diagnostic software. After completing this lab, you will be able to:

➤ Use TestDrive to examine and diagnose problems with floppy drives and floppy disks

➤ Describe errors reported by TestDrive

Materials Required

This lab will require the following:

➤ Windows 98 or Windows 2000 operating system

➤ Internet access

➤ A floppy disk

Activity Background

MicroSystems Development provides a diagnostic program called TestDrive for examining and diagnosing problems with floppy drives and floppy disks. You will learn to use some functions of this utility in this lab. You will begin by downloading a demo version from the company's Web site. Note that most of the options on the TestDrive menu require that you have a DDD (digital diagnostic disk) for testing the drive, but you can perform a few tests without one.

6

Estimated completion time: **30 minutes**

ACTIVITY

To download and install a demo copy of Test Drive:

1. Open your browser and go to **www.msd.com/diags/**.

2. Download the TestDrive software.

3. Insert a disk containing no important data into the floppy drive. Open a command prompt window and switch to the directory containing the Testdriv.exe program. Type **testdriv.exe** and press **Enter** to launch the program. When the program launches, press any key to continue.

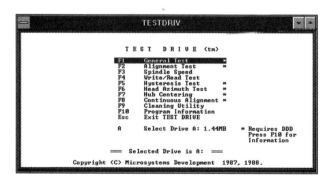

Figure 6-1   TestDrive main menu

Now that you have installed the TestDrive software, you can begin using it. Note that the main screen tells you which Function key to press in order to perform various tasks. Follow these steps:

1. Press the **F4** key to perform the Write/Read test. The warning box shown in Figure 6-2 appears.

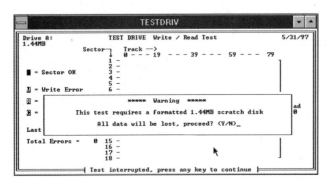

Figure 6-2   TestDrive's Write/Read Test

2. Press **Y** to continue. While the test is running, answer these questions:

   ■ In what order are these components of the floppy disk tested: heads, tracks, and sectors.

   _____

   _____

   ■ Did you get any errors? If so, describe each error?

   _____

   _____

3. If you got a significant number of errors, try another disk. Do you see any consistency in errors when switching from one disk to another? If there is a pattern of errors when using several disks, the problem is most likely with the drive. If the errors are isolated to only one disk, the problem is most likely with the disk and not the drive.

   _____

4. Press any key to return to the Main Menu.

5. Select the Spindle speed test and record the spindle speed below. What is the acceptable range for spindle speed?

_____

_____

6. Press any key to return to the Main Menu.

7. Select Program Information and answer the following questions:

   - What type of disk do most of the TestDrive tests require?

   _____

   - What is one function of the software that is not a test?

   _____

   - What type of disk is required for this function?

   _____

   - What five measurements of floppy disks can be diagnosed by TestDrive?

   _____

   _____

Review Questions

1. What type of drive is TestDrive designed to test?

_____

2. What are the only two tests that can be run without a special disk?

_____

_____

3. What is the symbol that TestDrive uses to indicate a write error?

_____

4. Suppose you run the Write/Read test with several floppy disks, and receive the same errors with each of the disks. What might you conclude?

_____

_____

5. Why do you think TestDrive allows you to try some free tests before you must purchase the software?

___

LAB 6.4 FORMAT A FLOPPY DISK

Objectives

The goal of this lab is to help you use various format options available from the MS-DOS Prompt and in Windows Explorer. After completing this lab, you will be able to:

➤ Use switches for different format options

➤ Format a floppy disk using Windows Explorer

Materials Required

This lab will require the following:

➤ Windows 98 operating system

➤ Blank unformatted floppy disk

Activity Background

Floppy disks must be formatted before you can use them. These days, floppy disks usually come preformatted from the factory. But you may often be required to re-format a used disk. The formatting process defines track and sector spacing so that data can be written to a known location. Formatting also creates the File Allocation Table, or FAT, which lists the locations of files on the disk. You can format a disk from within Windows Explorer or from the command line. When formatting disks from the command line, you can use switches to make decisions about exactly how the disk will be formatted. These switches allow you to cut some corners in order to speed up the formatting process, or to stream-line the process of making a bootable disk. In this lab you will format a floppy disk in several different ways.

Estimated completion time: **30 minutes**

ACTIVITY

To practice formatting a floppy disk from the command prompt, follow these steps:

1. Insert a blank, unformatted floppy disk into drive A.

2. Open a command prompt window. Use the **Dir** command to examine drive A. Describe what you see on the screen.

_____

_____

3. The system cannot provide information about the contents of the disk because the disk has not yet been formatted. Type **Format /?** and press **Enter**. This displays a list of eleven switches that you can use to modify the Format command. What is the correct syntax for a Format command to test clusters on the disk in drive A: that are currently marked as bad?

_____

6

4. To format the disk, type **Format A:** and then press **Enter**.

5. When prompted, press **Enter**. The format process begins. Throughout the process, you see a message indicating the percent completed.

6. When the format reaches 100%, the system gives you the opportunity to name the volume. Name the volume **FTEST** and then press **Enter**.

7. Next the system displays the format summary and asks you if you want to format another.

8. Type **n** and press **Enter**.

9. Use the **Dir** command to examine drive A. Now the system is able to give you information about the floppy disk because it has been formatted.

10. A quick format does not write track and sector markings on the disk and is a quick way to re-format a previously formatted disk. To do a quick format, type **Format A: /q** and press **Enter**. Compare the time it took to do a quick format to the time it took to do a full format:

_____

11. Again, use the **Dir** command to examine drive A:. Is there a difference between the outcome of the quick format and the full format?

_____

You can use more than one switch at a time with most commands. To demonstrate this fact with the Format command, complete the following:

1. Type **Format a: /q /s** and then press **Enter**. This command instructs the system to do a quick format and then to copy the system files required to make the disk bootable.

2. Describe the format process.

_____

_____

_____

_____

3. How many bytes of free space are now included on the disk? What command did you use to get your answer?

_____

_____

4. Close the MS-DOS prompt window.

To practice formatting a floppy disk from within Windows Explorer, follow these steps:

1. Open Windows Explorer.

2. With the floppy inserted in drive A, right-click on drive A and then click **Format** in the shortcut menu. The Format window opens.

3. Observe the layout of the Format window, and describe the options provided by the Format window.

_____

Review Questions

1. Suppose you formatted a floppy disk on a Windows 98 system. Would you then be able to re-format the same disk using the /q switch on another Windows 98 system? Why or why not?

_____

_____

2. Suppose you want to format a disk in drive B, making it a bootable disk. What command would you use?

_____

3. In general, what difference did you see in a disk's directory listing after formatting the disk with the /s switch?

_____

_____

4. What is the maximum number of characters a volume name can contain?

_____

LAB 6.5 USE THE DISKCOPY AND XCOPY COMMANDS

Objectives

The goal of this lab is to help you observe differences in the Diskcopy and Xcopy commands. After completing this lab, you will be able to:

> ➤ Copy files and folders using the Xcopy command

> ➤ Duplicate a disk using the Diskcopy command

> ➤ Explain when to use Xcopy and when to use Diskcopy when copying files and folders

Materials Required

This lab will require the following:

> ➤ Windows 98 operating system

> ➤ 2 blank floppy disks

> ➤ Safety pin

Activity Background

The Copy command simply allows you to copy files from one folder to another folder. Using a single Xcopy command, however, you can copy files from multiple folders, duplicating an entire file structure in another location. The Diskcopy command, meanwhile, allows you to make an exact copy of a floppy disk. You will learn to appreciate the differences between these commands in this lab.

Estimated completion time: **45 minutes**

ACTIVITY

Before you begin using the Xcopy and Diskcopy commands, you need to create a test directory to use when copying files. Follow these steps:

1. Open a command prompt window and make the root of drive C: the current directory. Note that the quickest way to change to the root of a drive is to type *X*: (where *X* is the drive letter) and then press Enter.

2. Make a directory in the drive C root called **copytest**.

Now you can begin experimenting with the Xcopy command. Follow these steps:

1. Type **Xcopy /?** and press **Enter**. Xcopy Help information appears. Notice all the switches that you can use to modify the Xcopy command. In particular, you can use the /e switch to instruct Xcopy to copy all files and all subdirectories in a directory, including the empty subdirectories, to a new location.

2. Type **Xcopy C:\"program files"\"internet explorer" C:\copytest /e** and then press **Enter**. You see a list of files scroll by as they are copied from the C:\program files\internet explorer folder to the C:\copytest folder. Notice in the command line, you had to use quotation marks to surround a folder name that contains spaces.

3. When the copy is complete, check the **copytest** directory to see that the files have been copied and the subdirectories created.

4. Insert a blank floppy disk into drive A:, type **md A:\copytest** and then press **Enter**. This creates a directory named **copytest** on drive A:.

5. To copy all the files in the Copytest directory on the hard drive to the Copytest directory on drive A, type the command **Xcopy C:\"program files"\ "internet explorer" A:\copytest** and then press **Enter**.

6. The system begins copying files, but the floppy disk lacks the capacity needed to hold the entire \Internet Explorer directory. As a result, the system displays a message indicating that the disk is out of space and asking you to insert another disk. What is the exact error message?

_____

_____

7. In this case, you do not really want to copy the entire directory to the floppy disk, so you need to stop the copying process. To do that, hold down the **Ctrl** key and then press the **Pause/Break** key. You return to the command prompt.

You have used the Xcopy command to copy some files to a floppy disk. Next, you will use the Diskcopy command to make an exact copy of that floppy disk, which is referred to as the source disk. (The disk you copy files to is known as the target disk.) You'll begin by writing down a list of the files and directories on the source disk. Later, you will compare this list to the list of files actually copied to the target disk. Follow these steps:

1. Display a directory listing for the **A:\copytest** directory.

2. Write the complete summary of files, directories and space on the A: drive here:

_____

_____

_____

_____

3. Verify that the floppy disk you used in the preceding set of steps is inserted in drive A, type **Diskcopy A: A:** and press **Enter**. This instructs the system to copy files from one floppy disk to another using a single floppy disk drive. (If your system contained a drive B:, you could copy files from a disk in drive A: to a disk in drive B: or vice versa.)

4. Press **Enter** to begin copying.

5. Because you are copying from drive A: to drive A:, the system prompts you to remove the source disk and to insert the target disk. When prompted, insert a blank floppy and press **Enter**.

6. When the copy operation finishes, a message appears asking if you want to copy another. Type **n** and press **Enter** to indicate that you do not wish to copy another disk. (When using Windows 98, you must also say that you do not wish to make another duplicate.)

7. With the target disk still in drive A:, use the **Dir** command to compare the newly copied files with the file list from the source disk, which you recorded in step 2. The disks should be identical.

CRITICAL THINKING (additional 30 minutes)

1. Format one floppy disk. Use any method from Lab 6.4 to format the disk.

2. Use a safety pin to damage one of the floppy disks created in this lab by sliding back the disk's protective guard and punching a small hole about ½ an inch from the edge of the disk.

3. Use Xcopy to attempt to copy the files on the damaged disk to the newly formatted disk by first copying them to a folder on the hard drive. List the steps you used to do this and the outcome.

_____

6

_____

_____

4. Attempt to recover the files from the damaged disk that the system could not copy. Explain how you were able to do this.

_____

_____

5. Run TestDrive on the damaged disk and describe the outcome.

_____

_____

Review Questions

1. Can a single Copy command copy files from more than one directory?

_____

2. What switch can you use with Xcopy to copy subdirectories?

_____

3. What is the complete Diskcopy command required to copy files on a disk in drive A: to a disk in drive B:?

_____

4. What is one disadvantage of using the Diskcopy command with only one floppy disk drive?

_____

5. What Xcopy switch suppresses overwrite confirmation?

_____

UNDERSTANDING AND SUPPORTING HARD DRIVES

Labs included in this chapter

- ➤ Lab 7.1 Install and Partition a Hard Drive
- ➤ Lab 7.2 Format a Drive and Test it with ScanDisk
- ➤ Lab 7.3 Test Hard Drive Performance Using SANDRA
- ➤ Lab 7.4 Research Data Recovery Options on the Internet
- ➤ Lab 7.5 Troubleshoot Hard Drives
- ➤ Lab 7.6 Critical Thinking: Sabotage and Repair a Hard Drive Subsystem

LAB 7.1 INSTALL AND PARTITION A HARD DRIVE

Objectives

The goal of this lab is to help you master the process of installing a hard drive in a computer. After completing this lab, you will be able to:

➤ Physically install a drive

➤ Set CMOS to recognize the drive

➤ Partition the drive

Materials Required

This lab will require the following:

➤ Windows 9x operating system

➤ Hard drive with unpartitioned drive space

Activity Background

As a technician, you definitely need to know how to install a hard drive in a computer. You might have to replace a failed drive with a new one, or, if you have a hard drive that is running out of storage space, you might need to install an additional drive. In either case, you need to know the steps involved in installing a new hard drive.

In this lab you will install and partition a new hard drive. Ideally, you would install a second hard drive in a system that already has a working drive. However, this lab also gives you the option of removing the hard drive from your system, trading your hard drive for another student's hard drive, and then installing the traded hard drive in your computer. Ask your instructor which procedure you should perform. Because the steps in this lab allow for both possibilities, you need to read the steps carefully to make sure you are performing the right steps for your particular situation.

In any case, after you install the hard drive, you will have to partition it. If you are installing a hard drive that has been used as a boot device, the drive will already have a primary DOS partition. In that case, you need to verify that the drive contains at least some unpartitioned space. If it does contain unpartitioned space, you can add an extended partition to the drive. Again, ask your instructor for specific directions.

Estimated completion time: **45 minutes**

ACTIVITY

Do the following to physically install the drive in the computer case:

1. Remove the case cover. Remove the hard drive and exchange it for another student's hard drive. (If your instructor has provided you with a second hard drive to install in your system, simply open the case cover.)

2. Examine the case and decide where to place the drive. Consider whether to place the drive on the primary or secondary IDE channel, and if you will need a bay kit to fit a 3½-inch drive into a 5-inch drive bay.

3. Place the drive in or near the bay to test its position. Make sure that all cables will reach in that position. If the cables won't reach, try a different bay or obtain longer cables.

4. When you are satisfied everything will fit, remove the drive and set the jumpers to their proper setting. If the jumpers are not marked on the drive, consult the drive documentation for jumper configuration. You might have to go to the Web site of the drive manufacturer and search for information on the drive.

5. Install the drive in the bay and secure it with screws on each side of the drive.

6. Attach the power cord and data cable and close the case.

Now that you have physically installed your hard drive, you need to configure CMOS to recognize the new hard drive. Follow these steps:

1. Attach the keyboard, monitor and mouse.

2. Boot your computer and enter the CMOS setup utility.

3. If IDE hard drive autodetect is not enabled, enable it now. In CMOS, what is the name of this entry? If you have just enabled autodetect, reboot the system so the drive can now be detected.

---

4. Check the drive parameters that were set by autodetect and change them if they were not detected correctly. If your system does not have autodetect, set the drive parameters now. When in doubt use Logical Block Addressing (LBA) or consult the drive documentation. What are the drive parameters in CMOS?

---

5. Save and exit CMOS setup.

6. The system reboots. While the system boots, hold down the **Ctrl** key to activate the Windows Startup Menu and watch for the drive to appear during POST.

Now that the drive has been recognized, use the Fdisk utility to create or delete partitions. The following sections show you how to create and delete the primary partition, an extended partition, and a logical DOS drive.

Enter Fdisk by following these steps:

1. Turn on your computer and hold down the **Ctrl** key while the computer boots. This will activate the Startup Menu.

2. From the Startup menu, select **Command Prompt Only**.

3. Type **Fdisk** and then press **Enter**.

4. Select **Y** and then press **Enter** to enable Large Disk Support. Large Disk Support uses FAT32 to enable partition sizes above 2GB. The Fdisk Options menu appears as shown in Figure 7-1.

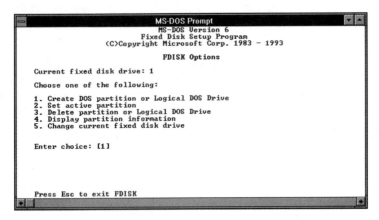

Figure 7-1 Fixed Disk Setup Program (FDISK) menu

On the Fdisk screen, the current fixed disk drive is drive 1. If you are installing a second hard drive, you must first change to drive 2 by following the steps below. (If you are installing the only drive in the system, skip these steps and go to the next section, where you will determine what types of partitions currently exist on your newly installed drive.)

1. Select option **5** on the menu and then press **Enter**. A list of drives appears.

2. Select drive **2** and then press **Enter**. You return to the Fdisk Options menu shown earlier in Figure 7-1.

Now that you have the correct drive selected, you need to find out what kind of partitions currently exist on the drive. Whether you are installing the only drive on the system, or a second drive, follow these steps:

1. To display partition information, select option **4** on the menu and then press **Enter**. Answer these questions about your drive:
   - What is the total disk space reported?

   _____

   - What is the available disk space reported?

   _____

   - Do any partitions currently exist?

   _____

   - If partitions exist, what kind of partitions are they?

   _____

2. Press **Escape** to return to the Fdisk Options menu.

If you are installing a second hard drive on your system, you need to create a primary DOS partition on the second hard drive, by following the steps below. (If you only have one hard drive installed or your second hard drive has a primary partition containing an operating system, skip these steps and move on to the next section, where you will create an extended partition.)

1. To select the second hard drive, from the Fdisk options menu, select option **5** on the menu and then press **Enter**.

2. To select the second hard drive, select option **2** on the menu and then press **Enter**. You return to the Fdisk Options menu.

3. To create a DOS partition, from the Fdisk Options menu, select option **1** on the menu and then press **Enter**. The Create DOS Partition or Logical DOS Drive menu appears.

4. To create a primary DOS partition, select option **1** and then press **Enter**.

5. The system verifies disk space and displays a progress update. When space on the drive has been verified, Fdisk asks if you want to use the maximum available space for the primary DOS partition. Type **N** and then press **Enter**.

6. Fdisk again verifies disk space and asks for the amount of disk space that you want to use for the primary partition. Type a numerical value that is half of the total available space and then press **Enter**.

7. Fdisk tells you that the primary DOS partition has been created. It displays a summary of the new partition and assigns the partition a drive letter. Record the summary below.

_____

_____

Note that Fdisk may slightly increase the partition size to accommodate the disk's geometry.

8. Press **Escape** to return to the Fdisk Options menu.

With a primary partition in place, you are ready to install an extended partition on the last part of the drive. Follow these steps to create an extended partition and one logical DOS drive within that extended partition:

1. In the Fdisk Options Menu, select option **1** and then press **Enter**.

2. To create an extended DOS partition, select option **2** and then press **Enter**.

3. Fdisk verifies disk space and prompts you to enter the amount of disk space to use for the extended partition. Press **Enter** to use the remaining disk space to create the extended partition.

4. Fdisk displays a summary of the extended partition. Note that the extended partition has no drive letter assigned.

5. Press **Escape**. A message appears indicating that no logical drives are defined, and Fdisk again verifies disk space.

6. Fdisk prompts you to enter the amount of space to use for a logical drive. Press **Enter** to use the maximum amount of disk space to create a logical drive.

7. Fdisk assigns a drive letter and displays a summary. Press **Escape** to return to the Fdisk Options menu.

8. Select option **4** and then press **Enter** to display the disk summary. Note that the system column displays "Unknown" because the drive has not been formatted.

9. Press **Escape** to return to the Fdisk Options menu.

You will now practice deleting partitions. Fdisk is particular about the order in which you create and delete partitions. To delete a primary partition, you must delete an extended partition, and in order to delete an extended partition, you must delete all the logical DOS drives in the extended partition. A word of warning; if you have an operating system installed on the drive and you have only a single hard drive, *do not delete the primary partition*! Doing so will destroy the operating system installed on the drive.

To delete the extended partition you just created, you must first delete the logical DOS drive in that partition. Follow these steps:

1. From the Fdisk Options menu, select option **3**, and then press **Enter**.

2. On the next screen, select option **3** and then press **Enter** to indicate that you are about to delete a logical DOS drive

3. Type the drive letter assigned to the logical DOS drive and then press **Enter** to confirm that you wish to delete that drive.

4. Enter the volume label (or leave it blank) and then press **Enter**. Select **Y** and then press **Enter** to confirm that you wish to delete the drive. Fdisk confirms that the drive has been deleted.

5. Press **Escape** once. The No Logical Drive Defined message appears.

6. Press **Escape** to return to the Fdisk Options menu.

Now that you have deleted the logical DOS drive, you can now delete the extended partition. Follow these steps:

1. From the Fdisk Options menu select option **3**, and then press **Enter**.

2. On the next screen, select option **2** and then press **Enter** to delete an extended partition.

3. Type **Y** and then press **Enter** to confirm that you want to delete an extended partition. Fdisk confirms that the partition has been deleted.

4. Press **Escape** to return to the Fdisk Options Menu.

If you are working with a second hard drive, you can now delete the primary partition. (Remember, do not delete the primary partition if you are working with a single hard drive.) Follow these steps:

1. From the Fdisk Options menu, select option **3**, and then press **Enter**.

2. On the next screen, for the first partition select option **1**, and then press **Enter**.

3. Enter the volume label (or leave it blank if there is no volume label) and then press **Enter**.

4. Select **Y** and then press **Enter** to confirm that you wish to delete the partition. Fdisk confirms that the drive or partition has been deleted.

5. Press **Escape** to return to the Fdisk Options menu.

   Based on what you have learned, re-create a partition using half of the total disk space. If you have only a single hard drive, create an extended partition. If you have a second hard drive, create only a primary partition, thus leaving half of the drive space unused. Answer these questions:

   ■ What kind of partition did you create (primary or extended)?

   _____

   ■ How much space did you use for your partition?

   _____

   ■ What drive letter was assigned to the logical drive on the new partition?

   _____

To exit the Fdisk utility, follow these steps:

1. With the Fdisk Options menu displayed, press **Escape**.

2. A message displays indicating that the system must be rebooted in order for the changes to take effect. Reboot the system while holding down the **Ctrl** key.

3. Select **Command Prompt Only**.

4. To confirm the drive is set up correctly, type the drive letter followed by a colon and then press **Enter**. The command prompt now includes the drive's letter.

Review Questions

1. When physically installing a hard drive, what steps should you take before you permanently fix the drive in place with screws?

   _____

   _____

2. What CMOS setup tool can recognize a new hard drive?

_____

_____

3. What are two types of partitions?

_____

_____

4. What must you do before you can delete an extended partition?

_____

_____

5. What must you do before you can delete a primary partition?

_____

_____

6. What would prevent your partitions from being recognized after you exit Fdisk?

_____

_____

LAB 7.2 FORMAT A DRIVE AND TEST IT WITH SCANDISK

Objectives

The goal of this lab is to help you prepare a partitioned drive for use. After completing this lab, you will be able to:

➤ Format a drive

➤ Use ScanDisk to test the drive's condition

Materials Required

This lab will require the following:

➤ Windows 98 operating system

➤ Floppy disk containing no essential data

Activity Background

Before your computer can read from and write to a drive, you must format the drive. It is also a good idea to test a drive to ensure that it's in working order before you put it to use. In this lab, you will format and test your newly partitioned drive. You will begin by creating a bootable floppy and adding some important utility files to it. Then you will use the disk to boot your computer and then format and test your drive. The utility files you will include are:

➤ ScanDisk.exe, which is used to detect and repair hard drive errors

➤ Himem.sys, which is used to manage memory above 1 MB

➤ Format.com, which is used to format a drive

You will also include the system file, Config.sys, which contains configuration settings.

7

| Estimated completion time: **30 minutes** |

ACTIVITY

Follow these steps to create a bootable disk and then copy the necessary files to it:

1. Create a bootable floppy disk. If you need help, see Lab 2.2.

2. Copy the file named **ScanDisk.exe** from **C:\Windows\Command** to the bootable floppy disk.

3. Copy the file named **Himem.sys** from **C:\Windows** to the bootable floppy disk. Himem.sys is necessary to run Scandisk on a hard drive.

4. Copy the file named **Format.com** from **C:\Windows\Command** to the bootable floppy disk.

5. Edit or create the **Config.sys** file on your floppy disk. Add the line: **Device=A:\himem.sys**. (Note that if you fail to edit the config.sys file on your boot disk, when you attempt to start Scandisk you will receive a message indicating it is necessary to do so.)

Now that you have prepared a bootable disk, follow these steps to format your new drive:

1. Boot from the floppy disk.

2. At the command prompt, type **Format _x_:** (where _x_ is the drive letter assigned to the partition you created in Lab 7.1) and then press **Enter**.

3. The system warns you that all data will be lost and asks whether you want to continue. Type **Y** and then press **Enter** to confirm that you want to format this drive.

4. The system begins formatting the drive. When the format process is complete, you are asked to enter a volume label. You will name the volume "New."

5. Type **New** and then press **Enter**.

6. At the command prompt, type the drive letter followed by a colon and then press **Enter**. The newly formatted drive is now the current directory.

7. Use the DIR command to view the drive summary. Record the summary information here:

_____

_____

_____

_____

_____

Now that the drive has been formatted, you can use ScanDisk to check the condition of the drive. Follow these steps:

1. Type **A:\ScanDisk *x:*** (where x is the drive letter of the volume named "New").

2. ScanDisk begins checking the following:
   - Media descriptor
   - File Allocation Table
   - Directory structure
   - File system
   - Free space

3. If ScanDisk finds any file fragments or errors, it will give you the option of correcting the problem. If no errors are found (or after all errors are corrected), ScanDisk displays a summary and gives you the option of running a surface scan.

4. A surface scan is a lengthy process in which the disk is scanned block by block until the surface condition of each platter has been checked. Type **Y** to begin a surface scan.

5. ScanDisk begins the surface scan and displays an illustration of the process. While the surface scan continues examining the disk, answer the following questions. ScanDisk can take a large amount of time to complete. For the purposes of this lab, you can press **X** to cancel the surface scan once you've answered the questions.
   - How many total clusters does the disk contain?

_____

- How many clusters does each block represent?

_____

- What symbol indicates a bad cluster?

_____

Review Questions

1. Suppose you need to format drive D:. Write the command you would use.

_____

2. When is himem.sys required in order to run ScanDisk?

_____

3. By default, does ScanDisk run a surface scan automatically?

_____

4. Why should you run a surface scan?

_____

5. What happens when Scandisk finds errors during its automatic check?

_____

LAB 7.3 TEST HARD DRIVE PERFORMANCE USING SANDRA

Objectives

The goal of this lab is to help you use SANDRA to compare the performance of your system's drives against similar drives. After completing this lab, you will be able to:

➤ Use SANDRA to test your drive's performance
➤ Use SANDRA to compare your system's drives with similar drives

Materials Required

This lab will require the following:

➤ Windows 9x operating system
➤ SiSoft SANDRA 2001te standard software installed in Lab 2.5

Activity Background

You can use SANDRA to run a routine of several tests on your drive, report the results, and compare your drive to a selection of comparable drives. This will give you an indication of how your drive is performing and whether another product is available that better meets your performance needs. Some tasks, such as video editing, are very demanding on the drive where the files are stored; a faster drive can increase productivity. When making an upgrade decision, it's helpful to compare results reported by SANDRA to information on other hard drives. In this lab you will use SANDRA to test your drive.

> Estimated completion time: **30 minutes**

ACTIVITY

Follow these directions to test your drive:

1. Start SANDRA.

2. Double-click the Drives Benchmark icon. The Drives Benchmark window opens. (If you don't see the Drives Benchmark icon, you installed the wrong version of Sandra. You should be using the 2001te standard version.)

3. Click the **Select Drive** list arrow, and then click the letter of the drive you are testing from the drop-down menu. What message appeared after you selected drive C?

   _____

   _____

4. Wait until SANDRA has finished testing your drive before moving your mouse or doing anything else with the system. After the test is finished, a summary appears. Use the summary to answer the following questions:
   - In the Current Drive field, what drive index is reported?

     _____

   - What drives were compared to the Current Drive?

     _____

     _____

5. Click the drop-down menu of one of the compared drives and note that you can compare your drive against several drives.

6. One by one, select each of the drives and note their performance ratings. List those drives with a lower performance rating than the current drive:

_____

_____

7. List the size and rpm of the two drives with the lowest performance.

_____

_____

8. Use the bottom field of the Drives Benchmark window to complete the following table. (Scroll down as necessary to display the information you need.)

7

Category	Value
Drive Class	
Total Space	
Sequential Read	
Random Read	
Buffered Write	
Sequential Write	
Random Write	
Average Access Time	

Review Questions

1. Why might you want to test your drive with SANDRA?

_____

_____

2. Based on the drive ratings information from SANDRA, do you think a drive performs better if it spins faster or slower?

_____

3. Based on the drive ratings information from SANDRA, do you think a drive performs better if it reads data randomly or sequentially?

_____

4. Why shouldn't you use the system when SANDRA is testing a drive?

_____

_____

Lab 7.4 Research Data Recovery Options on the Internet

Objectives

The goal of this lab is to help you explore options for recovering data from a malfunctioning hard drive. After completing this lab, you will be able to:

➤ Search the Internet for recovery services

➤ Search *www.ontrack.com* to learn about data recovery

➤ Use EasyRecovery to locate files for possible recovery

Materials Required

This lab will require the following:

➤ Windows 98, Windows 2000, or Windows XP operating system

➤ Internet access

Activity Background

Probably nothing makes a computer user panic more than the prospect of losing important data. As a technician, you have to be prepared to recover data from a variety of storage media; most often, however, you will be asked to recover it from a hard drive. Data on a hard drive may be lost for a variety of reasons ranging from human error to a natural disaster that renders the drive inoperable. In this lab you will investigate various data recovery options.

Estimated completion time: **60 minutes**

Activity

When you need to find information on the Internet, it's often helpful to start with a broad search via a search engine such as Google (*www.google.com*) or Alta Vista (*www.altavista.com*). To learn more, follow these steps:

1. Open your browser and go to your favorite search site on the Internet.

2. Search for information on data recovery services.

3. Explore as many links as you have time for. Then, list five sites that offer data recovery services:

_____

_____

_____

_____

_____

One major data recovery company is called Ontrack. You'll explore the Ontrack Web site in the following steps:

7

1. Open your Internet browser and go to *www.ontrack.com*.

2. Answer the following questions, using the links on the Ontrack site. If you cannot obtain all the answers from this site, supplement it with information from one or more of the sites you found in your earlier search process. Print pages supporting all of your answers.

   ■ According to the information you printed, what are the two top causes of data loss?

   _____

   _____

   ■ What data recovery options are available?

   _____

   _____

   _____

   ■ What solutions will work with your operating system?

   _____

   ■ What should you do if a hardware malfunction is detected?

   _____

   _____

   ■ Is Internet access necessary for this recovery option?

   _____

- Will this option work if you cannot boot from the hard drive?

_____

3. Return to the Ontrack home page.

4. Locate and follow the link that leads to information about easy recovery software.

5. Click the **Key Features** link. Using information on the Key Features page, answer the following questions.

- What is the name of the easy recovery software package that Ontrack offers?

_____

- Does this software need to be installed prior to the data loss?

_____

- Does this software require that your system be healthy enough to boot from the hard drive?

_____

- Can this product recover data from a deleted partition? Print the Web page supporting your answer.

_____

To download the EasyRecoverySoftware, follow these steps:

1. Click the **Try Before You Buy** link.

2. Click the link for downloading the **Free Version Professional Edition – English**.

3. Download the **ERPerfus.exe** file to your hard drive.

4. Open Windows Explorer and double-click the **ERProfus.exe** icon. The EasyRecovery window opens.

   Note that installing the EasyRecovery software on the partition containing the data you want to recover may in fact overwrite the lost data. To avoid this problem, you should install EasyRecover on a separate partition or PC and then create an EasyRecovery Emergency Boot Disk. For the purpose of this lab, however, it's okay to install on your current PC. Click **Next** to continue.

5. To continue installing EasyRecovery, accept the End-User License Agreement (EULA).

6. Click **Next** to install EasyRecovery in the Program Files folder.

7. When prompted, click **Finish** to complete and close the EasyRecovery installation. The EasyRecovery Personal Trial Edition window opens displaying shortcuts.

Now that EasyRecovery has been installed, you can run it. Follow these steps:

1. Double-click the EasyRecovery Personal Trial Edition shortcut in the EasyRecovery Personal Trial Edition window (which remained opened after the installation process ended). An EasyRecovery Personal Trial Edition notice opens and informs you that the trial edition can identify recoverable files but that you must purchase the full version to recover files. Click **OK** to close the notice. The EasyRecovery Data Recovery application launches.

2. Click **Next** to begin the EasyRecovery process. Notice that EasyRecovery graphically displays partition information along with a legend defining partition information and use.

3. Had you actually lost data you would select the partition with the lost data. For the purpose of this lab select any partition and click **Next**. EasyRecovery displays a summary confirming the selected partition, start sector, end sector, and FAT type. Click **Next**. EasyRecovery displays the file system type.

4. Click **Next** to continue. EasyRecovery begins searching the partition for recoverable files.

5. When the search is complete, click **OK** to review the results.

   In the left pane, a hierarchical list of folders is displayed. The right pane shows recoverable files within those folders. If this were a full version of EasyRecovery, you would be able to select Folders on the menu bar, click Files, and then specify a destination for the files. These files would then be copied from their current location to the specified destination.

6. Using procedures listed in earlier labs, print a screen shot of this EasyRecovery window.

7. Click **Cancel** to end the recovery process.

8. When asked if you want to save the recovery, click **No**.

9. Click **Exit** and then click **OK** to exit EasyRecovery.

Review Questions

1. What are three causes of data loss?

   _____

   _____

2. Which of these causes would Remote Data Recovery and EasyRecovery fail to overcome?

   _____

3. Is it normally possible to recover lost data that has been overwritten by other data?

_____

4. What are some symptoms of a hardware malfunction that would result in data loss?

_____

_____

5. List some steps to prevent mechanical drive failure.

_____

_____

LAB 7.5 TROUBLESHOOT HARD DRIVES

Objectives

The goal of this lab is to help you troubleshoot common hard drive problems. After completing this lab, you will be able to:

➤ Simulate common hard drive problems

➤ Diagnose and repair common hard drive problems

➤ Document the process

Materials Required

This lab will require the following:

➤ A computer with a hard drive subsystem that you can sabotage

➤ Bootable disk

➤ PC toolkit

➤ Workgroup of 2-4 students

Activity Background

This lab will give you practice diagnosing and remedying common hard drive problems.

Estimated completion time: **60 minutes**

ACTIVITY

1. Verify that your hard drive is working by using a command prompt or Windows Explorer to display files on the drive.

2. Switch computers with another team.

3. Sabotage the other team's computer by doing one of the following:
   - Remove or incorrectly configure the drive jumpers
   - Remove the power connector from the drive
   - Switch data cables to place devices on incorrect IDE channels
   - Disable IDE controllers in CMOS setup
   - If allowed by your instructor, delete partitions on the hard drive

4. Return to your computer and examine it for any symptoms of a problem.

5. On a separate piece of paper, answer the following questions relating to the problem's symptoms:
   - What symptoms would a user notice? (Describe the symptoms as the user might describe them.)
   - Does the system boot from the hard drive?
   - Does POST display the hard drive?
   - Can you boot from a floppy disk and change to the drive in question?
   - Does the CMOS HDD Autodetect option detect the hard drive?

6. On a separate piece of paper, before you actually begin your investigation, state your initial diagnosis.

7. Diagnose and repair the problem.

8. On a separate piece of paper, list the steps required to confirm your diagnosis and solve the problem.

9. Answer the following questions relating to your final conclusions:
   - What was the problem?

   _____

   - What did you do to correct the problem?

   _____

   _____

   _____

7

■ Was your preliminary diagnosis correct?

_____

10. Repeat Steps 1–8, choosing actions at random from the list in Step 2, until your team has performed all the items listed in Step 2. Be sure to write down the relevant information (as instructed in the steps) for each problem.

Review Questions

1. What was the first indication that the power was disconnected from your drive?

_____

_____

2. What incorrect drive configuration would still allow you to access files on the hard drive by booting from the floppy?

_____

_____

3. What incorrect configurations have similar symptoms?

_____

_____

4. What problem resulted in no drives being detected except for the floppy drive?

_____

_____

5. List the steps required to use a drive whose partitions have been deleted.

_____

_____

_____

_____

LAB 7.6 CRITICAL THINKING: SABOTAGE AND REPAIR A HARD DRIVE SUBSYSTEM

Objectives

The goal of this lab is to learn to troubleshoot a hard drive by repairing a sabotaged system.

Materials Required

This lab will require the following:

➤ A PC designated for a sabotage (containing no important data)

➤ Workgroup of 2–4 students

Activity Background

You have learned about several tools and methods for troubleshooting and recovering from a hard drive failure. This lab gives you the opportunity to use these skills in a troubleshooting situation. Your group will work with another group to first sabotage a system and then recover your own sabotaged system.

> Estimated completion time: **45 minutes**

ACTIVITY

1. If your system's hard drive contains important data, back up that data to another media. Is there anything else you would like to back up before the system is sabotaged by another group?

   _____

2. Trade systems with another group and sabotage the other group's system while they sabotage your system. Do one thing that will cause the hard drive to fail to work or give errors after the boot. Use any of the problems suggested in Lab 7.5 or you can introduce a new problem (do *not* alter the operating system files). What did you do to sabotage the other team's system?

   _____

   _____

3. Return to your system and troubleshoot it.

4. Describe the problem as the user would describe it to you if you were working at a help desk.

_____

_____

5. What is your first guess as to the source of the problem?

_____

6. List the steps you took in the troubleshooting process.

_____

_____

_____

_____

_____

7. What did you do that finally solved the problem and returned the system to good working order?

_____

_____

Review Questions

1. Now that you have been through the troubleshooting experience above, what would you do differently the next time the same symptoms present themselves?

_____

2. What software utilities did you use or could you have used to solve the problem?

_____

3. What third-party software utility might have been useful in solving this problem?

_____

4. In a real-life situation, what might happen that would cause this problem to occur? List three things.

_____

_____

_____

7

ALL ABOUT SCSI

Labs included in this chapter

➤ Lab 8.1 Compare SCSI to Competing Technologies

➤ Lab 8.2 Compare SCSI Standards

➤ Lab 8.3 Install a Host Adapter and Hard Drive

➤ Lab 8.4 Install an External Drive

 ➤ Lab 8.5 Critical Thinking: Plan a SCSI System

LAB 8.1 COMPARE SCSI TO COMPETING TECHNOLOGIES

Objectives

The goal of this lab is to compare the price of a SCSI system to a similar system without SCSI. After completing this lab, you will be able to:

➤ Recognize the cost of SCSI components

➤ Explain how SCSI components can improve performance

Materials Required

This lab will require the following:

➤ Internet access

Activity Background

SCSI components, in general, cost significantly more than non–SCSI components but offer similar basic functionality. At one time SCSI performance and capabilities far exceeded those of other devices. Due to the emergence of new technologies and the refinement of other technologies, this is not necessarily true today. In this lab you will compare the cost and performance of SCSI components to similar non–SCSI components.

Estimated completion time: **30 minutes**

ACTIVITY

1. Most motherboards come with embedded EIDE controllers. Generally speaking, they do not come with embedded SCSI controllers or FireWire ports. Use Pricewatch.com and various manufacturers' Web sites to compare controllers for each technology. For each technology, select one mid–price device and record the information for that device in this table.

	SCSI host adapter	EIDE adapter	FireWire adapter
Model and Manufacturer			
Cost			
Number of devices supported			

2. Use *www.pricewatch.com* to compare hard drives that use SCSI, IDE, and FireWire. Decide on a drive capacity to use for your comparisons (for example 50 GB). Try to use drives that are within approximately 5 GB of each other. Also, when comparing drives, try to compare drives with similar rotation

speed. For each technology, pick one mid–price drive and complete the tables below. For EIDE, use the most common speed, 7200 rpm. Use manufacturer Web sites for any information not available on Pricewatch.com:

	SCSI Drive	EIDE Drive	FireWire Drive
Model and Manufacturer			
Capacity (GB)			
Cost			
Rotation speed (rpm)		7200 rpm	
Avg. access time (ms)			
Max. transfer speed (ms)			

3. Use Pricewatch.com and manufacturer Web sites to compare CD-RW drives. Pick one mid–price drive for each technology and complete the following table:

	SCSI CD-RW	EIDE CD-RW	FireWire CD-RW
Model and Manufacturer			
Cost			
Read speed			
Write speed			
Rewrite speed			
Avg. access time (ms)			
Max. transfer speed (ms)			

Review Questions

1. What advantages does SCSI hold over EIDE?

_____

_____

2. What advantage over EIDE do SCSI and FireWire share?

_____

3. What are two advantages EIDE has over SCSI?

_____

_____

4. What technology is appropriate for an office PC that only needs one hard drive and would mainly be used for word processing? Explain your answer.

_____

5. What technology is appropriate for a video editing workstation requiring 200 GB of disk space, a high-speed CD-RW drive, and a DVD drive? Assume that the workstation would play video files directly from the hard drives. Explain your answer.

_____

LAB 8.2 COMPARE SCSI STANDARDS

Objectives

The goal of this lab is to familiarize you with the various SCSI standards. After completing this lab, you will be able to:

➤ Identify key specifications of various SCSI standards

Materials Required

This lab will require the following:

➤ Internet access

Activity Background

SCSI standards are a clear illustration of the principle that every improvement to a particular technology complicates the official standard for that technology. For example, the SCSI-1 standards (introduced in 1986) were relatively straightforward because they were established before refinements to SCSI technology had been introduced. However, SCSI-2 (introduced in 1994) was more complicated, reflecting various improvements to SCSI technology. At this stage, you shouldn't expect to be an expert on everything related to SCSI technology. For that, you'll need to investigate one of the many books devoted to the topic. In this lab you will concentrate instead on the basic differences in SCSI specifications.

Estimated completion time: **30 minutes**

ACTIVITY

1. Use the *A+ Guide to Hardware* and the Web site *www.pcguide.com* to complete the following tables:

SCSI-1

Date introduced	ANSI standard	Bus width	Max # of devices	Max transfer rate

SCSI-2

Version	Date introduced	ANSI standard	Bus width	Max # of devices	Max transfer rate
Fast					
Wide					
Fast/Wide					

SCSI-3

Version	Date published	ANSI standard	Bus width	Max # of devices	Max transfer rate	Cable length	
						Single ended	Differ-ential
Fast							
Wide							
Fast/Wide							

Use the *A+ Guide to Hardware* and the Web site *www.pcguide.com* to answer the following questions:

1. What organization actually researches and develops SCSI standards?

2. What signaling specification is used with Ultra 160 SCSI?

3. What does the symbol in Figure 8-1 mean?

_____

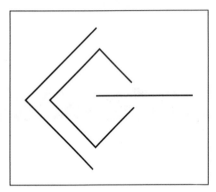

Figure 8-1

Review Questions

1. What does SCSI stand for?

_____

2. Can SCSI devices built to differing standards be used on the same bus? Explain.

_____

3. Define the term "active termination."

_____

4. What are four organizations that govern SCSI standards?

_____

5. What SCSI standard has a max transfer rate of 80 Mbps?

_____

LAB 8.3 INSTALL A HOST ADAPTER AND HARD DRIVE

Objectives

The goal of this lab is to familiarize you with the process of installing SCSI devices. After completing this lab, you will be able to:

➤ Install and configure a SCSI host adapter

➤ Install and configure a SCSI hard drive

Materials Required

➤ Windows 9x or Windows 2000 operating system

➤ SCSI host adapter and documentation

➤ Drivers, cables and terminators

➤ SCSI hard drive and documentation

➤ PC toolkit

➤ Workgroup of 2-4 students

Activity Background

A basic SCSI subsystem consists of one or more SCSI devices attached to a SCSI host adapter. The device can be attached either internally or outside the computer case. Recall that if you have more than one SCSI device on a SCSI subsystem, the devices are daisy-chained together, with a terminator at each end of the end of the chain. In this lab, you will learn how to set up a basic SCSI subsystem.

Estimated completion time: **45 minutes**

ACTIVITY

Follow these steps to install a SCSI host adapter and hard drive:

1. Remove the case cover and determine which expansion slot will be used for the host adapter.

2. Consult the host adapter documentation and then configure the host adapter to SCSI ID 7. Enable any onboard termination.

3. Install the host adapter in the expansion slot and secure it with a screw.

4. Consult the hard drive documentation and set the jumper on the drive to assign the hard drive as SCSI ID 6.

5. Physically install the SCSI hard drive in the case. If you think you might want to add a second SCSI drive later, place the drive in a bay that is next to a vacant bay.

6. Attach one terminator to one end of the cable.

7. Attach the cable to the host adapter using the connector closest to the terminator.

8. Attach the SCSI data cable to the hard drive.

9. Attach the terminator to the connector that is closest to the hard drive. Note that the terminator should not be placed between the drive and host adapter (even if that's where the closest connector happens to be located).

10. Attach a power cable to the hard drive.

11. Use rubber bands or cable ties to secure the ends of the SCSI data cable so that it does not fall into other components.

12. Boot the PC and follow the manufacturer's instructions to install drivers for the SCSI host adapter.

13. When the installation process is complete, reboot the PC.

14. Observe the boot process and notice that before Windows loads, the SCSI host adapter initializes, scans the bus and reports devices found.

15. Partition and format the hard drive using the same methods that you would use to partition and format an EIDE hard drive.

16. Verify that Windows recognizes the drive and that you can read from and write to it.

17. If asked to do so by your instructor, remove the SCSI components.

Review Questions

1. What SCSI ID should be assigned to the host adapter?

_____

2. Why didn't you need to use the CMOS setup to identify the hard drive?

_____

3. In what situation would you need to adjust the CMOS setup to use the newly installed hard drive?

_____

4. Where should terminators not be placed? Why?

_____

5. According to the documentation, how many devices will the host adapter support?

_____

LAB 8.4 INSTALL AN EXTERNAL DRIVE

Objectives

The goal of this lab is to give you experience configuring an external SCSI drive. After completing this lab, you will be able to:

➤ Identify the advantages of an external drive

➤ Install the drive in the external chassis

➤ Connect the drive to the system

Materials Required

This lab will require the following:

➤ Windows 9x or Windows 2000 operating system

➤ External chassis and drive with documentation

➤ Drivers if necessary

➤ External cable and terminator

➤ PC toolkit

➤ Workgroup of 2-4 students

Activity Background

Suppose you need to add a drive to your SCSI-equipped PC, but have no free drive bays in the case. One option is to upgrade the case, which involves totally disassembling and reassembling the PC, not to mention the cost of the case and drive. The simpler and often cheaper option is to install an external SCSI drive. Most commonly this is accomplished by installing an internal SCSI component in an external chassis, which includes its own power supply (thus eliminating the need for the PC's power supply to power the device). In addition to the external chassis and SCSI drive, you will also need an external SCSI cable and a terminator. The combined cost of these components is usually about the same or less than a new case and eliminates the need to totally rebuild the system. Another advantage of using an external drive is that it can be moved to any compatible SCSI system with a minimum of effort. In this lab you will assemble, configure and install an external SCSI drive.

Before you begin, note that the designs of external chassis vary from one manufacturer to the next. Review the documentation for your external chassis, and look for any required steps that are not included here. Be sure to perform those additional steps when assembling your external SCSI drive.

Note that in a real-world situation, you would first have to decide which SCSI standard you wanted to follow. Then you would have to decide which components and adapters (if any) you needed. Then, of course, you would have to purchase the components. This lab assumes that your instructor has selected compatible standards for each component and that you already have the necessary devices on hand.

Estimated completion time: **45 minutes**

ACTIVITY

To install the internal drive in the external chassis, follow these steps (as well as any additional steps specified in your documentation):

1. Determine what SCSI IDs are available on the bus, and if necessary, disable termination on the host adapter so you can use the external connector.

2. Consult the drive documentation and then set the jumper on the new drive to assign the SCSI ID.

3. Open the external chassis and examine the cabling. Decide which cable to attach first and whether to secure the drive in the chassis or attach the cabling first. It is usually best to connect the data cable, followed by the power cable, before securing the drive in the chassis.

4. Install and secure the drive in the chassis.

5. Close and secure the external chassis.

6. Attach the SCSI cable to the chassis.

7. Attach the terminator to the chassis.

   Note that many SCSI devices now have internal termination available. This feature is usually activated and deactivated by a jumper setting. In general, using an actual terminator is considered more reliable than internal termination.

8. Attach the power cable to the chassis and to a power source.

Follow these steps to set up the drive and verify that it is functioning:

1. Switch on power to the external drive assembly.

2. Boot the PC and observe the boot process. Did the host adapter detect the new drive?

_____

3. As necessary, partition and format the new hard drive or follow the manufacturer's instructions to install drivers for the drive.

4. When the drive is fully configured, verify that you can read from and write to the drive.

5. If instructed, remove and disassemble the external assembly.

Review Questions

1. What are some advantages of using an external SCSI drive?

   _____

   _____

2. What should you do before you purchase SCSI components?

   _____

   _____

3. Did you find it easier to connect cabling before securing the drive in the chassis or after securing the drive?

   _____

4. Is it preferable to use internal or external termination?

   _____

5. Does the process of partitioning a SCSI hard drive differ from partitioning an IDE hard drive? Why or why not?

   _____

   _____

   _____

8

LAB 8.5 CRITICAL THINKING: PLAN A SCSI SYSTEM

Objectives

The goal of this lab is to use your knowledge to plan a SCSI-based system. After completing this lab, you will be able to:

➤ Identify and select the best components to meet your performance requirements

➤ Plan the configuration of the system

➤ Estimate the cost of the system

Materials Required

This lab will require the following:

➤ Internet access

Activity Background

Often a customer will give a technician a set of performance requirements and then explain that she wants to upgrade her PC to meet those requirements. The technician then has to design a configuration that meets the requirements and also estimate the cost of the upgrade. You'll practice doing that in this lab.

Estimated completion time: **45 minutes**

ACTIVITY

1. Review the following information about the customer's existing system:
   - Windows 2000 Professional
   - Pentium 4 1.8 GHz with 256 MB Rambus RAM
   - Mini ATX motherboard with AGP, 3 PCI slots, no embedded SCSI adapter
   - Standard 3.5-inch floppy and internal EIDE Zip drive
   - Internal 40 GB EIDE hard drive, DVD-ROM drive, CD-RW drive
   - Mid-tower case with 350 Watt power supply, three 5-inch drive bays and three 3.5-inch drive bays
   - AGP video adapter, PCI MPEG card, and PCI Ethernet NIC
   - USB mouse and Microsoft keyboard

2. Review this list summarizing the customer's upgrade requirements:
   - Two identical 50 GB SCSI hard drives
   - Transfer rate of at least 40 Mbps
   - Compatibility with a SCSI 10 disk array that will eventually be installed in a server room that is 20 feet away

3. Design an upgrade configuration that is compatible with the customer's existing system. Explain your configuration on a separate piece of paper. You may, if necessary, remove one (but only one) component of the existing system. In your design notes, report both the physical and logical configuration, including termination and ID assignments. Also include an estimated cost of parts for the upgrade. Use the *A+ Guide to Hardware* and the Internet for research. Print any documentation that supports your final configuration.

Review Questions

1. How did you determine which SCSI standard to base your upgrade on?

   _____

   _____

   _____

2. Did you decide to remove any existing components? Why or why not?

_____

_____

_____

3. How did you determine if your host adapter was compatible with Windows 2000?

_____

_____

4. How many IRQs would the SCSI system use with a total of one host adapter and three SCSI devices?

_____

5. How many devices will your selected host adapter support?

_____

8

MASS STORAGE AND MULTIMEDIA DEVICES

Labs included in this chapter

➤ Lab 9.1 Install a Sound Card

➤ Lab 9.2 Install a PC Camera

➤ Lab 9.3 Compare CD and DVD Technologies

➤ Lab 9.4 Install Dual Monitors in Windows 9x

➤ Lab 9.5 Research Digital Cameras

➤ Lab 9.6 Explore Windows 98 Audio Features

LAB 9.1 INSTALL A SOUND CARD

Objectives

The goal of this lab is to help you install a sound card. After completing this lab, you will be able to:

➤ Physically install a sound card

➤ Install device drivers

➤ Test the card and adjust the volume

Materials Required

This lab will require the following:

➤ Windows 98 operating system

➤ Windows 98 installation CD or installation files stored in another location as specified by your instructor

➤ Empty expansion slot

➤ Compatible sound card with speakers or head phones

➤ Sound card device drivers (on an installation floppy disk, CD, or stored in other location as specified by your instructor)

➤ PC toolkit

Activity Background

One of the most popular multimedia devices is the sound card. A sound card enables a computer to receive sound input and to output sound such as when playing a music CD. As an A+ computer technician you will need to know how to install a sound card, either when you are putting together a computer from scratch or when you are upgrading components on an existing system. In this lab, you will install, configure, and test a sound card.

Estimated completion time: **45 minutes**

ACTIVITY

Follow these steps to physically install a sound card:

1. Disconnect all external cables from the case.

2. Remove the case cover.

3. Locate an empty expansion slot that you can use for the sound card. On some systems, expansion cards are attached to a riser card, which you might have to remove at this time. If necessary, remove the expansion slot faceplate on the case so that the sound card will fit into the expansion slot.

4. Insert the sound card into the expansion slot on the motherboard (or insert the sound card into the riser card and the riser card into the motherboard). Line up the sound card on the slot and press it straight down, making sure that the tab on the backplate (the metal plate on the rear of the card where sound ports are located) fits into the slot on the case. It normally requires a little effort to seat the card, but do not force it. If the card does not insert with just a little effort, something is preventing the card from seating. Check for obstructions and try again, removing components that are in the way if necessary.

5. Once the card is installed, secure it with a screw. The screw goes through a hole in the card's backplate, securing the backplate to the case.

6. Attach any cable required to carry an audio signal from other multimedia devices, such as a CD-ROM drive.

7. Replace any components that you removed while installing the sound card, and replace and secure the cover on the case.

8. Reattach all cables from external devices to the appropriate ports. Attach speakers or headphones. (Some speakers receive power from the computer, and others have to be plugged into an external power source such as a wall outlet.)

9

Next, you will configure the drivers and other software for your sound card. If you have the documentation for your sound card, follow the exact instructions given in the documentation. Otherwise, follow these general steps to install software for most sound cards, keeping in mind that your sound card might require a slightly different procedure.

1. Start the computer, and if necessary, log on. Windows displays a Found New Hardware window and attempts to determine what type of new hardware is present.

2. The Add New Hardware Wizard launches, displaying the name of the device it found, and indicating that it will search for drivers for the device. In this case, the new device is the sound card you just installed. The wizard might refer to the sound card as a PCI Multimedia Audio Device or something similar. Click **Next** to continue.

3. The Add New Hardware Wizard displays a message asking how you want to install the software. Click the **Search for the best driver for your device (Recommended)** option button, and click **Next** to continue.

4. The Add New Hardware Wizard displays a message asking where the drivers for the new device are located. Insert the floppy disk or CD containing the drivers and select the appropriate check box to indicate the location of the drivers. (If the CD Autorun program launches when you insert the CD, close the application.) Click **Next** to continue.

5. If the Add New Hardware Wizard is able to locate the correct driver, it displays a message identifying the sound card model name, driver location, and driver file name. Click **Next** to continue and then skip to Step 7. If the wizard reports that it is unable to find the drivers, proceed to Step 6.

6. If the Add New Hardware Wizard reports that it was unable to locate the drivers, click **Back** and repeat Step 4, but this time select the **Specify Location** option and then click **Browse**. This opens the Browse for a Folder window. Browse to the location of the setup files, expanding folders as necessary, and look for a folder named Win98, Win9x, or similar. After you select the correct folder, click the **OK** button to close the Browse for Folder window, and then click **Next** in the Add New Hardware Wizard. If the wizard finds the driver, continue to Step 7; otherwise, consult the documentation for the correct installation procedure.

7. After locating and installing the drivers, the Add New Hardware Wizard displays a message notifying you that the installation of the device is complete. Click **Finish** to close the Add New Hardware Wizard. At some point during the process, you may be required to supply the Windows 98 installation CD or the location of installation files.

8. After the sound card is completely installed, Windows may detect additional devices. Sound cards sometimes include embedded features such as MIDI Wave Audio, SB16 Emulation, Game Port, etc. The Add New Hardware Wizard will launch as necessary to install each of these devices separately. Follow the preceding steps to install each device.

9. When Windows finishes installing software, the Updating Settings dialog box appears. After the settings are updated, the Updating Settings dialog box closes, and the Windows desktop appears. You should hear the Microsoft sound (the default sound played on startup).

Follow these steps to test the sound card and customize Windows sound settings. You will start by adjusting the volume.

1. On the right side of the task bar, you should see the speaker volume setting represented by a speaker icon. Click the speaker icon. A pop-up window opens where you can adjust speaker volume.

2. Drag the volume slider all the way to the top, and then click on the desktop. The pop-up window closes.

3. Double-click the speaker icon. The Volume Control dialog box opens. Note that this dialog box gives you more control than the pop-up window you used in Step 2. Among other things, it allows you to adjust the volume of various inputs including the master volume which controls the actual volume of the signal fed to the speakers. List the various volume controls from left to right and identify two settings (other than volume) that can be changed here.

_____

_____

_____

_____

_____

4. Set the master volume slider (the one on the far left) to half volume and close the Volume Control window.

Follow these steps to control what sounds will play for certain Windows events:

1. Open the Control Panel, and double-click the **Sounds** icon. The Sounds Properties dialog box opens. Scroll down the Events list box, and note that a speaker icon next to an event indicates that a specific sound will play when that event occurs. Complete Table 9–1 by clicking each event listed in the table and noting the sound associated with that event. (The name of the sound file associated with the selected event appears in the Name list box.) Also note that not all Windows events are assigned a sound.

Table 9-1

Event	Sound Name
Start Windows	
Empty Recycle Bin	
Critical Stop	

2. In the Event list box, click **Empty Recycle Bin** and then click the **Play** button to the right of the Preview pane. The recycle sound plays.

3. Use the Name list arrow to select and play several different sounds until you find one that you like better than the recycle sound. Click **Save As** in the Schemes section, type **Custom**, and then click **OK**. What sound did you choose?

_____

4. Click **OK** to apply and save the revised Sounds Properties. Next, you will test the new sound by emptying the Recycle Bin.

5. Right-click the **Recycle Bin** on the desktop, and then click **Empty Recycle Bin** in the shortcut menu. Note that if there are no files in the Recycle Bin, this option is unavailable.

6. Using the Sounds applet in Control Panel, change the sound that plays when Windows starts. What sound did you use?

_____

7. Restart Windows and listen to the new sound.

8. After you have verified that the sound plays, repeat the process and return the sound to the original settings.

Review Questions

1. What Windows feature walks you through the process of installing drivers for a new device?

   _____

2. Other than driver files included with the sound card, what other software might be requested by Windows when configuring a new sound card?

   _____

3. What other devices embedded on the sound card might Windows detect after the sound card installation is finished?

   _____

   _____

4. How does Windows handle the installation of these additional devices?

   _____

   _____

5. What Control Panel applet allows you to test the sound card by playing sounds for Windows events?

   _____

   _____

LAB 9.2 INSTALL A PC CAMERA

Objectives

The goal of this lab is to help you complete the process of installing and testing a PC camera. After completing this lab, you will be able to:

➤ Install a PC camera

➤ Install NetMeeting

➤ Configure NetMeeting to test your PC camera

Materials Required

This lab will require the following:

➤ Windows 98 operating system

➤ Windows 98 installation CD or installation files stored in another location as specified by your instructor

> ➤ PC camera compatible with your system

> ➤ Device drivers for the camera

> ➤ Sound card, speakers and microphone (optional)

> ➤ Internet access (optional)

Activity Background

PC cameras are becoming increasingly popular. Using these cameras, you can set up a video conference, record or send video images to your family and friends, and monitor your house over the Internet. You can even detach some PC cameras and use them to take still pictures while away from your system, uploading them to the computer when you return. Most PC cameras install via the USB port, making physical installation a relatively simple process. In this lab, you will install, configure, and test a basic PC camera.

Estimated completion time: **45 minutes**

ACTIVITY

Follow these steps to install a PC camera:

1. Start the computer and log on if necessary.

2. Insert the PC camera's installation CD or floppy disk. (If the CD Autorun program launches, close it).

3. Locate an unused USB port. Insert the PC camera's cable into the USB port. (Do not force it; if the cable does not insert easily, flip the connector over, and try again; it should insert easily.)

4. Windows detects the new USB device and the Found New Hardware window opens, informing you that a USB device has been detected. A second window opens, informing you that Windows is forming a New Driver Database; when the new database is finished, the second window closes. The Found New Hardware window closes as well. (If Windows does not detect the camera, check the Device Manager or BIOS settings to discover whether the USB controller has problems or has been disabled. If necessary, enable the USB controller in Device Manager and CMOS setup and begin again with Step 1.)

5. The Add New Hardware Wizard opens and indicates that it will begin searching for drivers for a USB device. Click **Next** to continue.

6. The Add New Hardware Wizard asks if you want to specify a driver or search for the best driver. Click the **Search for the Best Driver for Your Device (Recommended)** option button and click **Next** to continue.

7. Locate the installation files as you learned how to do in Lab 9.1 and click **Next**.

8. The wizard indicates that it has found the driver for the PC camera and displays the driver's location and file name. Click **Next** to continue.

9. The wizard copies all necessary files and then displays a message indicating that the installation is complete. Click **Finish** to close the wizard. Many PC cameras have built-in microphones as well as other devices. If this is the case, the wizard may launch again for each device. It is also possible that during any installation, the wizard will prompt you to provide the location of Windows 98 installation files.

Now you will use NetMeeting to test your camera. NetMeeting is video conferencing software included with Windows 98. To perform a full video conference with two or more people, can use a directory service, an online database that NetMeeting uses to locate participants in a NetMeeting conference. One such directory service is Microsoft Internet Directory. When you install NetMeeting, you are asked to enter information about yourself, and are then given the opportunity to be added to the Microsoft Internet Directory. The following steps tell you to use the Microsoft Internet Directory, although your instructor might ask you to use a different directory service. Follow these steps to install NetMeeting if it is not already installed:

1. Open the Control Panel, open the **Add/Remove Programs** applet and then click the **Windows Setup** tab. Windows searches for Windows Components.

2. Double-click the **Communications** group in the Components list box. The Communications dialog box opens.

3. Scroll down the Components list box, select the **Microsoft NetMeeting** checkbox, and then click **OK**. The Communications dialog box closes.

4. Click **OK** to close the Add/Remove Properties dialog box. The Copying Files dialog box appears, indicating that the copying process has begun. If prompted, supply the location of Windows 98 installation files. When the files are copied, the Copying Files dialog box closes. Reboot your PC if prompted to do so.

Now you will launch NetMeeting and configure it. Follow these steps:

1. Click **Start** on the task bar, point to **Programs**, and then look for Microsoft NetMeeting on one of the submenus. You might find it located under Internet Explorer, or under Accessories\Communications.

2. Click **Microsoft NetMeeting**.

3. Microsoft NetMeeting begins configuring your connection. Click **Next** to continue.

4. In the NetMeeting dialog box shown in Figure 9-1, **accept** Microsoft Internet Directory as the server name (unless your instructor gives you different directions) and then click **Next**.

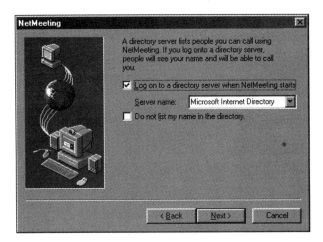

Figure 9-1   By default, installing NetMeeting adds you to the Microsoft Internet Directory

5. Supply the requested identification information, including your name and e-mail address and then click **Next** to continue. (Keep in mind that your identification information will be available to other NetMeeting users on the directory server.)

6. What you see on the next screen depends on the version of NetMeeting installed. You might see a screen asking you what category to use for your personal info (personal use for all ages, business use for all ages or adults-only use). Select a category and click **Next**. For some versions of NetMeeting, the screen will give you the option of selecting a directory server. In this case, the default is Microsoft Internet Directory. Leave the default selected and click **Next**.

7. On the next screen, you are asked to specify your connection speed. Select **Local Area Network** (or other speed as specified by your instructor) and then click **Next** to continue.

8. You are asked to specify your video capturing device. Select your camera from the drop-down menu, if it is not already selected, and then click **Next** to continue.

9. NetMeeting informs you that it will help tune your audio settings. Click **Next** to continue.

10. Set and test your audio settings. When they are satisfactory, click **Next** to continue.

11. When the installation is complete, click **Finish**. NetMeeting launches.

12. Click **Current Call** and then click the **Play** button in the My Video frame. You should be able to see video supplied by your PC camera in the My Video screen. This demonstrates that your video camera was installed correctly.

CRITICAL THINKING (additional 20 minutes)

If others in the lab are connected to NetMeeting and you have access to a sound card, speakers, and microphone, join someone else in a video conference. To make the connection, you can use an IP address of another computer on the LAN, instead of using a directory server. To use Windows 98 to determine the IP address of a workstation: Enter Winipcfg in the Run dialog box and then select the network adapter from the drop-down list. Figure 9-2 shows a full NetMeeting video conference complete with shared whiteboard, chat window and video.

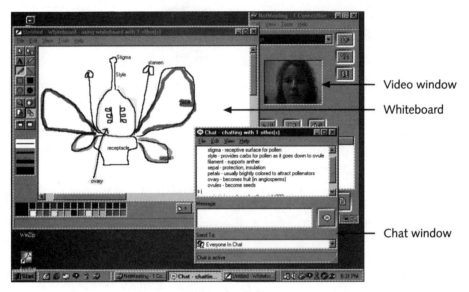

Video window
Whiteboard
Chat window

Figure 9-2   NetMeeting provides three windows during a session

Review Questions

1. Typically, via what type of port do PC cameras attach to a system?

_____

2. What type of audio device may be embedded in a PC camera?

_____

_____

3. Do you have to power down the system before connecting a USB camera? Why or why not?

_____

_____

4. What should you do if Windows fails to detect a USB device?

_____

_____

_____

5. What application can you use to test the video supplied by your PC camera?

_____

_____

LAB 9.3 COMPARE CD AND DVD TECHNOLOGIES

9

Objectives

The goal of this lab is to help you use the Internet to research CD and DVD standards. After completing this lab, you will be able to:

➤ Recognize CD and DVD specifications

Materials Required

This lab will require the following:

➤ Internet access

Activity Background

Many multimedia PCs include CD or DVD drives (and sometimes both). These drives may be of three types: read-only (ROM), write/record (R) and write/record and re-write (RW or RAM). (The last two types can only write and record to specialized disks.) You will research the features and limitations of CD and DVD standards in this lab.

Estimated completion time: **60 minutes**

ACTIVITY

Use the Internet and your favorite search sites such as Google (*www.google.com*) or Yahoo! (*www.yahoo.com*) to answer the following questions on CD standards. Print the source page or pages supporting your answers.

1. What is the maximum storage capacity of a CD?

_____

2. Briefly, how is information recorded on a CD–ROM disk?

_____

_____

3. Are CDs capable of storing data on both sides of the disk?

_____

4. What type or color of laser is used in a CD drive?

_____

5. What is a limitation of a CD–R drive that is not an issue with a CD–RW drive?

_____

_____

6. What kind of problems might occur if you tried to use an older CD–ROM drive or a CD player to play a CD–R or a CD–RW disk?

_____

_____

7. Define "constant angular velocity" and explain how it applies to CD standards.

_____

_____

8. Define "constant linear velocity" and explain how it applies to CD standards.

_____

_____

9. What term is used to refer to the process of writing data to a disk?

_____

10. Can any CD hold video data? Explain.

_____

11. On a CD disk, is data written in concentric circles or in a continuous spiral track?

_____

12. What are three common standards CD drives used to interface with a system?

_____

13. What does the X factor of a drive indicate? What is the specification of one X?

_____

_____

14. Briefly describe how a CD-RW writes data to a disk and how it is able to re-write data.

_____

_____

_____

_____

_____

15. How much would you pay for a package of CD-R disks? How much for a package of CD-RW disks? How many disks are in a package of each type?

_____

Use the Internet and your favorite search sites to answer the following questions on DVD standards. Print the source page or pages to support your answers.

1. What is the maximum storage capacity of a DVD disk?

_____

2. What two characteristics give a DVD disk more storage capacity than a CD disk?

_____

_____

_____

3. Describe the difference between DVD-R and DVD-RAM.

_____

_____

_____

_____

4. Explain how DVD audio and CD audio differ.

_____

_____

_____

5. How many CD's worth of data can a single DVD hold?

_____

6. How many layers of data can be stored on one side of a DVD?

_____

7. How many data areas are on a single side of a DVD-R?

_____

8. List the versions and maximum capacities of DVD-RAM.

_____

_____

9. Can DVDs be used in CD devices? Explain.

_____

10. Explain the use of the UDF file system and how it applies to a DVD.

_____

_____

_____

_____

_____

Review Questions

1. What factors give a DVD greater storage capacity than a CD?

2. What factors, other than storage capacity, would you consider when choosing between a DVD drive and a CD drive?

3. What characteristics do DVD and CD drives share?

9

4. If you wanted to create a disk that would never need to be altered and could be used on the maximum number of systems, what type of disk would you use and why?

5. Why do you think motion pictures are released on DVDs instead of CDs?

LAB 9.4 INSTALL DUAL MONITORS IN WINDOWS 9x

Objectives

The goal of this lab is to help you set up a second monitor on a system. After completing this lab, you will be able to:

➤ Install a display adapter and its drivers

➤ Attach a second monitor

➤ Configure the system to use both monitors at the same time

Materials Required

This lab will require the following:

➤ Windows 9x operating system

➤ PC toolkit

➤ Second display adapter with drivers

➤ Second monitor

Activity Background

It is often quite handy to have two monitors on a system. For instance, if you have a second monitor, you can have a Web browser maximized on one and a video editing application maximized on the other. This has the effect of making your desktop larger and making it easier to work with multiple applications simultaneously, which is often very useful when developing multimedia presentations. In this lab, you will install and configure a second monitor on a computer.

```
Estimated completion time: 45 minutes
```

ACTIVITY

It is important to verify that the original hardware is working properly before you try to add a second display adapter and monitor. That way, if a problem arises after you install new hardware, you can be pretty sure that something is amiss with the newly added components rather than with the original equipment.

Follow these steps to physically install the second display adapter:

1. Check to make sure that the original display adapter uses the PCI or AGP standard, and decide whether it will be the primary or secondary monitor.

2. Install the second adapter card in the PCI slot nearest to the AGP slot (if the original is an AGP adapter) or in the PCI slot immediately next to the original PCI adapter (if the original is a PCI adapter). If you need additional guidance on installing a card, refer to Lab 9.1.

3. Attach the second monitor to the port on the back of the display adapter.

4. Boot your PC and enter CMOS setup. If your setup has the display settings for dual monitors, adjust them so that the primary display adapter is initialized first. For a system with an AGP slot, make sure the AGP adapter is selected as your primary adapter and the PCI adapter as the secondary adapter. For a system that uses two PCI adapters, it does not matter which adapter is the primary one; you can leave the setting as is. For additional guidance on adjusting BIOS settings refer to Lab 4.1. Exit CMOS setup and wait for your system to reboot.

Follow these steps to install device drivers and adjust Windows display settings:

1. When the system reboots, Windows recognizes the new adapter and may prompt you for the location of the drivers. The Found New Hardware wizard launches. Complete the steps in the wizard to install the adapter. When installation is complete, reboot. Refer to Lab 9.1 if you need additional information on using the wizard.

2. Windows starts and the original monitor displays the messages related to the boot process. At this time a message will appear on the new monitor indicating that if you can see the message, installation was successful. The message also tells you to use the second screen to adjust display properties.

3. The system might recognize the monitor connected to the second adapter and attempt to install the monitor even though it has already installed the adapter. (If the monitor is Plug and Play, this will definitely be the case.) If your system does recognize the monitor, follow the directions on screen to install the monitor.

Before you use a second monitor, you must activate it. You'll activate your second monitor in the following steps:

1. With the desktop active, open the Control Panel and double-click the **Display** icon. The Display Properties dialog box appears, similar to the lower window showing in Figure 9-3.

2. Click on the image of the monitor with the number 2 in it, or select the correct adapter from the Display list box.

3. When prompted, click **Yes** to enable the monitor.

4. Adjust the resolution and color settings to your preference, and then select the **Extend My Windows Desktop Onto This Monitor** check box.

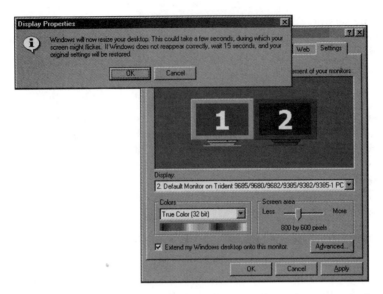

Figure 9-3   You must choose to activate a second monitor before it can be used
by Windows

5. Click **Apply** to apply the settings.

6. If you are asked if you want to restart your computer, choose to apply the settings without restarting. A message (similar to the one at the top of Figure 9-3)
appears warning that your screen may flicker and that if the settings render the
display unreadable then the original settings will be restored in 15 seconds.
Click **OK** to apply the settings.

7. If you are satisfied with the new settings, click **Yes** to keep the settings. If you
are not happy with the settings continue adjusting them until you are. You
must apply the new settings each time. Note that each display adapter's settings
must be saved and applied individually. Up to nine separate adapters can be
added to a single system.

Follow these steps to test your dual-monitor configuration:

1. Open Paint, and then drag and drop it to the second monitor. Does your desktop extend to the second monitor as expected?

_____

2. Open Windows Explorer and maximize it on the original monitor. Can you
see your mouse move as expected from one monitor to the next? Does the
mouse interact with applications on each monitor?

_____

3. Close Paint and Windows Explorer and open Device Manager.

Follow these steps to remove the second adapter and return to a single monitor configuration:

1. Open Device Manager, find the second display adapter and highlight it. (Make sure you are looking at the second adapter and not the first!)

2. Click **Remove.** If prompted, verify that you do wish to remove the device, and when asked if you want to restart the computer, click **No**.

3. Shut down the computer. Do not restart the computer at this time.

4. Remove the secondary monitor and adapter card. If necessary, reverse any BIOS changes you made that affect the display initialization sequence, and reboot the system to verify that the adapter card is no longer recognized by the system.

Review Questions

1. Before installing a second monitor, why is it important to know if your existing configuration is working properly?

_____

2. Why might it be necessary to change the sequence in which the system initializes display adapters?

_____

_____

3. In Display Properties, what is one way to select the monitor you wish to adjust?

_____

4. How many display adapters can be installed on a single system?

_____

5. Does adjusting the settings of one monitor affect the settings of the other?

_____

9

LAB 9.5 RESEARCH DIGITAL CAMERAS

Objectives

The goal of this lab is to help you research digital cameras and learn how you might integrate them with a multimedia PC. In this lab, you will research:

➤ Camera picture quality and compatibility

➤ Camera storage technology

➤ Methods of transferring images to a PC

Materials Required

This lab will require the following:

➤ Internet access

Activity Background

As digital cameras have become more common and popular, they have also become more refined. Their special features, image quality, methods of file storage, and methods of transferring image data to the PC have improved over earlier models. Also, the prices of digital cameras have decreased significantly. In this lab, you will research digital cameras and learn how they are used with multimedia PCs.

Estimated completion time: **60 minutes**

ACTIVITY

Research digital photography on the Internet. Try searching for "digital camera" or "digital photography" on your favorite search engine. Sites that might be useful include:

➤ *www.cnet.com* by CNET Networks, Inc.

➤ *www.dpreview.com* by Digital Photography Review

➤ *www.shutterline.com* by Shutterline

➤ *www.keyworlds.com/d/digital_photography.htm* by KeyWorlds.com

Answer these questions about general camera topics. Print the Web page or pages supporting your answer.

1. How is image quality measured? Will all digital cameras produce the same image quality?

_____

_____

2. What are three storage technologies that digital cameras might use to store images in a camera?

_____

_____

_____

3. Name four technologies a camera might use to transfer images to a PC. What requirements must a PC meet for each?

_____

_____

_____

_____

4. Name and print information about at least two digital cameras that offer features such as changeable lenses, manual focus, aperture settings (F stops), and shutter speed settings (exposure).

_____

_____

Answer these questions regarding basic image characteristics.

1. What three file types might a digital camera use to store images?

_____

2. Name three factors that affect the number of images that a camera can store on a single storage device.

_____

_____

_____

3. Do most digital cameras offer the ability to control image quality? Explain.

_____

4. Can you remove an image that you do not like from a camera without transferring the image to a PC? Explain.

_____

5. What are three means of obtaining an actual printed photo of an image taken by a digital camera?

_____

_____

_____

6. Will any digital cameras record images other than still shots?

_____

Answer these questions about how cameras transfer images to a PC.

1. Which means of transfer offers the highest transfer speed and what is that speed?

_____

_____

2. Which means of transfer requires the least specialized hardware on the PC?

_____

3. Which storage technologies allow the direct transfers of images by removing the storage device from the camera and inserting it in the PC?

_____

_____

4. What devices can be added to a PC to allow them to directly read flash memory cards?

_____

_____

_____

_____

5. What means of image transfer does not require you to remove a device from the camera or use cabling to the PC?

_____

6. Does image resolution have any effect on transfer speed?

_____

_____

_____

_____

Review Questions

1. What are three advantages of a digital camera over a 35mm camera?

_____

_____

_____

2. What are some disadvantages of a digital camera as compared to a 35mm camera?

_____

_____

3. What are some features that you would like on a digital camera if you were to buy one? Explain your choices.

_____

_____

_____

4. What could be done to maximize the number of images stored on the camera without modifying the storage device capacity?

_____

_____

_____

5. Typically, would a 3.1 mega-pixel camera have a superior or inferior picture quality as compared to a 4.9 mega-pixel camera?

LAB 9.6 EXPLORE WINDOWS 98 AUDIO FEATURES

Objectives

The goal of this lab is to let you experiment with different audio features and capabilities of Windows 98. After completing this lab, you will be able to:

➤ Identify audio media types

➤ Download and install Nullsoft Winamp, a third-party sound software application

➤ Control audio CD playback with Windows CD Player and Realplayer

➤ Customize sounds that Windows plays for events

Materials Required

This lab will require the following:

➤ Windows 98 operating system

➤ Windows 98 CD or installation files

➤ Internet access

➤ CD-ROM drive and an audio CD

Activity Background

Windows 98 provides various features that let the user experience and use audio files in different ways. Various Windows events may be configured to play a certain sound when the event occurs. These features can be used simply to make using Windows more enjoyable to the average user, but to a sight-impaired user they can be vital tools.

Windows 98 provides Windows CD Player and Windows Media Player to provide a means to experience audio CDs as well as other multimedia types. In this lab you will experiment with Windows audio capabilities and use Nullsoft's Winamp, a third-party sound software application.

Estimated completion time: **60 minutes**

ACTIVITY

Follow these steps to adjust the Windows volume level:

1. On the right side of the task bar, you should see the Windows volume represented by a speaker symbol. Click once on the speaker symbol. This opens the Volume Control pop-up window.

2. Drag the volume slider all the way to the top, and click on the desktop. The Volume Control dialog box disappears.

3. Double-click on the speaker symbol. This opens the Volume Control window. Note that this window lets you adjust the volume of various inputs independent of and including the master volume. The number of volume controls offered here depend on the capabilities of your sound card. List the various volume controls from left to right and identify two settings (other than volume sliders) that can be made here.

_____

_____

_____

_____

_____

4. Set the "master" volume slider (the one on the far left) to half volume and close the Volume Control window.

Follow these steps to customize Windows sound settings:

1. From the Control Panel, double-click the **Sounds** icon to open the Sounds Properties dialog box. Scroll down the Events field, and note that each event for the speaker symbol has a sound assigned to play when the event occurs.

2. Click **Start Windows** in the Event field, and then click the **Play** button to the right of the Preview field. The Microsoft sound plays. If you do not hear the sound, check your volume levels and make sure that the volume is not muted.

3. From the drop-down menu of the Name field, select and play several different sounds until you find one that you like better than the Microsoft sound. Click **Save As** in the Schemes section, type **Custom**, and click **OK** to save the new settings. (You could also apply the Windows Default scheme by selecting it from the Schemes drop-down menu.)

9

4. Click **OK** to apply and save Sound Properties. Restart Windows to hear the new sound.

5. Using procedures learned in earlier labs, open the Add/Remove Programs applet from the Control Panel, and then add Multimedia Sound Schemes under the Multimedia group. Open the Sounds Properties window again and list the Schemes added.

_____

_____

_____

Follow these steps to play an audio CD with Windows CD player:

1. Insert the audio disk in the CD-ROM drive. Windows CD Player should launch (in a minimized window) and automatically begin playing the CD. Adjust the volume so it is not distracting to others.

2. On the task bar, double-click the **Windows CD Player** button to restore the Windows CD Player window.

3. From the CD Player menu bar, click **View** and then click **Toolbar**. This adds the Toolbar to the CD Player dialog box.

4. Take and print a screenshot of the CD player dialog box. Explore the CD Player and label the screenshot to define what each display component and each button does. Answer these questions about the CD Player.

   ■ What opens when you select View and Volume Control from the menu bar?

   _____

   ■ How are the controls of the Windows CD Player similar to an actual CD player? How are they different?

   _____

   _____

Follow these steps to install Winamp and use it to play the audio CD:

1. In your Web browser, go to the Nullsoft Winamp Web site at *www.winamp.com*. Follow the Download link and download the Standard version of Winamp. (This file will be named winamp278_std.exe or something similar.)

2. In Windows Explorer find your download location and double-click **winamp278_std.exe** to launch Winamp Setup and begin the installation process. The Winamp Setup process is very similar to other installation wizards you have previously completed. Work through the installation using default settings for everything. If you do not wish to receive email from Nullsoft,

select the **Stop Bugging Me** check box if it appears on the information screen for Winamp Setup. When prompted, click **Run Winamp** to launch Winamp Lite, which will download additional information in the Winamp Browser.

3. Close Winamp and the Winamp browser. Remove the audio CD and then insert the Audio CD again. Winamp will automatically launch again and begin playing your audio CD.

4. Experiment with Winamp to answer these questions:

   ■ Does Winamp have the same basic features as Windows CD Player?

   _____

   ■ What feature does Winamp provide that allows you to customize the sound tone?

   _____

   ■ Name three popular music file types that Winamp supports.

   _____

   ■ Could you set up a play list that would play all the files on your CD in an order that you chose, instead of first to last? Explain your answer.

   _____

   _____

   _____

9

Review Questions

1. What icon do you single click to access the Windows volume control?

   _____

2. Will Windows CD Player support streaming audio or MP3?

   _____

3. Besides CD Player, what other player does Microsoft offer for playing audio CDs and other multimedia files?

   _____

   _____

4. Which player provided more features, and which was easier to use? Explain your answers.

_____

_____

_____

_____

5. How can you lower the volume of CD playback while keeping the Windows event sounds volume the same?

_____

_____

CHAPTER TEN

SUPPORTING MODEMS

Labs included in this chapter

➤ Lab 10.1 Simulate Serial Port Communication

➤ Lab 10.2 Install and Test a Modem

➤ Lab 10.3 Use AT Commands to Control a Modem

➤ Lab 10.4 Simulate Modem Problems

 ➤ Lab 10.5 Critical Thinking: Use Two Modems to Create a Multilink Connection

LAB 10.1 SIMULATE SERIAL PORT COMMUNICATION

Objectives

The goal of this lab is to illustrate serial communication using a game. After completing this lab, you will be able to:

➤ Identify pin arrangements

➤ Explain which pins are used for handshake and data transfer

Materials Required

This lab will require the following:

➤ Eight pieces of string, each approximately four feet long

➤ Workgroup of eight students

Activity Background

RS-232 standards specify cabling and communication methods for the PC. Among other things, they specify the sequence of signals that must travel across a serial cable in order to complete a handshake and transmit data between devices. In this lab, to keep things simple, you will simulate a handshake and data transfer on a null modem cable. You and your fellow students will play the part of the serial ports, using pieces of string for the cable.

Estimated completion time: **30 minutes**

ACTIVITY

Follow these steps to simulate a cable connection between two devices:

1. Position eight students in two rows facing each other, with four on each side. Designate the students on one side as Students A through D. Designate the students on the other side as Students E through H. Students E and A should be facing each other, as should Students B and F, and so on down the line. The two groups of students make up Computer ABCD and Computer EFGH.

2. Stretch seven strings between the eight students as shown in Figure 10-1. Student A's left hand and Student E's right hand are Pin 1 on their respective serial ports. The numbers should proceed down the line until Pin 8 is Student D's right hand and Student H's left hand. Table 10-1 describes the null modem cable communication you are simulating. Notice that Pins 1 and 9 are not used in a null modem cable communication and are therefore omitted from this simulation.

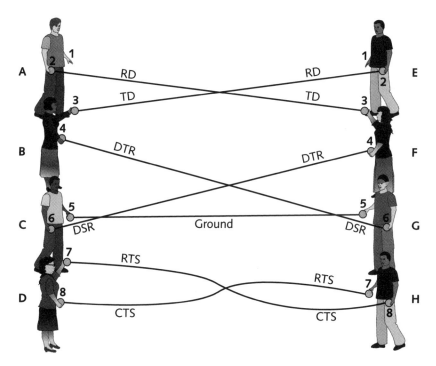

Figure 10-1   Simulating null modem cable communication

Table 10-1   Pin connections for a 9-pin null modem cable

Pin number on one connection	Pin number of the other connector	How the wire connecting the two pins is used
1	1	Not used
2 (RD)	3 (TD)	Data sent by one computer is received by the other
3 (TD)	2 (RD)	Data received by one computer is sent by the other
4 (DTR)	6 (DSR)	One end says to the other end, "I'm able to talk"
5 (Ground)	5 (Ground)	Both ends are grounded
6 (DSR)	4 (DTR)	One end hears the other end say, "I'm able to talk"
7 (RTS)	8 (CTS)	One end says to the other, "I'm ready to talk"
8 (CTS)	7 (RTS)	One end hears the other say, "I'm ready to talk"
9	9	Not used

Follow these steps to perform the handshake and then to send and receive data. Suppose that Computer EFGH has initiated communication to Computer ABCD, and that Computer ABCD is ready to receive data from Computer EFGH.

10

1. Student G raises his left hand indicating that he is able to talk (DSR high).

2. Student B raises his hand on the other end of the same string to indicate that he has received Student G's communication.

3. Student C raises his right hand, indicating he understands that Computer EFGH is able to talk (DTR high).

4. Student F raises his left hand indicating he has received the communication.

5. Student H raises his right hand indicating he is ready to talk (RTS high).

6. Student D raises his hand indicating he has received the communication.

7. Student D raises his left hand indicating he is ready to receive data from Computer EFGH.

8. Student H raises his hand indicating he has received the communication.

Computer ABCD has just indicated that it is able and ready to have a conversation. (As you'll recall, DTR indicates that Computer ABCD is open to having a conversation, and RTS tells Computer EFGH to go ahead and start talking.) Computer EFGH is now ready to start talking to Computer ABCD.

9. Student F repeatedly raises and lowers his hand—which represents the TD (TXD) pin—to indicate that data is being sent. (Each raise of the hand represents one bit transmitted.)

10. Student A sees this signal and repeatedly raises and lowers his right hand—which represents the RD (RXD) pin—to indicate the reception of each bit.

Now suppose that computer EFGH has been transmitting for a while and Computer ABCD has noticed that its buffer is getting full. (That is, it has to process what Computer EFGH has said.) This ability of the receiving computer to stop transmission so it can catch up is called flow control.

11. Student D lowers his left hand (RTS) to indicate that Computer ABCD is processing and doesn't want to hear any more right now.

12. Student H quits receiving CTS high and lowers his hand to indicate he has received the communication.

13. Other students keep their hands raised, indicating that the conversation is still not yet over.

14. Student F quits sending data and keeps his hand down.

At this point, computer EFGH has quit talking, but has not yet finished sending all the data. After a pause, computer ABCD finishes processing and the buffer is empty. Computer ABCD is now ready to listen again.

15. Student D raises his hand, raising RTS high.

16. Student H raises his hand, indicating CTS high. In response, Student F starts sending data again until all data is sent.

17. Students H and G lower their hands indicating that Computer EFGH has nothing more to say and wants to end the conversation.

18. All students then lower their hands in response to Students H and G. The conversation is ended.

    Now that you have seen how Computer EFGH sends data to Computer ABCD, answer the following questions regarding communication from Computer ABCD to Computer EFGH.

    ■ Which hands should be raised to indicate that Computer EFGH is able to communicate with Computer ABCD?

    _____

    ■ Which hands should raise to indicate that Computer EFGH is ready to receive data?

    _____

    ■ Which hands should raise to indicate data flowing from Computer ABCD to Computer EFGH?

    _____

    ■ Which hands should be lowered when Computer EFGH's buffers are full?

    _____

    ■ Which hands should be lowered when the communication is finished?

    _____

19. Now raise and lower your hands to simulate communication from Computer ABCD to Computer EFGH.

Review Questions

1. Pins 1 and 9 are not used for communication via a null modem cable. How are they used by a modem?

    _____

    _____

2. What is indicated by a signal raised on Pin 8?

    _____

3. Pin 4 on one end of the cable is connected to Pin _____ on the other end of the cable.

4. Data passes from Pin _____ on one end of the cable to Pin _____ on the other end of the cable.

5. What is the sole purpose of Pin 5's participation in the network communication?

_____

LAB 10.2 INSTALL AND TEST A MODEM

Objectives

The goal of this lab is to help you install and test a modem. After completing this lab, you will be able to:

➤ Physically install a modem

➤ Test the modem using Modem Properties

Materials Required

This lab will require the following:

➤ Windows 98 operating system

➤ Windows 98 installation CD or installation files stored in another location

➤ Modem with drivers

➤ PC toolkit

Activity Background

Most users dial in to their ISP using a modem and Plain Old Telephone Service (POTS). Such dial-up connections can be unreliable, for several reasons. So as an A+ technician, you need to be prepared to install modems and troubleshoot modem connections. In this lab, you will install a modem and then run some simple diagnostics to test the modem.

Estimated completion time: **30 minutes**

ACTIVITY

Follow these steps to install a modem:

1. Remove all cables from the case and remove the case cover.

2. Locate the expansion slot that you will use to install the modem and then remove the slot's cover.

3. Install and secure the modem card.

4. Replace the case cover and reattach all cables including the telephone cable to the Line-In port on the back of the modem card.

5. Boot the computer and log on, if necessary. The Found New Hardware Wizard launches, and informs you that it is ready to search for drivers. Click **Next** to continue.

6. The wizard asks how you want to locate the drivers. Select the **Search for the Best Driver for Your Device (Recommended)** option button and click **Next** to continue.

7. The wizard asks you to specify a location for the drivers. Insert the floppy disk or CD containing the drivers and select the appropriate check box to indicate the location of the drivers. (If the CD Autorun program launches when you insert the CD, close the application.) Note that you can temporarily disable Autorun by holding down the Shift key while you insert the CD.

8. The wizard reports the device name and location of the driver. Click **Next** to continue.

9. The wizard informs you that the installation was successful. Click **Finish** to close the Found New Hardware Wizard.

10. Additional Found New Hardware Wizards might launch for any devices embedded in the modem, such as voice or fax devices. Complete the wizards for these devices. Be prepared to provide any Windows 98 installation files as necessary.

10

Follow these steps to verify that your modem is working properly:

1. Check that your modem is displayed in Device Manager. Device Manager should report no problems with the modem. If necessary, review Lab 1.1 for a reminder of how to use Device Manager.

2. Open the Control Panel, double-click the **Modems** icon to open the Modems Properties dialog box, and then select the **Diagnostics** tab. What type of port information does the Diagnostics tab provide?

_____

3. Select the modem you just installed, and note the port it is associated with. Record that information here.

_____

4. Click the **More Info** button.

5. The More Info dialog box opens. The system uses its modem diagnostic tool to test the modem and then displays the test results. Take and print a screen shot of this dialog box and then click **OK** to close the More Info dialog box.

Answer these questions:

- When you open the More Info dialog box, what type of commands are used to test the modem?

  _____

- List two commands and the purpose of each command.

  _____

  _____

6. Click **OK** to close the Modems Properties dialog box.

Leave the modem installed for use in upcoming labs in this chapter.

Review Questions

1. Were any devices embedded in your modem? How could you tell?

   _____

   _____

2. What are two system resources that a modem requires?

   _____

3. What is the format of the diagnostic commands shown in your screen shots?

   _____

4. In what situation might you use the modem diagnostic tool?

   _____

LAB 10.3 USE AT COMMANDS TO CONTROL A MODEM

Objectives

The goal of this lab is to help you use AT commands to initiate and receive calls. After completing this lab, you will be able to:

➤ Install HyperTerminal

➤ Use several modem commands to control a HyperTerminal session, dial a number, receive a call and test your modem.

Materials Required

This lab will require the following:

➤ Windows 98 operating system

➤ Windows 98 installation CD or installation files in another location

➤ Access to a phone line that can send and receive calls

➤ The line's telephone number

➤ A lab partner to whom you can make modem calls

Activity Background

By using HyperTerminal, you can test a newly installed modem with AT commands. These commands allow you to control virtually every aspect of modem behavior and are useful in troubleshooting modem hardware and connections. In this lab, you will use AT commands to make and receive calls and to adjust modem settings.

Estimated completion time: **45 minutes**

10

ACTIVITY

Follow these steps to install HyperTerminal:

1. Open the Control Panel, double-click the **Add/Remove Programs** icon and then click the **Windows Setup** tab.

2. In the Components list box, double-click the **Communications** group. The Communications dialog box opens.

3. Select the **HyperTerminal** checkbox and then click **OK**. The Communications dialog box closes and you return to the Add/Remove Programs dialog box.

4. Click **OK** to close the Add/Remove Programs dialog box. Supply Windows 98 installation files as necessary.

Follow these steps to use AT commands in HyperTerminal:

1. Click **Start** on the task bar, point to **Programs**, point to **Accessories**, point to **Communications**, and then click **HyperTerminal**. This opens the HyperTerminal folder.

2. Double-click **HyperTrm.exe**. HyperTerminal starts, with the Connection Description dialog box displayed.

3. In the Connection Description dialog box, type **Test 1** in the Name field and then click **OK**. The Connect To dialog box opens.

4. Select your modem from the drop-down list and then click **Cancel** to close the Connect To dialog box. The Connect To dialog box closes, and the main HyperTerminal window is active.

5. Click in the blank field in HyperTerminal to position the cursor there.

At this point, if you start typing AT commands, the commands will be executed but you might not actually be able to see the commands as you type them in the HyperTerminal window. To make it possible to see the AT commands as you type them (if displaying commands has not already been enabled), you must begin with the AT echo command: ATE1. To practice using this command, follow these steps:

1. Type **ATE1** and press **Enter**. The modem's response (OK) appears under the cursor. Note that you couldn't see the command, ATE1, as you typed it. But from now on you should now be able to see commands as you type.

2. Type **ATE0** and press **Enter**. (Be sure to type a zero and not the letter "o.") The command, ATE0, appears on the screen as you type. OK appears below ATE0 after you press Enter.

3. Type **AT** and press **Enter**. The AT command issued by itself should always return an OK response, and, in fact OK does appear on the screen. But this time the command you typed is not displayed on the screen. Which command caused the text not to appear as you typed (i.e., caused the text not to "echo")?

_____

4. Execute the ATE1 command to again echo the commands as you type.

Now that you know how to make commands appear as you type, you are ready to test your modem using HyperTerminal. Follow these steps:

1. To verify that a working phone line is connected to the modem, type **ATD** followed by your computer's telephone number and then press **Enter**. You should hear the modem dial. What message does HyperTerminal return?

_____

2. Type **ATL3**, press **Enter**, and then use the ATD command to dial your computer's number again.

   ■ What difference do you notice from the first time you dialed the number?

_____

_____

   ■ What do you think the L in the ATL command stands for?

_____

3. HyperTerminal can also be controlled via commands on its menu bar. Click **Call** on the HyperTerminal menu bar and then click **Wait for a Call**.

4. Give your lab partner your computer's number and have him or her dial and connect to your computer. What messages does HyperTerminal display on your computer?

_____

_____

_____

5. Click the button that shows the phone handset hanging up on the phone cradle (shown in Figure 10-2). Your modem disconnects.

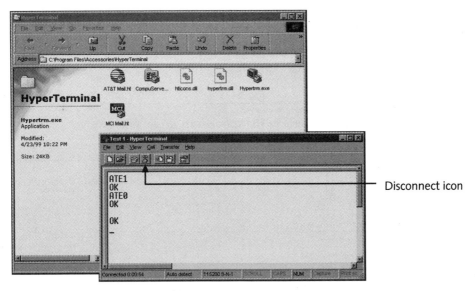

Figure 10-2   HyperTerminal window

6. Type **AT&T1** and press **Enter**. HyperTerminal runs a local analog loop to make sure the modem is working correctly. Record the results below.

_____

_____

_____

_____

7. To end the test, type **AT&T0** and press **Enter**. (Ending the test might take a few moments.)

8. Click the disconnection button on the toolbar.

9. If you begin testing a working modem with AT commands and the modem begins to experience problems, you can use the AT&F command to reset the modem to factory settings. Type **AT&F** and press **Enter**. The modem's default settings are restored.

10. To close HyperTerminal, click **File** and then click **Exit**. When asked if you wish to disconnect, click **Yes**. When asked if you wish to save the session, click **No**.

Review Questions

1. What Windows application is commonly used for working with AT commands?

2. What command turns on the text echo so that you can see what you are typing?

3. What command dials a number?

4. What command returns the modem to its default settings?

5. What method, other than an AT command, can be used to receive an incoming call?

LAB 10.4 SIMULATE MODEM PROBLEMS

Objectives

The goal of this lab is to help you simulate, diagnose, and remedy common modem problems. After completing this lab, you will be able to:

➤ Diagnose problems with a modem

➤ Remedy problems with a modem

Materials Required

This lab will require the following:

➤ Windows 98 operating system

➤ Modem installed in a PC and connected to a phone line

➤ PC toolkit

➤ Modem installation drivers

➤ Windows 98 installation CD or installation files

➤ Standard phone

➤ Lab partner with whom you can swap PCs

Activity Background

Dial-up connections are notoriously unreliable. One of the challenges of troubleshooting such connections is determining whether a dial-up failure is related to a problem with the modem itself or to a problem with the phone line. In this lab, you will diagnose and remedy common modem problems. Mastering these skills will make it easier for you to determine when the modem itself is the source of trouble in a dial-up connection.

Estimated completion time: **90 minutes**

10

ACTIVITY

1. To verify that your modem is working, start HyperTerminal, dial any reliable phone number and listen for the sound of the modem dialing and attempting to connect. (The actual connection is not necessary at this point.) Disconnect the call and close HyperTerminal.

2. Sabotage your modem by introducing one of the problems listed below:
   - If your modem has jumpers or DIP switches, record the original settings and then change the settings.
   - In BIOS or Device Manager, disable the modem's COM port.
   - Loosen the modem card in the expansion slot so that it does not make good contact.
   - Unplug the phone cord from the wall.
   - Change the port the phone line connects to on the back of the modem.
   - Uninstall the modem in Device Manager.
   - Using Device Manager, disable the modem in the current hardware configuration.

3. Swap PCs with your partner and then troubleshoot and repair your partner's PC.

4. Answer these questions:
   - What is the initial symptom of a problem as the user would describe it?

_____

_____

■ How did you discover the source of the problem?

_____

_____

_____

_____

■ What did you do to resolve the problem?

_____

_____

_____

_____

5. Introduce another problem from the list in Step 2 and swap again. Continue this process until you have introduced and remedied all of the problems listed in Step 2.

Review Questions

1. What was the easiest problem to diagnose and why?

_____

_____

2. Which problems would not be apparent when you tested the modem but would result in no dial tone when dialing?

_____

_____

3. Did all of the problems listed in Step 2 actually prevent the modem from working? Which (if any) were not actually "problems"?

_____

4. Which problem prevented the modem from being displayed in Modems Properties?

_____

_____

_____

5. What was the simplest way to determine if there definitely was a dial tone?

_____

_____

6. Suppose a user says, "I can't dial out using my modem." List the first three things you would check, in the order you would check them.

_____

_____

_____

LAB 10.5 CRITICAL THINKING: USE TWO MODEMS TO CREATE A MULTILINK CONNECTION

10

Objectives

The goal of this lab is to help you setup a Dial-Up Networking connection involving two modems in order to increase connection performance. After completing this lab, you will be able to:

➤ Install a second modem

➤ Create a Dial-Up Networking connection

➤ Configure a Dial-Up Networking connection for multilink

➤ Download a file to compare single modem and multilink connection performance

Materials Required

This lab will require the following:

➤ Windows 98 operating system

➤ Two modems and any necessary drivers

➤ Two phone lines and phone jacks

➤ ISP that allows multilink connections

➤ User name and password for your ISP connection, as provided by your instructor

➤ Dial-up phone number for your ISP, as provided by your instructor

Note that if you don't have a second modem and phone line and an ISP that supports multilink connections, you can still do most of this lab to create and test a singlelink connection.

Activity Background

A broadband connection is the best option when you need to transfer lots of data at high speeds. But if you don't have access to a broadband connection, you can make do by using two phone lines and two modems to create a multilink connection. (Note that not all ISP's support multilink connections, and those that do will charge extra for the service.) Assuming both modems connect at the same speed, a multilink connection can roughly double your usual dial-up connection speed. In this lab, you will configure a multilink connection and compare its performance to a single modem connection. You will start by creating a dial-up connection for the modem you installed in Lab 9.2. You will then install a second modem and combine the two modems in a multilink connection.

Estimated completion time: **90 minutes**

ACTIVITY

Follow these steps to create a Dial-Up Networking connection using the modem you installed in Lab 10.2:

1. In Windows Explorer, double-click the **Dial-Up Networking** icon to open the Dial-Up Networking window.

2. Double-click the **New Connection** icon to open the Make New Connection dialog box.

3. Type in the name for the connection you are about to create, select the modem to use in the drop-down menu if it is not already selected, and then click **Next** to continue.

4. The Made New Connection dialog box opens. Here you need to specify the number your computer will dial to complete the dial-up connection. Enter your ISP's area code and phone number (as provided by your instructor), and select the country code from the drop-down menu. Click **Next** to continue.

5. The Make New Connection dialog box informs you that the connection was created successfully. Click **Finish** to close the Make New Connection dialog box. Your new connection appears in the Dial-Up Networking window.

Follow these steps to configure and test your connection:

1. Double-click your connection in the Dial-Up Networking window.

2. The Connect To dialog box opens, showing the connection name. Enter the User Name and Password supplied by your instructor, and then click **Dial Properties** to open the Dialing Properties dialog box.

3. Click the **I am Dialing From:** text box and then type **LAB**.

4. Click **Area Code Rules** to open the Area Code Rules dialog box, select the **Always Dial the Area Code (10–digit dialing)** check box and then click **OK**. The Area Code Rules dialog box closes.

Note that creating multiple dial-up connections is a useful technique on a portable computer. You can configure a separate connection for each location where you intend to travel, with separate dialing rules for each connection. For example, suppose you live in Kentucky and have a dial-up connection to a local ISP. You could create one dial-up connection for your home office that does not require an area code (because the ISP is local). You could also create a connection for dialing into your ISP from a hotel in Boston. This connection might include dialing 9 for an outside line as well as dialing your ISP's area code. You could create yet another connection for dialing into your ISP from a private home in Orlando where you have the local phone number for your ISP's point of presence (POP) in Orlando.

5. Adjust the appropriate settings in the "When Dialing From Here:" section as necessary to reach an outside line or to disable call waiting. What other options can you adjust in the Dialing Properties dialog box?

_____

_____

_____

6. Click **OK** to close the Dialing Properties dialog box.

7. In the Connect To dialog box, notice that the Dialing From: field has changed to "Lab."

8. Select the **Save Password** check box so that you won't have to enter your password each time you connect.

9. Click **Connect** to dial.

10. The Connecting To dialog box appears and displays messages indicating what task is currently being performed ("Dialing…" and "Verifying User Name and Password…," and so forth). When the connection is completed, a connection symbol appears in the system tray as shown in Figure 10-3.

Connection icon

Figure 10-3   A connection icon appears in the system tray when the connection is completed

11. Double-click the connection symbol in the system tray. The Connected To dialog box opens. Record your connection speed and any other information provided in this dialog box.

_____

_____

_____

Now that you have established a dial-up connection, you can use it to download the driver required by your second modem (which you will install in this lab).

12. Open your Web browser and find the Web site for the manufacturer of your second modem.

13. Download the latest driver for this modem. As the file is being downloaded, take and print a screen shot of the download progress indicator.

Now that you have created a Dial-Up connection and tested it using a single modem, you will create a multilink connection. Do the following:

1. Install a second modem using the driver you just downloaded

2. Create a Dial-Up connection for the second modem and test it by dialing up your ISP and completing the connection.

Next, you need to adjust the connection properties of your first Dial-Up connection to allow a multilink connection. Follow these steps:

1. Right-click the connection's icon in the Dial-Up Networking window and then click **Properties** in the shortcut menu. The connection's Properties window opens.

2. Click the **Multilink** tab

3. Select the **Use Additional Devices** check box and then click **Add**.

4. Select the second modem from the list of available devices, and then click **OK**.

Now you are ready to use the multilink connection.

1. Following the directions given above, use the multilink connection to dial up your ISP.

2. Compare the speed of this connection to that of a single connection by downloading the same driver file as you did in step 13 above, taking and printing a screen shot of the download progress. What are the differences in the connection speed and process?

_____

_____

_____

_____

   3. Uninstall the second modem and reconfigure the original modem connection.

Review Questions

   1. What Windows feature allows you to configure and save connection information?

_____

   2. List the steps required to adjust the number of digits required to dial a local phone number.

_____

_____

   3. How does a multilink connection improve performance?

_____

_____

_____

   4. What are the requirements for a multilink connection?

_____

_____

   5. What is the advantage of creating several Dial-Up connections for a single modem?

_____

_____

10

CONNECTING A PC TO A NETWORK

Labs included in this chapter

➤ Lab 11.1 Install and Test an Ethernet NIC

➤ Lab 11.2 Inspect Cables

➤ Lab 11.3 Compare Options for a Home LAN

➤ Lab 11.4 Troubleshoot with TCP/IP Utilities

➤ Lab 11.5 Practice Solving Network Connectivity Problems

LAB 11.1 INSTALL AND TEST AN ETHERNET NIC

Objectives

The goal of this lab is to install and configure an Ethernet Network Interface Card (NIC). After completing this lab, you will be able to:

> ➤ Remove a NIC (and network protocols if necessary)

> ➤ Install a NIC and network protocol

> ➤ Perform a loopback test

Materials Required

This lab will require the following:

> ➤ Windows 98 operating system with no modem or dial-up networking installed

> ➤ NIC and drivers

> ➤ Windows 98 installation CD or installation files stored in another location

> ➤ PC toolkit

> ➤ Cross-over cable

> ➤ Workgroup partner

Activity Background

A computer connects to a wired network via a Network Interface Card (NIC). In this lab, you will install a NIC, configure necessary network settings, and verify that the NIC is functioning properly. Working with a partner, you will create a simple network of two PCs.

Estimated completion time: **30 minutes**

ACTIVITY

If your computer does not already have a NIC installed, skip to the next section. Otherwise, follow these steps to remove the computer's networking components:

1. Right-click the **Network Neighborhood** icon and select **Properties** in the shortcut menu. The Network dialog box opens.

2. If necessary, click the Configuration tab, click **Client for Microsoft Networks** and then click **Properties**. The Client for Microsoft Networks Properties dialog box opens.

3. In the General section, make sure that the **Log on to Windows NT Domain** check box is deselected. Click **OK** to close the Client for Microsoft Network Properties dialog box. Then close the Network Properties dialog box and reboot when prompted.

4. After the computer has rebooted, open the Network dialog box again by right-clicking the **Network Neighborhood** icon and selecting **Properties**. On the Configuration tab of the Network Properties dialog box, click your NIC (indicated by an adapter symbol) and then click **Remove**. The NIC and any protocol associated with it are uninstalled; Client for Microsoft Network is also uninstalled.

5. Click **OK** to close the Network dialog box. You might see a message indicating that the network is incomplete.

6. Click **Yes** to continue. You are prompted to restart your computer.

7. Click **No**.

8. Shut down your computer, but do not reboot.

9. Remove your computer's NIC and proceed to the next set of steps in this lab. Or, if your instructor directs you to do so, remove the network cable but leave the NIC in place and proceed to Step 2 in the next set of steps.

Follow these steps to install and configure your NIC:

1. Physically install the NIC as you would other expansion cards. If you need a refresher on the process, review Labs 4.4, 8.3, or 9.1.

2. Boot the system. The Add New Hardware Wizard detects the NIC and begins the driver installation process. Complete the Add New Hardware Wizard as in previous labs. Reboot when prompted.

3. The Network Neighborhood icon reappears on the desktop. Right-click the **Network Neighborhood** icon and then click **Properties**. The Network dialog box opens.

4. Select the **Configuration** tab and examine the Network Components displayed on the tab. List the installed components.

_____

_____

_____

_____

_____

11

5. Verify that your NIC appears in the list and that TCP/IP is installed and bound to the NIC, as indicated by an item in the list that includes TCP/IP with an arrow that points to the name of your NIC. Select this item and then click **Properties**. The TCP/IP dialog box opens.

6. On the IP Address tab of the TCP/IP dialog box, click the **Specify an IP Address** option button.

7. In the IP Address field of the TCP/IP Properties dialog box, type **192.168.1.1** or **192.168.1.2**. (Your lab partner should use one and you the other.) In the Subnet Mask field, click **255.255.255.0**. (Both you and your partner should do this.) Note that it is possible for a server (called a DHCP server) to assign these two necessary values (which enable TCP/IP communication), but in this lab, you'll assume no such server is available.

8. Click **OK** to close the TCP/IP dialog box.

9. To identify each computer on the network, click the **Identification** tab in the Network dialog box. Record the computer name displayed in the Computer Name field. Replace this name with either the name **Lab 1** or the name **Lab 2**. (Again, your partner should use one of these names while you use the other.) In the Workgroup field, type **NIC Lab**. Although it's not necessary, you can type a description for your computer if you want. When you are browsing the network, this description will appear in the computer's Properties dialog box (under the Comment Heading). This description can help users determine what resources might be available on the computer.

---

10. Click **OK** to close the Network window and save your settings. Supply the Windows 98 CD or the location of the installation files when prompted. If you receive a message indicating that a file being copied is older than the current file, click **Yes** to keep the current file. (This is usually the best practice, unless you suspect that the newer file has been the source of any existing problem.)

11. Click **Yes** when prompted to restart the computer.

Follow these steps to test your NIC:

1. Open an MS-DOS prompt window.

2. Type **ping 127.0.0.1** and press **Enter**. Ping is a TCP/IP utility used to test whether an address is reachable and able to respond. Any 127.x.x.x address is a loopback address. Essentially, a loopback address is a stand-in for your computer's own address. When you use a loopback address in a ping test, the Ping utility sends packets to your local computer's NIC, thereby allowing you to verify that your computer's NIC has a functioning TCP/IP connection. If your computer is connected to a printer, take and print a screen shot of the results of the loopback ping command.

3. Examine the results of the loopback test and answer these questions:

- How many bytes were sent in each packet?

_____

- How many packets were sent with one ping command?

_____

- How many responses were received from one ping command?

_____

- Were any packets lost?

_____

Another way to test a NIC is to use its assigned IP address in a ping test.

1. Use the ping command with the IP address you assigned to your computer. The results should be similar or identical to the loopback test results, except for the address listed in the ping results.

2. Now ping your partner's IP address. Describe what happened to the request.

_____

_____

_____

You will now connect the two PCs using the cross-over cable. Then you will test your network.

1. Close the command prompt window and shut down both computers.

2. Connect one end of the cross-over cable to the NIC on your partner's computer and the other end to the NIC on your computer.

3. Reboot the computers and open a command prompt window.

4. Ping your partner's IP address. If your computer is connected to a printer, take and print a screen shot of the results. How do these results differ from your earlier attempt to ping your partner's IP address?

_____

_____

_____

Review Questions

1. What window is used to configure network adapters and protocols?

_____

11

2. What two name fields are used to identify a computer on a workgroup?

_____

_____

3. Other than the IP address, what other information is required for TCP/IP communication?

_____

4. What are two ways to use the ping utility to test the local computer's NIC?

_____

_____

5. What conclusion should you draw from a loop-back test that reports dropped packets or an unreachable host?

_____

_____

LAB 11.2 INSPECT CABLES

Objectives

The goal of this lab is to help you visually inspect and use a multimeter to test a set of cables. After completing this lab, you will be able to:

➤ Identify two CAT-5 wiring systems

➤ Test cables with a multimeter

➤ Draw pin-outs for cable connectors

➤ Determine if a cable is a patch cable (also known as a straight-through cable) or a cross-over cable

➤ Visually inspect cables and connectors

Materials Required

This lab will require the following:

➤ A variety of cables including a patch cable and a cross-over cable

➤ Multimeter

➤ Internet access

Activity Background

Once you narrow down a problem to physical connectivity, you must inspect the connections to verify that they are not loose. If you eliminate that possibility, then you can assume that the cable is the problem. In this lab, you will physically inspect the cables and the connector and then test the cable for continuity and pin-out using the multimeter.

Estimated completion time: **45 minutes**

ACTIVITY

1. Consult the information available at
   www.atcomservices.com/highlights/cat5notes.htm or search the Internet for information about a patch cable diagram, a crossover cable diagram, and a CAT-5 wiring diagram. List the two standards of CAT-5 wiring schemes. What Web site did you use?

   _____

   _____

   _____

2. Print a wiring diagram for a patch cable wired to each scheme and for a crossover cable using each scheme.

Follow these steps to visually inspect cables:

1. Examine the length of the cable for obvious damage. The damage could be in the form of a cut or abrasion in the outer sleeve with further damage to the twisted pairs inside. A completely cut strand is an obvious problem but the proper conductor inside the cable might be broken even if the insulator is intact. Any visible copper is an indication that you need a new cable.

2. Inspect the RJ-45 connectors. Particularly look for exposed twisted pairs in between the clear plastic connector and the cable sleeve. This is an indication that the cable was assembled improperly or that excessive force was used when pulling on the cable. The cable sleeve should be crimped inside the RJ-45 connector. It is sometimes possible to identify a nonconforming wiring scheme by noting the color of the insulation through the clear connector, but the cable should be checked with a multimeter to verify the condition.

3. Next verify that the retaining clip on the connector is present. Often when an assembled cable is pulled, this clip will snag on carpet or other cables and break off. This results in a connector that is likely to become loose or fall out of the jack. Worse still, this connection may be intermittent. Some cables have hooded guards to prevent the clip from snagging when pulled. These guards themselves can cause problems when seating the connector in the jack if the guard has slid too far toward the end of the cable.

4. Test your cables using a multimeter and complete Table 11-1.

11

Table 11-1

	End A		End B		Questions about the Cable
Pin #	Insulator Color	Pin Tied to at End B	Insulator Color	Pin Tied to at End A	Is the cable good or bad?
1					
2					Wired with what scheme?
3					
4					
5					Is the cable a
6					crossover or a
7					patch cable?
8					
Pin #	Insulator Color	Pin Tied to at End B	Insulator Color	Pin Tied to at End A	Is the cable good or bad?
1					
2					Wired with what scheme?
3					
4					
5					Is the cable a
6					crossover or a
7					patch cable?
8					
Pin #	Insulator Color	Pin Tied to at End B	Insulator Color	Pin Tied to at End A	Is the cable good or bad?
1					
2					Wired with what scheme?
3					
4					
5					Is the cable a
6					crossover or a
7					patch cable?
8					

Cable 1 spans the first block, *Cable 2* the second block, and *Cable 3* the third block.

Review Questions

1. If you can see a copper conductor in a cable, what should you do with the cable?

_____

_____

2. What type of connector is used with CAT 5 cable?

_____

3. Based on your research, what cabling scheme is more common?

_____

4. On a patch cable, pin 3 on one end connects to pin ____ on the opposite end of the cable.

5. On a cross-over cable, pin 2 on one end connects to pin ____ on the other end of the cable.

LAB 11.3 COMPARE OPTIONS FOR A HOME LAN

Objectives

The goal of this lab is to help you research the costs and capabilities of both a wired and a wireless home LAN. After completing this lab, you will be able to:

➤ Research wired and wireless Ethernet

➤ Research 802.11 standards

➤ Identify the strengths and weaknesses of each option

11

Materials Required

This lab will require the following:

➤ Internet access

Activity Background

As the price of equipment and computers fall, installing a home LAN has become increasingly popular. In this lab, you will research wired and wireless Ethernet and determine which option is best in certain situations.

Estimated completion time: **30 minutes**

ACTIVITY

Use your favorite search site to investigate and answer the following questions regarding wireless LAN standards.

1. List the 802.x standards used to specify wireless networks.

   _____

   _____

2. What industry name is associated with 802.11b?

   _____

3. What is the simplest form of a wireless network? What devices are needed to create this type of network and what mode does this type of network use?

   _____

   _____

   _____

4. What device connects wireless users to a wired network?

   _____

5. What standard speeds are supported by 802.11x?

   _____

   _____

   _____

6. What kind of encryption is used with 802.11b?

   _____

   _____

7. Give four examples of devices (besides PCs) that will probably eventually run on wireless LANs.

   _____

   _____

   _____

   _____

8. What does the acronym WI-FI stand for?

   _____

9. What is the approximate maximum range for 802.11b technology?

_____

10. What inherent feature of 802.11b, seen as a significant problem by businesses, might affect your decision to not use WI–FI at home as well?

_____

_____

11. In the context of how they physically interface with a computer, what are the three basic types of wireless adapters?

_____

_____

_____

12. What mode requires a wireless access point?

_____

13. How many 802.11b devices can be used at one time with a single access point?

11

_____

14. What radio band and speed does 802.11a use?

_____

_____

15. Which standard offers a faster transfer rate, 802.11a or 802.11b? List their transfer rates.

_____

_____

16. List components and prices required to connect four PCs in ad hoc mode. List the device and extra expense necessary to connect the same four PCs to a cable modem.

_____

_____

_____

_____

_____

Use the Internet to research and answer these questions on an Ethernet home LAN:

1. What is the maximum cable length for a 100BaseT Ethernet LAN?

_____

2. Must you use a hub to connect three PCs? Two PCs? Explain.

_____

_____

_____

3. What type of cabling is typically used for 100BaseT?

_____

4. Are special tools required when working with CAT 5 cabling to create patch or cross-over cables?

_____

5. What feature included with Windows allows more than one computer to share a connection to the Internet?

_____

6. What type of cable connector is used for fast Ethernet?

_____

7. What standard supports a speed of 100 Mbps using two sets of CAT-3 cable?

_____

8. What is the name for a cable that connects a computer to a hub?

_____

9. Suppose you have a LAN consisting of a 100BaseT hub, two computers with 10BaseT NICs, and a computer with a 10/100BaseT NIC. At what speed would this LAN operate? Why?

_____

_____

10. Given a budget of $200 to connect five computers, would you choose 100BaseT or 10BaseT? Explain your choice.

_____

_____

_____

11. What is the name for a cable that connects a hub to a hub?

_____

12. In theory, if File X is transferred in 4.5 seconds on a fast Ethernet LAN, how long would the same file transfer take on a 10BaseT LAN?

_____

13. Give three examples of ways to physically interface a NIC to a computer?

_____

_____

_____

14. What device might you use to connect two or more PCs to a single cable modem?

_____

15. List the components, including cables, required to connect four PCs. Include the price of each component. List the changes and additional devices required to connect all four PCs to a cable modem and provide a hardware firewall.

_____

_____

_____

_____

_____

11

Review Questions

1. Based on your research, does wireless or 100BaseT offer the best performance for the money?

   _____

   _____

2. Would wireless or 100BaseT be easier to configure in a home? Why?

   _____

   _____

3. What factors dictate the transmission range of 802.11x?

   _____

   _____

   _____

4. What determines the speed of a LAN that consists of both 10Mbps and 100Mbps devices?

   _____

   _____

5. Would a wired or wireless LAN offer better security?

   _____

LAB 11.4 TROUBLESHOOT WITH TCP/IP UTILITIES

Objectives

The goal of this lab is to help you use Windows 2000 TCP/IP utilities to troubleshoot connectivity problems. After completing this lab, you will be able to:

➤ Use IPConfig

➤ Use the Ping utility

➤ Use Tracert

➤ Identify the point at which your packets will no longer travel

Materials Required

This lab will require the following:

➤ Windows 2000 operating system

➤ DHCP server

➤ Internet access

Activity Background

Perhaps nothing frustrates users more than a suddenly unavailable network connection. As a PC technician, you might be asked to restore such a connection. In some cases, in fact, you may have to deal with multiple failed connections at one time. When troubleshooting network connections, it helps to know if many users in one area of a network are having the same connection problem. That information can help you narrow down the source of the problem. Once you have an idea of what machine is causing the problem, you can use a few TCP/IP utilities to prove your theory without actually physically checking the system. In this lab, you will learn to use TCP/IP utilities to isolate connection problems.

Estimated completion time: **30 minutes**

11

ACTIVITY

Follow these steps to display IP settings in Windows 2000:

1. On the Windows 2000 desktop, right-click the **My Network Places** icon and select **Properties** from the shortcut menu. The Network and Dialup Connections window opens.

2. In the Network and Dialup Connections window, right-click **Local Area Connection** and select **Properties** from the shortcut menu. The Local Area Connection Properties dialog box opens.

3. Click **Internet Protocol (TCP/IP)** and then click **Properties**. The Internet Protocol (TCP/IP) dialog box opens. In the Internet Protocol (TCP/IP) dialog box, notice the different options. What two ways can you set up the IP configuration?

_____

_____

4. Verify that **Obtain an IP address automatically** is selected.

5. Click **OK** to close the Internet Protocol (TCP/IP) dialog box, and then click **Close** to exit the Local Area Connection Properties dialog box. Close the Network and Dialup Connections window.

Follow these steps to adjust the command prompt so that you can view more informa-tion at a time:

1. Open a command prompt window.

2. Right-click on the title bar of the command prompt window and select **Properties** from the shortcut menu. The MS–DOS Prompt Properties dialog box opens.

3. In the Screen Buffer size section of the Layout tab, specify **150** for width and **300** for height. This will allow you to scroll in the command prompt window and view the last 300 lines of 150 characters. If you wish you can adjust the Window Size section but it is generally best to wait to adjust each command prompt window after it opens. This ensures that you do not make the window too large for your monitor's display settings. Click **OK** to save the settings.

4. The Apply Properties to Shortcut dialog box appears. To specify that you wish to apply the properties every time you open a command prompt window, select **Modify the shortcut that started this window** and then click **OK**.

Follow these steps to learn how to display IP information from the command line:

1. Open a command prompt window.

2. Type **IPConfig** and press **Enter**. Displayed are three types of information. List them below.

_____

_____

_____

3. To get more information about your IP settings, type **IPConfig /all** and press **Enter**. Take and print a screen shot of these results and answer these questions.

   ■ Is your system using DHCP?

   _____

   ■ What is the purpose of DHCP?

   _____

   _____

   ■ What is the address of the DHCP server?

   _____

4. Because your system is using DHCP to obtain an IP address, type **IPConfig /renew** and press **Enter**. The command prompt window again displays IP information.

5. Again, type **IPConfig /all** and press **Enter**. Compare the current lease information to the information in the screen shot. What information changed?

_____

_____

6. Next type **IPConfig /release** and press **Enter**. What message is displayed? What implications do you predict this will have on connectivity?

_____

_____

7. Using your screen shot as a reference, attempt to ping the DHCP server and the DNS server. What are the results?

_____

_____

8. Type **IPConfig** and press **Enter**. Note that your adapter has no IP address and no subnet mask. These two parameters are necessary to communicate using TCP/IP.

9. To re-obtain an IP address lease, type **IPConfig /renew** and press **Enter**. New IP information is assigned which may or may not be the same address as before.

10. Find your new lease information. List the command you used to obtain this information. Also list the lease information itself.

_____

_____

_____

11

Follow these steps to determine what route your packets take to reach an Internet address:

1. Open a command prompt window.

2. Type **Tracert** followed by a single space, followed by a domain name on the Internet that you seldom use, and then press **Enter**. (You need to use a domain name you don't regularly access, because any recently accessed addresses might be cached on your system.)

3. The domain name is resolved by the DNS server and an associated IP address is listed, indicating that you can reach at least one DNS server. This tells you that your packets are travelling at least that far. Next, each hop (or router your packet passed through) is listed with the time in milliseconds the packet took

to reach its destination. How many hops will Tracert list? How many hops did the packet take to reach the domain you specified?

_____

4. Now use the Tracert command with an illegal name such as *www.mydomain.c.* What are the results of this command?

_____

When troubleshooting connectivity problems, always consider the number of users experiencing the problem. If many users have similar difficulties, it is unlikely the problem lies with any one user's computer. Thus, you can probably eliminate the need to run extensive local tests on each computer. Instead, you can examine a device that all the computers commonly use.

As a general rule, when troubleshooting, you should start by examining devices close to the computer that is experiencing problems, and then move further away. The following steps show you how to apply this principle, by first examining the local computer, and then moving outward to other devices on the network.

1. Verify that the computer is physically connected (that is, that both ends of the cable are connected).

2. Verify that the NIC is installed and that TCP/IP is bound to the NIC.

3. Perform a loop-back test to verify that the NIC is functioning properly.

4. Check the IP settings with the following command: **IPCONFIG /ALL**. Verify that an IP address is assigned.

5. Ping other computers on the local network. If you get no response, begin by examining a hub or punch-down panel (a panel where cables convene before connecting to a hub).

6. If you can ping other computers on the local network, then ping the default gateway, which is the first stop for transmissions being sent to addresses that are not on the local network.

7. Continue troubleshooting connections, beginning with nearby devices and working outward until eventually you discover an IP address that returns no response. That will be the source of the trouble.

8. If the device is under your supervision, take the necessary steps to repair it. If the device is out of your control, contact the appropriate administrator.

Review Questions

1. Name four additional pieces of information that the IPCONFIG command with the /ALL switch provides that the IPCONFIG command alone does not.

_____

_____

_____

_____

2. What type of server resolves a domain name to an IP address?

_____

3. Using Windows 2000, what command discards the IP address?

_____

4. What command would you use to determine whether you are able to reach another computer on the local network? Would this command work if the Default Gateway were down?

_____

_____

5. If many users suddenly encountered connection problems, would you suspect problems with their local computers or problems with other devices on the network? Explain.

_____

_____

_____

11

LAB 11.5 PRACTICE SOLVING NETWORK CONNECTIVITY PROBLEMS

Objectives

The goal of this lab is to troubleshoot and remedy common network connectivity problems. After completing this lab, you will be able to:

➤ Diagnose and solve connectivity problems

➤ Document the process

Materials Required

This lab will require the following:

➤ Windows 98 or Windows 2000 operating system connected to a network and to the Internet

➤ Windows 98 or Windows 2000 installation CD or installation files stored in another location

➤ PC toolkit

➤ Workgroup partner

Activity Background

To a casual user, Internet and network connections can be confusing. When users experience a connectivity problem, they usually have no idea how to remedy the situation. In this lab, you will introduce and solve common connectivity problems.

Estimated completion time: **30 minutes**

ACTIVITY

1. Verify that your network is working correctly by browsing the network and connecting to a Web site.

2. Do one of the following:
   - Change your PC's IP address
   - Change your PC's subnet mask
   - Remove your PC's network cable
   - Remove TCP/IP from your PC
   - Remove your PC's adapter in the Network dialog box
   - Unseat or remove your PC's NIC, but leave it installed in the Network window
   - Disable your PC's NIC in the Device Manager
   - Release your PC's IP address (if DHCP is enabled)

3. Swap PCs with your partner and troubleshoot your partner's PC.

4. On a separate sheet of paper, answer these questions about the problem you solved:
   - What is the initial symptom of the problem as the user might describe it?

   _____

   _____

   - What steps did you take to discover the source of the problem?

   _____

   _____

_____

_____

■ What steps did you take to resolve the problem?

_____

_____

_____

_____

5. Repeat Steps 1–4 until you and your partner have each used all the options listed in Step 2. Be sure to answer the questions in Step 4 for each troubleshooting scenario.

Review Questions

1. What problem could you resolve by issuing only one command? What was the command you used?

_____

2. Which problem (or problems) forced you to reboot the computer after repairing it?

_____

_____

_____

_____

3. What two pieces of information are necessary for TCP/IP communication on the local network?

_____

4. When using Windows 98, what problem (or problems) caused the Network Neighborhood icon to disappear?

_____

_____

_____

11

5. What TCP/IP utility was the most useful, in your opinion, for troubleshooting these problems? Why?

_____

_____

6. What situation would not necessarily cause a communication problem if a network protocol other than TCP/IP (such as NetBEUI) were installed on this and other computers on the network?

_____

CHAPTER TWELVE

NOTEBOOKS, PDAS, AND PRINTERS

Labs included in this chapter

➤ Lab 12.1 Examine Notebook Documentation

➤ Lab 12.2 Compare Notebooks and Desktops

➤ Lab 12.3 Replace a Notebook Hard Drive

➤ Lab 12.4 Research Software Available for PDAs

➤ Lab 12.5 Install and Share a Printer

➤ Lab 12.6 Critical Thinking: Sabotage and Repair a Network Printer

LAB 12.1 EXAMINE NOTEBOOK DOCUMENTATION

Objectives

The goal of this lab is to help you acquire documentation for a notebook from a manufacturer's Web site and become familiar with it. After completing this lab, you will be able to:

➤ Locate documentation for specific notebook computer models

➤ Download the documentation

➤ Use a notebook's documentation to find critical information

Materials Required

This lab will require the following:

➤ Internet access

Activity Background

Notebooks are designed for portability, compactness, and energy conservation, and their designs are often highly proprietary. Therefore, establishing general procedures for supporting notebooks is more difficult than for desktop computers. Often it is necessary to consult the documentation for a particular notebook computer in order to get information on technical specification and support procedures. In this lab, you will locate and download documentation for two different notebook computers and then use that documentation to answer questions about each model.

Estimated completion time: **30 minutes**

ACTIVITY

Follow these steps to locate and download documentation:

1. Choose two notebook manufacturers listed in Table 12-1, go to their Web sites, and select one model from each to research. List your two choices here.

_____

_____

Table 12-1   Notebook manufacturers

Manufacturer	Web Site
Acer America	global.acer.com
ARM Computer	www.armcomputer.com
Compaq Computer	www.compaq.com

Table 12-1 Notebook manufacturers (continued)

Manufacturer	Web Site
Dell Computer	www.dell.com
FutureTech Systems	www.futuretech.com
Gateway	www.gateway.com
Hewlett-Packard	www.hp.com
IBM	www.ibm.com
Micron Electronics	www.micronpc.com
PC Notebook	www.pcnotebook.com
Sony	www.sonystyle.com/vaio
Toshiba America	www.csd.toshiba.com
WinBook	www.winbook.com

2. On the support section of each Web site, search for documentation on each of the models you chose and follow the directions to download it. Were you able to find documentation for both models? If not, list the models for which you were unable to find documentation. Try other models until you have located documentation for two.

_____

_____

3. Using the documentation you located, answer the following questions for your first model. If you can't answer a question because the information is not included in the documentation, write "information unavailable."

- What type of processor does the notebook use and how much RAM is installed?

_____

- What operating system does the notebook support?

_____

- Could you download or save the documentation locally, or did you have to view it on the company's Web site?

_____

- Does the notebook offer quick-launch keys for commonly-used applications? If so, can you customize them? How? If they are not customizable, what buttons are offered, and which applications do they launch?

_____

_____

_____

12

■ List the functions assigned to keys F1 through F4.

_____

_____

_____

_____

■ Does the notebook have a sleep or hibernation mode? If so, how do you activate it? How does activating this mode differ from shutting down the computer?

_____

_____

_____

■ What other types of downloads are offered besides the manual?

_____

_____

4. Using the documentation you located, answer the following questions for your second model. If you can't answer a question because the information is not included in the documentation, write "information unavailable."

■ What type of processor does the notebook use and how much RAM is installed?

_____

■ What operating system does the notebook support?

_____

■ Could you download or save the documentation locally, or did you have to view it on the site?

_____

■ Does the notebook offer quick-launch keys for commonly-used applications? If so, can you customize them? How? If they are not customizable, what buttons are offered, and which applications do they launch?

_____

_____

_____

■ List the functions assigned to keys F1 through F4.

_____

_____

_____

_____

■ Does the notebook have a sleep or hibernation mode? If so, how do you activate it? How does activating this mode differ from shutting down the computer?

_____

_____

_____

■ What other types of downloads are offered on the Web site besides the manual?

_____

_____

Alternate Activity

If you have access to a notebook computer, do the following:

1. Go to the manufacturer's Web site for your notebook computer and download the user manual, if available. List other downloads that are available:

_____

_____

_____

2. From the list of available downloads, choose a device driver or system update for your notebook. Download and install it using instructions on the site. List the driver or update and the steps you took to install it on your notebook.

_____

_____

_____

_____

_____

12

Review Questions

1. On a manufacturer's Web site, where do you usually find support and documentation information?

   _____

   _____

2. For which model was it easiest to find documentation? Which manufacturer site did you feel was most user-friendly and, in general, offered the best support?

   _____

   _____

3. Besides the questions you researched in the lab, what other type of information is available in the manuals you reviewed?

   _____

   _____

4. If you were to purchase one of the notebooks you researched, which one would you choose? Explain your answer.

   _____

   _____

LAB 12.2 COMPARE NOTEBOOKS AND DESKTOPS

Objectives

The goal of this lab is to help you compare the specifications and costs of notebook and desktop computers. After completing this lab, you will be able to:

➤ Compile a list of specifications for a computer according to its purpose

➤ Locate a desktop computer and a notebook computer with similar specifications

➤ Compare the price of a desktop computer to a similar notebook computer and decide which you would purchase

Materials Required

This lab will require the following:

➤ Internet access

Activity Background

When you shop for and purchase a computer, your decisions are generally driven by questions like this: What will the computer be used for? What features are required to accomplish your goals, and what features would be nice to have but are not essential? What features are you willing to compromise on in order to gain others?

One of the most basic of these decisions is whether to choose a notebook computer or a desktop. Unlike desktops, notebooks are portable; however, in order to make notebooks portable, manufacturers often choose to sacrifice performance or other features. In addition, you'll usually pay more for a notebook than for a desktop computer with comparable features. In this lab, you will compile a list of requirements for a computer, locate a notebook and desktop computer with those features, and compare the two.

Estimated completion time: **30 minutes**

ACTIVITY

1. Determine your requirements by answering the following questions:

   - What will the computer mainly be used for? (Possible uses include office applications, graphics and multimedia, gaming, and software development.)

     _____

   - Based on the purpose listed above, what features are required? Include in your list the desired amount of memory and hard drive space. (Some features you might consider include wireless support, display/screen type, software packages supported, PC card support, and external device support.)

     _____

     _____

     _____

     _____

     _____

   - List any additional features that you would like but do not require.

     _____

     _____

     _____

     _____

12

2. Use computer manufacturer Web sites (such as the ones listed earlier in Table 12-1) or comparison sites (such as *www.cnet.com* or *www.zdnet.com*) to find one notebook and one desktop that fulfill as many of your requirements as possible and that are as similar to each other as possible. Summarize your findings by completing Table 12-2. Print the Web pages supporting this information.

Table 12-2

Features	Desktop Computer	Notebook Computer
Manufacturer and model		
Processor type and frequency		
Memory installed		
Hard drive space		
Operating system		
Drive 1		
Drive 2		
Drive 3		
External ports		
Preinstalled applications		
Cost		

3. Based on your research and the requirements you listed in Step 1, would you choose to purchase a desktop computer or a laptop? Explain your answer.

_____

_____

_____

Review Questions

1. Which computer was more expensive, the desktop or the laptop? What was the price difference?

   _____

   _____

2. What features, if any, were you unable to find information on?

   _____

   _____

3. What features, if any, were missing from the desktop and from the laptop? How did this influence your purchasing decision?

   _____

   _____

4. Did you find that you changed your requirements or expectations based on the products available? Explain your answer.

   _____

   _____

   _____

5. Was it easier to find a comparable desktop and laptop from the same manufacturer or from a different manufacturer? Why do you think this is the case?

   _____

   _____

   _____

12

LAB 12.3 REPLACE A NOTEBOOK HARD DRIVE

Objectives

The goal of this lab is to describe the process of replacing a hard drive in a notebook computer. After completing this lab, you will be able to:

➤ Locate the hard drive in a notebook computer

➤ Remove the hard drive from a notebook computer

➤ Replace the hard drive in a notebook computer

Materials Required

This lab will require the following:

➤ Notebook computer or Internet access

➤ PC toolkit

➤ Additional, smaller screwdrivers if necessary

Activity Background

Hard disk drives are by nature delicate devices. Dropping one, even if only a few inches, can cause permanent damage to the read/write heads, the platter surfaces, or both. Notebook systems are, of course, often moved and commonly subjected to forces that most 3.5-inch hard drives will never encounter. While drives intended for use in notebook systems are designed to be resistant to movement and shock, they are still more likely to fail than any other notebook components. In this lab you will remove a hard drive from a notebook computer and then re-install the same hard drive. If you do not have access to a notebook, perform the alternate activity at the end of this lab.

Hard drives designed for notebook computers tend to be 75% to 100% more expensive than the standard 3.5-inch drives of comparable capacity for desktop computers. Also, the majority of newer notebooks support most 2.5-inch drives designed for notebooks, but sometimes a notebook computer requires a proprietary hard drive. For these reasons, it is particularly important to research your replacement options carefully. Read the documentation that came with your notebook to determine what drives the notebook will support. If this information is not available in the documentation, search the manufacturer's Web site. For the purpose of this lab, you will remove the existing drive then re-install the same drive. The specific steps required for your notebook might be slightly different from the procedures given below, so, again, it's important to study the documentation before you begin.

Estimated completion time: **30 minutes**

ACTIVITY

1. What is the manufacturer and model of your notebook computer?

   _____

2. Based on the notebook's documentation or information on the manufacturer's Web site, what type hard drive can be used to replace the existing hard drive? Be as specific as the documentation or the Web site is.

   _____

   _____

3. Search the Internet for a replacement hard drive that meets the requirements for your notebook. Print the Web page showing the specifications for the drive and its cost. How much space does the hard drive have?

_____

4. Look for specific directions (in the documentation or on the Web site) for removing and replacing your notebook's hard drive. If you find any, summarize those directions here. (If you are using the Web site as your source of information, print any relevant Web pages.)

_____

_____

_____

_____

Follow these general steps to remove the hard drive in a notebook computer. Note that these directions might not list every single step necessary for your particular model. Refer to specific directions in the documentation or the company's Web site, as necessary.

1. Remove the main battery or batteries and, if necessary, unplug the computer from the AC adapter. Close the screen and turn the computer so that the bottom is facing up.

2. Locate and remove the access panel or component enclosing the drive bay. In many notebooks, the hard drive is located beneath a floppy drive or other removable device. For example, see Figure 12-1.

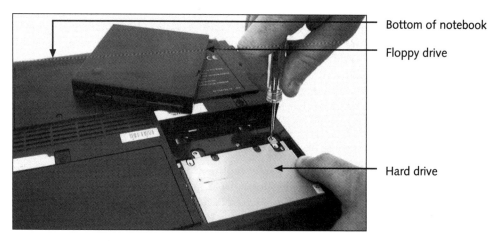

Bottom of notebook

Floppy drive

Hard drive

Figure 12-1   First remove the floppy drive to reveal the hard drive cavity

12

3. Once you have gained access to the drive, determine how it is secured within the system. The device is commonly attached to a frame or "cradle" by small screws. The cradle is in turn often attached directly to the system chassis. This cradle helps locate and support the drive inside the drive bay. Remove the screws securing the cradle.

4. In most notebooks, data cables do not connect the hard drive to the motherboard as in desktop computers. Instead, a hard drive connects to the notebook's motherboard by way of an edge connector, similar to those found on expansion cards in desktop computers. This type of direct connection has two advantages. First of all, it improves reliability because it reduces the total number of connection points; fewer connection points mean fewer connections that might possibly shake loose as the notebook is moved around in daily use. The second advantage of a direct connection is that the lack of data cables reduces the overall size and weight of the notebook. To remove the cradle/drive assembly, slide the cradle away from the connector. Slide the assembly back until all pins are clear of the connector. Once the pins are clear, lift the assembly straight up out of the drive bay.

5. Note the orientation of the drive in the cradle so that, when you reinstall the drive, you will be able to mount the drive in the same direction. Remove the screws securing the drive in the cradle, and then remove the drive.

Follow these general steps to re-install the hard drive in the notebook computer. Note that these directions might not list every single step necessary for your particular model. Refer to specific directions in the documentation or the company's Web site, as necessary.

1. If necessary, configure the jumper settings to indicate master or slave. Place the drive in the cradle so that the pins are correctly oriented and then secure with screws.

2. Set the drive-cradle assembly straight down into the drive bay. Gently slide the assembly to the connector and verify that the pins are correctly aligned with the connector. Slide the assembly until the drive is fully seated in the connector. The cradle should now align with the holes in the chassis. If the holes do not align, you should remove the assembly, loosen the drive retaining screws and adjust the position of the drive in the cradle. You should repeat this process until the drive is fully seated, so that there is no room for the drive to move once the cradle is secured. Once the assembly is seated, secure it with screws.

3. Replace any drives or access covers that you removed to get at the hard drive.

4. Reinstall any batteries and reconnect to AC power if necessary. As with any other hard drive, a notebook drive must be correctly recognized by BIOS, and then partitioned and formatted before it can be used. This process is not necessary in this lab because you have not installed a new hard drive.

Alternate Activity

If you do not have access to a notebook computer:

1. Using the documentation for one of the notebooks you selected in Lab 12.1 as your source, what is the exact requirements for a replacement hard drive for this notebook? Be as specific as the documentation is.

   _____

   _____

2. Search the Internet for information on replacement hard drives, and print the Web page showing the correct specifications for a replacement hard drive. What is the cost of the drive? How much space does the drive have?

   _____

3. Locate steps for replacing the hard drive. To find this information, use the manuals that you downloaded in Lab 12.1, the manufacturer Web sites, and other Internet resources (such as the Web sites of manufacturers of replacement notebook hard drives).

4. How do the steps you found differ from the steps provided in this lab? Note the differences here:

   _____

   _____

   _____

   _____

   _____

   _____

   _____

   _____

12

Review Questions

1. Why should you thoroughly research hard drives when replacing one in a notebook computer?

   _____

   _____

2. Why is cabling commonly not included in notebook systems?

_____

3. How was the installation procedure for your computer different from the one listed in this lab?

_____

_____

_____

4. Suppose you need to install a hard drive in a notebook that does not include an access panel for the hard drive. Where should you look for the hard drive inside the notebook?

_____

_____

_____

5. What do you have to do in CMOS setup before a new hard drive can be used?

_____

_____

LAB 12.4 RESEARCH SOFTWARE AVAILABLE FOR PDAs

Objectives

The goal of this lab is to help you research and compare PDAs. After completing this lab, you will be able to:

➤ Locate and compare information on available PDAs

Materials Required

This lab will require the following:

➤ Internet access

Activity Background

One common problem with PDAs (personal digital assistants) is finding compatible software (in addition to the software that comes preinstalled on the PDA). There are two basic OS choices for a PDA: Pocket PC and Palm OS. Before you can install additional software, you have to verify that the software is compatible both with the PDA's operating system and with the specific PDA model. Some basic models do not allow you to add any software. You also have to make sure that the software is compatible with the desktop PC that you want to synchronize with the PDA. Finally, some business organizations will not allow certain PDAs to synchronize with the business network. You will learn more about these issues in this lab, as you research software availability for two different PDA models.

Estimated completion time: **30 minutes**

ACTIVITY

1. Using the manufacturer sites listed in the Tables 12-3 and 12-4, select one Palm OS PDA and one Pocket PC PDA. Record the name and model number of your choices here:

_____

_____

Table 12-3   Manufacturers of Palm OS PDAs

Manufacturer	Web Site
HandEra	*www.handera.com*
Handspring	*www.handspring.com*
IBM	*www.ibm.com*
Palm	*www.palm.com*
Samsung	*www.samsung.com*

Table 12-4   Manufacturers of Pocket PC PDAs

Manufacturer	Web Site
Casio	*www.casio.com*
Compaq	*www.compaq.com*
Hewlett-Packard	*www.hp.com*
Toshiba	*www.toshiba.com*

2. On the manufacturer Web sites, search for technical specifications and lists of installed software for the first model you selected. Then answer the following questions for this model. Download and search user manuals if necessary.

 ■ What version of the operating system is installed?

_____

12

- What software comes installed on the PDA?

  _____

  _____

  _____

  _____

- Can you install other software? If so, list some available programs.

  _____

  _____

  _____

  _____

  _____

- Will the applications on the PDA synchronize with common office applications on a desktop PC or notebook? List the applications on the PDA and the
  applications on the desktop PC or notebook with which it can synchronize.

  _____

  _____

  _____

  _____

  _____

3. Answer the following questions for the second model PDA:

   - What version of the operating system is installed?

     _____

- What software comes installed on the PDA?

  _____

  _____

  _____

  _____

- Can you install other software? If so, list some available programs.

  _____

  _____

  _____

  _____

  _____

- Will the applications on the PDA synchronize with common office applications on a desktop PC or notebook? List the applications on the PDA and the applications on the desktop PC or notebook with which it can synchronize.

  12

  _____

  _____

  _____

  _____

  _____

Alternate Activity

If you have access to a PDA, perform the research suggested in this lab for your particular model. Try to locate, download, and install a trial version of an add-on software program for your PDA. Record the necessary steps and the name of the program you installed.

_____

_____

_____

_____

_____

_____

_____

_____

Review Questions

1. Was add-on software available for both of the PDA models you researched?

   _____

   _____

2. How easy was it to find the information you needed? List the Web sites you visited, ranking them from most user friendly to least user friendly.

   _____

   _____

   _____

   _____

3. Which PDA OS appears to support the most PDA applications? Explain your answer.

   _____

   _____

   _____

4. Are more or few software options available for the higher priced PDAs? Explain your answer.

   _____

   _____

5. Would you consider purchasing either of the PDAs you researched in this lab? Why or why not?

_____

_____

_____

_____

6. List three questions you should carefully research about software availability before selecting a PDA.

_____

_____

_____

LAB 12.5 INSTALL AND SHARE A PRINTER

Objectives

The goal of this lab is to help you install and share a printer. After completing this lab, you will be able to:

> Install a local printer on a computer

> Share that printer with other users on the network

> Using another computer on the network, install and use the shared network printer

Materials Required

This lab will require the following:

> A printer and its printer drivers

> Two or more Windows 9x or Windows 2000 computers connected to a network

> Windows installation CD or installation files stored in another location

> Workgroup of 3-4 students

12

Activity Background

A printer can be connected to and dedicated to one particular PC (in which case it is called a local printer), or it can be shared with other PCs on the network (in which case it is called a network printer). For a printer to be shared using a Windows operating system, it must be physically connected to and installed on one computer and then shared with others in the same Windows workgroup. All computers involved must have the Client for Microsoft Networks and Microsoft File and Printer Sharing components installed. In this lab, you will install and share a printer in a workgroup and then use the shared printer on the network.

Estimated completion time: **45 minutes**

ACTIVITY

You must first install Client for Microsoft Networks and File and Printer Sharing (if they are not already installed). Both of these components are installed on Windows 2000 computers by default. Client for Microsoft Networks is installed in Windows 98 by default. To install them on Windows 9x computers (if necessary), use these steps:

1. In the Control Panel, double-click the **Network** applet.

2. The Network dialog box opens. Click **Add**.

3. The Select Network Component Type dialog box opens. In the list box, click **Client** to select it and then click **Add**.

4. The Select Network dialog box opens. Click **Microsoft** on the left and **Client for Microsoft Networks** on the right. Click **OK** and then insert the Windows 98 installation CD. Reboot the PC when prompted.

5. Return to the Network dialog box. Repeat Steps 2 and 3, this time selecting **Service** instead of Client.

6. The Select Network Service dialog box opens. Click **File and printer sharing for Microsoft Networks** and then click **OK**. Click **OK** to close the Network dialog box and then insert the Windows 98 installation CD. Reboot the PC when prompted.

7. Return to the Network dialog box and then click **File and Print Sharing**.

8. The File and Print Sharing dialog box opens. Select the **I want to be able to give others access to my files** check box and the **I want to be able to allow others to print to my printer(s)** check box and then click **OK**. (You will not be practicing file sharing in this lab, but as a general rule you will usually set up files and print sharing at the same time.)

Next, you need to verify that all the computers that need to use the printer are in the same workgroup. Follow these steps:

1. Ask your instructor for the name of the workgroup you are to use for this lab and record the name here:

   _____

2. For Windows 98, right click on the **Network Neighborhood** icon on the desktop and select **Properties** from the shortcut menu. The network's Properties window appears. Click the **Identification** tab. (For Windows 2000/XP, right click on the **My Computer** icon and select **Properties** from the shortcut menu. In the System Properties window, click the **Network Identification** tab and then click the **Properties** button. The Identification Changes window appears.)

3. What workgroup does this computer belong to?

   _____

4. If necessary, change the workgroup assignment to match the one noted in Step 1.

You are now ready to install and share the printer. On a Windows 2000 computer that will be physically connected to the printer, follow these steps. Note that the steps for Windows 98 differ slightly but you can use these steps as a guide.

1. With the computer off, connect the printer cable to the parallel port on your computer, turn on the printer, and then boot up the computer.

2. If the Add Printer Wizard opens, click **Next** and then skip to Step 4.

3. If the wizard does not open, click **Start** on the taskbar, point to **Settings**, and then click **Printers**. The Printers window opens. Double-click **Add Printer**. The Add Printer Wizard opens. Click **Next**.

4. Click **Local printer**, select the **Automatically detect and install my Plug and Play printer** checkbox, and click **Next**.

5. A list of ports is displayed. Select **Use the following port**, select **LPT1:** and then click **Next**.

6. A list of manufacturers and printer models is displayed. Select first the manufacturer and then the model from the list. If your printer is not listed, and you have the correct printer driver on disk or CD-ROM, click **Have Disk**. Keep in mind that drivers designed for one Windows operating system might not work for a later version of Windows, so you need to make sure you have the correct drivers for your computer's version of Windows. (You can download printer driver files from the printer manufacturer's Web site.) If you select a manufacturer and model from the Windows list, a dialog box might appear to allow you to specify the location of the Windows setup files. In that case, insert the Windows setup CD or select another location for the files.

12

7. The next screen in the Add Printer Wizard asks for a name for the printer. This name will later appear in the list of available printers. Windows provides a default name. Accept the default name or enter your own, and then click **Next** to continue.

8. Click **Share as** to indicate that this printer will be shared with others on a network, and select the operating system that other computers on the network will be using. By selecting the operating system here, you ensure that your computer can communicate with the remote computers when they request access to the printer. Click **Next** to continue.

9. Select **Yes** to print the test page, and then click **Next**.

10. Windows displays the printer settings you selected. Click **Finish** to complete the installation.

Once the printer is installed, you need to make it possible for other computers in the network to access it. Follow these directions to share the printer with other computers in the workgroup:

1. On the computer that has the printer installed locally, click **Start** on the taskbar, point to **Settings**, and click **Printers**.

2. The Printers window opens, showing the printer you just installed. Right-click the printer and select **Sharing** in the shortcut menu.

3. The Properties window for the printer opens with the Sharing tab selected. Click the **Shared as** option button, type a share name for the printer, and then click **OK**.

4. For Windows 2000 computers, click **Additional Drivers**, select the operating systems used by the remote computers and then click **OK**. Windows can then provide the remote computers with the necessary driver files when they first attempt to connect to the shared printer. (Windows 98 does not provide this service.)

The printer is now listed in the Network Neighborhood window (or, for Windows 2000, in the My Network Places window) on all the other computers on the network. However, before the printer can be used by a remote computer, printer drivers must be installed on that computer. Follow these steps to install the shared printer on the other PCs:

1. On the computer that has the printer connected locally, share the **C:/Windows** folder so that the drivers in this folder will be available to the other computers. To do this, right-click the **C:/Windows** folder in Explorer, click **Properties** in the shortcut menu, click the **Sharing** tab, and select the option **Shared as** to share the folder. Do not require a password to access the folder. Click **OK**.

2. On the remote PCs, open My Network Places or Network Neighborhood and find the printer. Right-click the printer and click **Install** (for Windows 98) or **Connect** (for Windows 2000) on the shortcut menu.

3. Enter a name for the printer and print a test page to complete the installation.

4. After all remote computers have installed the printer, remove the shared option on the C:\Windows folder of the local computer in order to protect this important folder. To do this, right click on the folder in Explorer, click **Properties**, click the **Sharing** tab and select **Not Shared**. Click **OK**.

Review Questions

1. What two Windows components must be installed before you can share a printer in a workgroup?

   _____

   _____

2. What would happen if the C:\Windows folder on the host PC were not shared when you tried to install the printer on the remote PCs? How could you have installed the printer on a remote computer if you did not have access to the C:\Windows folder on the host computer?

   _____

   _____

3. Name an advantage of installing file sharing at the same time you install printer sharing.

   _____

   _____

4. Suppose you want to stop others on the network from using a shared printer, but you still want the printer to be available to the computer on which it is locally installed. What is the easiest way to accomplish this?

   _____

LAB 12.6 CRITICAL THINKING: SABOTAGE AND REPAIR A NETWORK PRINTER

Objectives

The goal of this lab is to learn to troubleshoot problems with a network printer.

Materials Required

This lab will require the following:

➤ Two or more computers connected to a network, one with a local printer attached

➤ Access to the Windows installation CD or installation files stored in another location

➤ Workgroup of 2–4 students

Activity Background

Problems with a network printer are common and a PC support technician is often called on to solve them. This lab will give you practice solving these types of problems.

Estimated completion time: **45 minutes**

ACTIVITY

1. Using the steps provided in Lab 12.5 as a guide, verify that each computer in a workgroup is able to print to a network printer, which is locally installed on one of the computers in the workgroup.

2. Trade systems with another group and sabotage the other group's system while they sabotage your system. Do one or more things that will prevent one or more computers in the workgroup from using the network printer. The following list offers some sabotage suggestions. Do something included in this list, or think of another option.

   ■ On the host computer, remove the sharing option for the printer

   ■ Uninstall the printer on a remote computer

   ■ Pause printing on one or more computers

   ■ Turn the printer off or offline

   ■ Disconnect the printer cable from the host computer

   ■ Remove paper from the printer

   ■ Introduce an error in the printer configuration on the host computer or a remote computer

3. What did you do to sabotage the other team's system?

   _____

   _____

   _____

4. Return to your system and troubleshoot it.

5. Describe the problem as the user would describe it to you if you were working at a Help desk.

_____

_____

6. What is your first guess as to the source of the problem?

_____

7. List the steps you took in the troubleshooting process.

_____

_____

_____

_____

_____

_____

12

8. How did you finally solve the problem and return the printing system to good
working order?

_____

_____

Review Questions

1. What would you do differently the next time you encounter the same symptoms?

_____

2. In a real–life situation, what are three easy things you could ask a user to check
or verify that does not require experience with Windows?

_____

_____

_____

3. In a real-life situation, what might cause this problem to happen? List three possible causes.

_____

_____

_____

13

TROUBLESHOOTING AND MAINTENANCE FUNDAMENTALS

Labs included in this chapter

➤ Lab 13.1 Produce Help-Desk Procedures

➤ Lab 13.2 Flash BIOS

➤ Lab 13.3 Troubleshoot General Computer Problems

➤ Lab 13.4 Troubleshoot Hypothetical Situations

 ➤ Lab 13.5 Critical Thinking: Update Motherboard Drivers

LAB 13.1 PRODUCE HELP-DESK PROCEDURES

Objectives

The goal of this lab is to demonstrate the process of setting up help desk troubleshooting procedures. After completing this lab, you will be able to:

➤ Identify problems that would prevent users from browsing the network

➤ Decide which problems can be solved over the telephone

➤ Decide which problems require administrative intervention

➤ Create a support matrix for telephone instruction

Materials Required

This lab will require the following:

➤ Windows 9x or Windows 2000 operating system

➤ PC connected to a working TCP/IP network

➤ Two workgroups with 2-4 students in each group

Activity Background

When a company sets up a help desk for computer users, it establishes a set of procedures to address common troubleshooting situations. These procedures should include instructions that the average user can be expected to carry out with telephone support. In this lab, you will design and create help desk procedures for one common problem, inability to connect to a network. In this lab, assume that you are working at the company help desk. Assume that, if you cannot solve the problem, you will escalate the problem to the network administrator or to another technician who will actually go to the computer that has the problem.

Estimated completion time: **45 minutes**

ACTIVITY

1. Assume that your company network is designed according to the following parameters. (Note that your instructor might alter these parameters so they more closely resemble the parameters of your working network.)

   ▪ Ethernet LAN that is using only a single subnet

   ▪ TCP/IP is the only protocol

   ▪ Workgroup name is ATLGA

   ▪ DHCP server assigns IP information

2. Assume that all users on your company network use computers with the following parameters. (Note that your instructor might alter these parameters so they more closely resemble your PC.)

- Pentium III 750 MHz
- Windows 98 operating system
- Internal NIC
- Category 5 cabling with RJ-45 connectors

3. As a group, discuss the various reasons a user might not be able to connect to the network, and then make a list of the four most common reasons a user might not be able to connect to a network. List the source of these problems below. Consider both hardware and software problems. In your list, include at least one problem that is difficult to solve over the phone by talking to the user, requiring, instead, that the network administrator or another technician actually go to the computer to solve the problem. Order the four problems from the least difficult to solve to the most difficult to solve. List the one problem that requires administrator intervention at the bottom of the list.

- Source of Problem 1:

  _____

- Source of Problem 2:

  _____

- Source of Problem 3:

  _____

- Source of Problem 4 (requires administrator or another technician to get involved):

  _____

For each problem, describe the symptoms as a user would describe them:

- Symptoms of Problem 1:

  _____

  _____

- Symptoms of Problem 2:

  _____

  _____

13

- Symptoms of Problem 3:

  _____

  _____

- Symptoms of Problem 4 (requires administrator or another technician intervention):

  _____

  _____

As a group, decide how to solve each of the problems. On separate pieces of paper, list the steps required to verify and resolve the problems. (Such a list of steps is sometimes referred to as a procedure, support matrix, or job aid.) Double-check each step by testing them on your computer. (In real life, you would actually test your steps using a computer attached to the network you are supporting.) When making your list of steps, allow for alternatives, based on how the user responds to your questions. For example, you might include one list of steps for situations in which the user says others on the network are visible in Network Neighborhood and another list of steps for situations in which the user says no remote computers can be seen in Network Neighborhood. Well written help desk procedures ensure that the help desk worker knows exactly what steps to perform; this in turn results in quicker and more confident user support. For any problem that cannot be solved by the procedure, the last step should be for the help desk personnel to notify the Administrator. In your procedure, include questions to the user where appropriate.

An example of one step that involves a question is:

➤ **Question:** Is your computer on?

➤ **Answer:** Yes, go to Step 3; No, go to Step 2

Now test your help desk procedures by using them on another workgroup. Follow these steps:

1. Introduce one of your four problems to a PC connected to a network.

2. Have someone from another workgroup sit at your PC. The remainder of these steps refer to this person as "the user."

3. Sit with your back to this person so you cannot see what he or she is doing. Place your step-by-step procedures in front of you, either on paper or on screen. (It's helpful if you can sit at a PC that is connected to the network, so that you can perform the same steps you ask the user to perform. But make sure you cannot see the other PC or see what the user is doing.)

4. The user should attempt to access the network and then "call" your help desk for assistance.

5. Follow your procedure to solve the problem.

6. Revise your procedure as necessary.

7. Test all four help desk procedures.

Review Questions

1. Can all user computer problems be resolved with help desk support? Explain.

   _____

   _____

2. After you first design and write your help desk procedures to resolve problems, what should you do next?

   _____

   _____

3. How should help desk procedures address complex problems that require administrative intervention?

   _____

   _____

   _____

4. How should you alter your procedures based on the technical experience of your users? Explain.

   _____

   _____

   _____

5. Why do you need to consider what the network and computer are like when creating your procedures?

   _____

   _____

   _____

13

LAB 13.2 FLASH BIOS

Objectives

The goal of this lab is to help you examine the process of flashing BIOS. After completing this lab, you will be able to:

➤ Gather motherboard information

➤ Gather BIOS string information

➤ Research correct BIOS update information

➤ Record current BIOS settings

➤ Flash your BIOS, if permitted by your instructor

Materials Required

This lab will require the following:

➤ Windows 9x or Windows 2000 operating system

➤ Motherboard documentation or SANDRA software installed in Lab 2.5

➤ Internet access

➤ Blank floppy disk

Activity Background

The BIOS on a motherboard controls many of the basic input/output functions of the system. The BIOS programming can be updated by downloading the latest update from the BIOS or motherboard manufacturer's Web site and then following specific procedures to update (or flash) the BIOS. Flashing a computer's BIOS is necessary when troubleshooting an unstable motherboard. You may also need to flash a computer's BIOS in order to provide support for new hardware (such as a processor, hard drive, or CD-ROM drive) or an operating system that you are about to install. For example, before upgrading your operating system to Windows 2000 Professional, you could update your BIOS to add support for ACPI power management. In this lab you will gather information about your system including what BIOS you are using and how to flash the BIOS. If you instructor permits, you will also flash your BIOS.

Estimated completion time: **45 minutes**

ACTIVITY

Before making hardware, software, or BIOS changes to a system, it's important to know your starting point so that, if problems occur, you will know if the problems already existed or you created them by what you did to the system. Do the following:

1. Verify that your computer can successfully boot to a Windows desktop with no errors.

2. Does the PC boot without errors?

It's critical that when flashing the BIOS you use the correct BIOS update. Using the wrong BIOS update can render your system inoperable. Follow these steps to gather information on the motherboard chip set and BIOS:

1. Use motherboard documentation or SANDRA to find and record the following:

   ▪ Motherboard manufacturer

   ▪ Motherboard model number and version/revision

   ▪ Chip set manufacturer

   ▪ Chip set model number and version/revision

   ---

2. Next, you need to record the BIOS string and manufacturer information that are displayed during the boot process. To make it possible to record this information, turn off the PC, unplug your keyboard and then turn on the PC. In most cases, the very first screen will contain video BIOS information from the video card and will be identified by "VGA BIOS" or "Video BIOS." Ignore this screen, and wait for the next screen, which indicates the start of POST. At this point, because you unplugged the keyboard, POST will stop and report the error about a missing keyboard. This freezes the screen so you can read the BIOS information.

3. The BIOS manufacturer and version can usually be found at the top left of the POST screen. You may also see a release date, which is useful in determining whether newer versions of the BIOS are available. The motherboard identification string will usually be located at the bottom left of the screen and usually contains dozens of characters. It is important to verify that this string is correct so that the exact BIOS update is obtained. Record your information below.

   ▪ BIOS manufacturer and version

   ▪ BIOS release date, if provided

13

- Motherboard identification string

If you have a name brand PC that does not identify BIOS information during the boot process, you should be able to locate BIOS information on the manufacturer's Web site by computer model number and serial number. Also, some newer computers will not halt the boot process if the keyboard is missing. For these computers, go to CMOS setup and look for the BIOS identifying information on the CMOS main menu screen.

Using the information you gathered, you can search the Web to determine what files you will need to update your BIOS.

1. Search first the motherboard manufacturer's Web site and then the BIOS manufacturer's Web site's support section for information on updating your BIOS. Alternately, search by motherboard model number or BIOS version number. Download the files required to update your BIOS or, if your computer is running the latest version of the BIOS, download the files required to refresh your existing BIOS. Answer the following questions:

   - Did you download files to update or refresh your BIOS?

   - Which manufacturer provided the BIOS: the BIOS manufacturer or motherboard manufacturer?

   - What is the name of the file you downloaded?

   - What is the release date of the latest version?

   ---

4. Search the manufacturer's Web site for the steps required to flash your BIOS. Print this procedure so you can use it during the upgrade. Does the procedure call for an additional BIOS utility or Flash utility? If so, download this utility as well. Research Flash utilities on *www.wimsbios.com*. Wim's BIOS is an excellent Web site for researching BIOS information in general. Print information on what BIOS utilities are available.

5. The next step is to record any changes you have previously made to CMOS settings. Generally, when BIOS is updated, settings are returned to their default state, so you will probably need to return the settings to their present state after you have flashed BIOS. In addition, you might need to manually input settings for all hard drives (or allow these settings to be detected automatically). Record any settings that you know you changed, as well as any hard drive settings that might have to be reconfigured after you update the BIOS. Also, record any additional settings specified by your instructor.

- Hard drive information

  _____

  _____

- Settings you've changed

  _____

  _____

  _____

  _____

- Settings specified by your instructor

  _____

  _____

  _____

  _____

6. At this point, if your update procedures require the use of a bootable floppy, verify that the boot order allows you to boot from drive A before drive C.

7. Prepare to update your BIOS. Decompress any files, double-check procedures and read any readme.txt files included in the upgrade files (which often contain last minute adjustments to the procedure) and create the upgrade boot disk if necessary.

8. If your instructor permits, follow the BIOS update procedure to update your BIOS. During the procedure, if you are given the opportunity to save your old BIOS, do so. This will make it possible to return to the previous BIOS version if you encounter problems with the new BIOS.

9. Reboot, verify CMOS settings, and verify that the computer will boot to a Windows desktop successfully.

13

Review Questions

1. At what point in the boot process is BIOS information displayed?

   _____

2. How can you freeze the screen during POST so that you can read the BIOS information?

_____

_____

3. Why is it so important to record BIOS and motherboard information correctly?

_____

_____

4. What files might contain last minute changes to the upgrade procedures?

_____

5. In what state are CMOS settings usually placed after a BIOS update?

_____

6. If given the opportunity during the update, what should you always do and why?

_____

_____

LAB 13.3 TROUBLESHOOT GENERAL COMPUTER PROBLEMS

Objectives

The goal of this lab is to troubleshoot and remedy general computer problems. After completing this lab, you will be able to:

➤ Diagnose and solve problems with various hardware devices

➤ Document the troubleshooting process

Materials Required

This lab will require the following:

➤ Windows 98 or Windows 2000 operating system

➤ Windows 98 or Windows 2000 installation CD or installation files stored in another location

➤ Drivers for all devices

➤ PC toolkit

➤ Workgroup partner

Activity Background

In previous labs, you have learned to troubleshoot problems in specific subsystems of a PC. This lab takes a comprehensive approach to troubleshooting an entire system, where the problem might relate to any subsystem. Troubleshooting a general problem is no different from troubleshooting a specific subsystem. You simply apply your troubleshooting techniques to a larger range of possibilities.

Estimated completion time: **120 minutes**

ACTIVITY

1. Verify that you and your partner's computers are working by verifying that the system runs smoothly, and that all drives are accessible. Browse the network and connect to a Web site.

2. Randomly pick one of the following problems and introduce it to your PC:
   - For PCs that have SIMMs installed, move the RAM to a different SIMM slot.
   - Change the boot sequence to boot from a non-existent device.
   - If both the mouse and the keyboard have PS/2 connectors, switch the connectors at the case.
   - Using Add/Remove Hardware, install a non-existing device.
   - Remove the data cable from the primary master hard drive.
   - Change the display settings to two colors that are hard to read.
   - Install the wrong type SIMM or DIMM or the wrong number of SIMMs or DIMMs on the motherboard. Or, for a system that uses SIMMs, remove one SIMM. Be sure to store all memory modules in an anti-static bag while they are outside the case.
   - Unplug the monitor from the video adapter.
   - Add Drive B: in BIOS but do not install a second floppy drive.
   - In BIOS, manually add information for a fictitious hard disk drive.
   - Unplug the network cable from the wall or hub.
   - Connect the floppy drive to the Drive B: connector on the data cable (the one without the twist).

3. Troubleshoot your partner's PC while your partner troubleshoots your computer. Verify that you can accomplish all the tasks that you could before the computer was sabotaged.

13

4. On a separate sheet of paper, answer these questions:

■ What is the initial symptom of a problem as the user would describe it?

_____

_____

■ How did you discover the source of the problem?

_____

_____

_____

■ How did you resolve the problem?

_____

_____

_____

5. Return to your computer and repeat Steps 2 through 4. Continue until you have solved all the problems listed in Step 2. For each problem, make sure to answer the questions listed in Step 4.

Review Questions

1. Which problems caused the computer to halt during the boot process?

_____

_____

_____

2. What problem was the most difficult to repair? Why?

_____

_____

_____

3. Of those problems that *allowed* the computer to boot, which problem was easiest to detect? Why?

_____

_____

_____

4. Of those problems that *prevented* the computer from booting, which problem was easiest to detect? Why?

_____

_____

_____

Lab 13.4 Troubleshoot Hypothetical Situations

Objectives

The goal of this lab is to help you think through the troubleshooting process using hypothetical situations. After completing this lab, you will be able to:

> Evaluate a troubleshooting situation

> Determine a likely source of a problem

> Explain how to verify the source of a problem

> Briefly explain a problem and the procedure required to remedy it

13

Materials Required

This lab will require the following:

> Workgroup of 2-4 students

Activity Background

One way to sharpen your troubleshooting skill is to think through the process of solving hypothetical problems. This lab will present situations that, while common, should present a challenge for your workgroup.

To complete this lab, imagine that you are in charge of repairs at a small computer shop. As part of your job, you first need to describe the symptoms of the problem on the repair work order and explain your initial guess or opinion as to the source of the problem. You must then write a short summary on the work order explaining what you did to repair the computer. The explanations you write on the work order should be as clear and precise as possible. Customers who know something about computers will appreciate your careful explanations. And even if the customer does not fully understand, a detailed work order will help assure the customer that you did a thorough job.

Estimated completion time: **30 minutes**

ACTIVITY

1. A customer installed a new 20 GB hard drive and complains that it will not work. He claims that he called the manufacturer's technical support, who walked him through BIOS setup. When he rebooted, POST did recognize the hard drive but Windows still did not. The customer then became frustrated and decided to bring the computer to you.

   ■ What are the possible sources of the problem?

   _____

   _____

   _____

   _____

   ■ What would you do to find out how to resolve the problem?

   _____

   _____

   _____

   _____

2. A customer brings in a computer and says that when she turns the computer on it will not boot. She says that a screen appears with an error message regarding something about the operating system. The customer claims that she has never modified the system, but that she does have children who use the computer and may have changed something inadvertently.

   When you boot the system, you get an invalid system disk error and you can hear the hard drive spin up when power is applied. You suspect that the BIOS settings are incorrect and that the hard drive is not being recognized. You successfully detect the hard drive using the BIOS autodetection feature. In standard CMOS setup you notice that the date and time are also incorrect, so you reset them. You save your changes and reboot. The system reboots to Windows.

You test the system for ten minutes, leave it on and come back to it after an hour, and it is still functioning correctly. You call the customer and tell her that you have fixed the situation and she can come and pick it up the next day. Then you shut the system off and eventually leave work.

The next day the customer comes in, and when you demonstrate that you have fixed the problem, you see the invalid system disk message again.

■ What do you suspect the problem is?

_____

■ How long will it probably take you to fix it?

_____

_____

3. A customer brings in a computer. The customer was trying to install a new U. S. Robotics modem, but the modem will not work even after trying several different ways to install the drivers for the new modem. When you boot and check Device Manager, you see two instances of U.S. Robotics modems, neither of which are functioning correctly. You also see one instance of a modem made by Creative Labs, which is reportedly functioning correctly. When you physically check the modem card, only the U.S. Robotics modem is present in the computer.

■ What is the source of the problem?

_____

_____

■ What steps would you take to install the U.S. Robotics modem?

_____

_____

_____

_____

_____

13

4. A customer brings in a computer with a new external modem and says that the computer is working fine but that the modem does not work. The customer wants you to get the modem to work with his computer. The customer says he tried attaching the external modem on both serial ports but to no avail. You decide to test the modem on a separate system and you find that it functions correctly. On the customer's computer, you check the Ports' Group in Device Manager and only the parallel port is present.

- What is likely the problem?

  _____

- What will you do to correct it?

  _____

  _____

5. A customer brings in a system and claims that it does not work after a thunderstorm. You open the case and immediately notice a burning smell. You test each component in a test system and find no functional components. You call and report the sad news to the customer. The customer is upset about the system but even more upset about the loss of important information on the hard drive for which he has no backup.

- What information or recommendation can you give the customer about what he can do now and what he should do in the future to safeguard important data?

  _____

  _____

  _____

  _____

- What advice can you give the customer about protecting his hardware?

  _____

  _____

  _____

Review Questions

1. How could a properly functioning hard drive, which is recognized by BIOS, fail to show up in Windows?

_____

_____

2. What device maintains CMOS settings even if the computer is totally unplugged from AC power?

_____

3. What Control Panel applet will let the inexperienced user forcibly install an incorrect device or non-existent device? What Windows feature will let you remove devices?

_____

_____

4. Suppose that the COM ports were enabled in BIOS. How could they be disabled in Windows, thereby preventing a modem from using a COM port?

_____

_____

_____

5. How, besides coming in through the roof and directly striking the computer, might lightning destroy a computer?

_____

Critical
Thinking

LAB 13.5 CRITICAL THINKING: UPDATE MOTHERBOARD DRIVERS

Objectives

The goal of this lab is to help you update the drivers for motherboard components. After completing this lab, you will be able to:

➤ Identify a motherboard and its embedded devices

➤ Search a motherboard's manufacturer's Web site for updated drivers

➤ Download all applicable drivers for a motherboard

➤ Install drivers

➤ Document the process of updating motherboard drivers

Materials Required

This lab will require the following:

➤ Windows 98 or Windows 2000 operating system

➤ Motherboard documentation or SANDRA software installed in Lab 2.5

➤ Internet access

➤ PC tool kit (if necessary)

➤ Blank floppy disk (if necessary)

Activity Background

Like other devices, components on the motherboard use drivers to interact with the operating system. These drivers may be updated from time to time to resolve newly discovered bugs or to conform to newly implemented industry standards. In this lab, you will use your experience researching and installing drivers to install all available drivers for the components embedded on your motherboard.

Estimated completion time: **90 minutes**

ACTIVITY

1. Using procedures you have learned in previous labs, provide the information requested below:

   ▪ Motherboard manufacturer:

   _____

   ▪ Motherboard model:

   _____

2. Using procedures you have learned in previous labs, identify the components on your motherboard and record the information in Table 13-1. In the "Included?" column, enter "Yes" or "No" to indicate whether or not a component is included on the motherboard. Enter the version number of each component if you have access to that information.

Table 13-1

Component	Included?	Version Number (if available)
CPU type		
Chip set		
IDE controller		
AGP controller		
Embedded audio		
Embedded NIC/LAN		
Embedded modem		
Embedded video		
Other		
Other		

3. Research the motherboard manufacturer's Web site for driver updates and documentation for performing the updates.

4. Download any necessary files, including any documentation. List the files you downloaded and the purpose of each file in Table 13-2.

Table 13-2

Downloaded File	Purpose of the File

5. Print any documentation describing how to perform the updates.

6. Update the drivers.

7. Briefly explain how you updated the drivers.

_____

_____

_____

_____

_____

13

Review Questions

1. What is an embedded device?

   _____

   _____

2. If your motherboard documentation covers different models of motherboards, some with more embedded components than others, how can you definitely determine which model is installed in your computer?

   _____

   _____

3. What embedded device controls non-SCSI hard drives?

   _____

4. If you connect your monitor to a PCI video card in an expansion slot, would downloading and installing drivers for embedded video or for an AGP controller likely resolve any problems related to video performance? Explain.

   _____

   _____

   _____

5. Why would you want to update motherboard drivers? Give two reasons.

   _____

   _____

CHAPTER FOURTEEN

PURCHASING A PC OR BUILDING YOUR OWN

Labs included in this chapter

➤ Lab 14.1 Choose a System

➤ Lab 14.2 Determine System Requirements

➤ Lab 14.3 Compare What You Need with What You Can Afford

➤ Lab 14.4 Check System Compatibility

➤ Lab 14.5 Evaluate an Upgrade

LAB 14.1 CHOOSE A SYSTEM

Objectives

The goal of this lab is to help you determine what system you might purchase or build to meet your needs and desires. After completing this lab, you will be able to:

> ➤ List applications you want to run on your system

> ➤ Determine the type of system required for several types of applications

Materials Required

This lab will require the following:

> ➤ Workgroup of 2–4 students

Activity Background

The goal of this chapter is to help you learn how to plan and build a new system from scratch. The first four labs in this chapter explore the various stages of creating a new system and each lab builds on the one before it.

One of the first steps in planning and constructing your own PC is deciding what you're going to use it for, and what applications you will be running on it. After you make these decisions, you can decide what components are required to meet your needs. In this lab, you will describe and discuss the kind of system you would build for particular uses. Most of the labs in this chapter will require research, but in this case, all you need to do is discuss issues with your workgroup partners.

Estimated completion time: **20 minutes**

ACTIVITY

In the following steps you will plan four different systems. Each member of the workgroup should work separately, with each member planning four systems. Follow these steps:

1. Plan a system that will be used for gaming and Web surfing. Complete the following:

   ■ Applications that you are likely to install:

   _____

   _____

   ■ Hardware needed:

   _____

   _____

2. Plan a system that will be used for programming. Complete the following:
   - Applications that you are likely to install:

   _____

   _____

   - Hardware needed:

   _____

   _____

3. Plan a system that will be used for office applications. Complete the following:
   - Applications that you are likely to install:

   _____

   _____

   - Hardware needed:

   _____

   _____

4. Plan a system that will be used for a company file server. Complete the following:
   - Applications that you are likely to install:

   _____

   _____

   - Hardware needed:

   _____

   _____

5. For each type of system, discuss the differences in the systems planned by each member of your group. List the major differences here:

   _____

   _____

   _____

   _____

14

6. As a group, agree on a set of specifications for each system. How does the specifications agreed on by your group differ from your original specifications?

_____

_____

_____

_____

7. Assign one type of system to each member of the group. List the assignments for each group member. In Lab 14.2 and Lab 14.3, each member of the group will continue planning the type of system assigned here:

_____

_____

_____

_____

Review Questions

1. What type of system was assigned to you?

_____

2. What resources will you need to produce a detailed design for this system?

_____

_____

3. Did you find the process of discussing the different types of systems helpful? Why or why not?

_____

_____

4. On which type of system was there the most disagreement on requirements?

_____

_____

LAB 14.2 DETERMINE SYSTEM REQUIREMENTS

Objectives

The goal of this lab is to help you determine the specific requirements for the system you plan to build. After completing this lab, you will be able to:

> ➤ List minimum software and hardware components required for a particular type of system

Materials Required

This lab will require the following:

> ➤ Internet access
>
> ➤ Workgroup of 2–4 students (different people from Lab 14.1)

Activity Background

In the previous lab, you were assigned a type of system to build and you made some preliminary plans for it. In this lab, you will make more specific decisions regarding the required software and hardware components.

> **Estimated completion time: 30 minutes**

ACTIVITY

1. Working from the preliminary requirements you formed in Lab 14.1, use the Internet to research system requirements for your assigned type of system. Complete the following list of requirements:

   - CPU speed _____
   - Memory _____
   - Hard drive size _____
   - Case _____
   - Motherboard _____
   - Monitor size and resolution _____
   - Type of printer _____
   - Expansion cards _____

     _____

     _____

14

_____

_____

■ Other peripheral hardware (such as keyboard, mouse, PC camera, speakers, etc.)

_____

_____

_____

_____

■ Drives needed (for example, hard drives, CD or DVD, tape backup, Zip, or floppy)

_____

_____

_____

_____

_____

■ Operating system

_____

■ Applications

_____

_____

_____

_____

■ Any other requirements not listed above

_____

_____

_____

_____

2. Use the Internet or your local computer store to learn more about each component. List the description and cost of each component below. If you are doing your research on the Internet, print the Web page describing each component. (The Web page you print should include the component's price.) If you are conducting your research at a computer store, take careful notes, and be sure to note a price for each component. At this point, you are interested in evaluating your options for each component, so collect information on more than one possibility. For example, for a motherboard, gather information for two or three different motherboards that all satisfy your system requirements. Although you need to list the price for each component, do not be concerned about total cost at this point in your research. The following Internet resources might be helpful in your search, though you can use others as well:

- *www.cnet.com*
- *www.tomshardware.com*
- *www.motherboards.com*
- *www.reviewbooth.com*
- *www.dirtcheapdrives.com*
- *www.zdnet.com*

3. After you have finished gathering system requirements, find another student from another group who planned the same type of system you did. Compare your plans and note the differences.

_____

_____

_____

_____

14

Review Questions

1. What sites did you use for your research besides the ones listed above?

_____

_____

2. Did you add any components to your list or remove any from it after researching the type of system you want to build? Explain.

_____

_____

_____

3. What processor speed, amount of memory, and hard drive size do you plan to use? How did you make your choices?

_____

_____

_____

4. What components did you decide to use in your system other than the ones listed in the lab? What purpose will they serve in the new system?

_____

_____

_____

5. List any differences between your plans and the other student's plans for the same type of system.

_____

_____

_____

_____

LAB 14.3 COMPARE WHAT YOU NEED WITH WHAT YOU CAN AFFORD

Objectives

The goal of this lab is to help you determine the cost of building your own PC. After completing this lab, you will be able to:

➤ Research and compare component prices

➤ Determine how to build a system within your budget

Materials Required

This lab will require the following:

➤ Internet access

➤ Workgroup of 2–4 students

Activity Background

When planning a system, it is important to consider the cost of the components that you want to include. You might not be able to afford everything that you'd like to have in the system, or you might have to buy less expensive versions of some components in order to get what you want in another area. In this lab, you will develop several versions of a budget for the system you want to build. You will begin without a budget—that is, by figuring out what your dream system would cost. Then you will prioritize your list of components, and determine ways to reduce the system's total cost.

Estimated completion time: **30 minutes**

ACTIVITY

1. Use the information regarding specific hardware components that you compiled in Lab 14.2, complete Table 14-1. List the price of each component in your dream system in Table 14-1. (Note that you might not use all the rows in the table.) At the bottom of the table, list the total cost for your dream system.

Table 14-1 Dream system

Component	Manufacturer and Model	Cost
Processor		
Memory		
Hard drive		
Case		
Motherboard		
Monitor		
Printer		
Expansion card 1		
Expansion card 2		
Expansion card 3		
Expansion card 4		
Keyboard		
Mouse		
Speakers		
CD or DVD drive		
Tape drive		

14

Table 14-1   Dream system (continued)

Component	Manufacturer and Model	Cost
Zip drive		
Floppy drive		
Other drive		
Operating system		
Application 1		
Application 2		
Application 3		
Application 4		
Other		
Other		
Other		
Total cost of the system		

2. Review your list of components in Table 14–1 and prioritize them. In Table 14–2, list the components in order of importance. In the Notes column of Table 14–1, make notes regarding how much you need each component, and whether you can use a lower-cost version or eliminate it altogether. Indicate which (if any) components you are most willing to sacrifice in order to be able to afford a better component in another area of the system.

Table 14-2   Priority of system components

Component	Notes

Table 14-2   Priority of system components (continued)

Component	Notes

3. Pare your list down to the absolute minimum for the type of system you are building: the lowest amount of memory and hard drive space, the cheapest monitor, and so on. In Table 14-3, list the lowest prices available for each component and calculate the total cost of your bare-bones system.

Table 14-3   Bare bones system

Component	Manufacturer and Model	Cost
Processor		
Memory		

14

Table 14-3 Bare bones system (continued)

Component	Manufacturer and Model	Cost
Hard drive		
Case		
Motherboard		
Monitor		
Printer		
Expansion card 1		
Expansion card 2		
Expansion card 3		
Expansion card 4		
Keyboard		
Mouse		
Speakers		
CD or DVD drive		
Tape drive		
Zip drive		
Floppy drive		
Other drive		
Operating system		
Application 1		
Application 2		
Application 3		
Application 4		
Other		
Other		
Other		
Total cost of the system		

4. In Table 14-4, list the components of a system that is a reasonable compromise between the dream system and the bare bones system. This mid-range system is the one you will work with in the next lab.

Table 14-4   Mid-range system

Component	Manufacturer and Model	Cost
Processor		
Memory		
Hard drive		
Case		
Motherboard		
Monitor		
Printer		
Expansion card 1		
Expansion card 2		
Expansion card 3		
Expansion card 4		
Keyboard		
Mouse		
Speakers		
CD or DVD drive		
Tape drive		
Zip drive		
Floppy drive		
Other drive		
Operating system		
Application 1		
Application 2		
Application 3		

14

Table 14-4   Mid-range system (continued)

Component	Manufacturer and Model	Cost
Application 4		
Other		
Other		
Other		
Total cost of the system		

5. Compare your results from Steps 1–4 with the results of another student who is planning the same type of system. Compare cost estimates and note differences in the components you both planned to include. Note how you arrived at your calculation.

_____

_____

_____

_____

6. Repeat Step 5 with at least one student who is planning a different type of system.

_____

_____

_____

_____

Review Questions

1. What was the cost difference between your dream system and the bare-bones version?

_____

2. Which components were you willing to compromise on and why?

_____

_____

3. Which components were you *not* willing to compromise on and why?

_____

_____

4. How would the performance of your mid-range system compare to the dream system? How would the performance of the mid-range system compare to the bare-bones system? How would the performance of the dream system compare to the bare bones system?

_____

_____

_____

LAB 14.4 CHECK SYSTEM COMPATIBILITY

Objectives

The goal of this lab is to help you verify that the components in a proposed system are compatible. After completing this lab, you will be able to:

> ➤ Find incompatibilities between components in a proposed system

> ➤ Suggest an alternative system of approximately the same price

Materials Required

This lab will require the following:

> ➤ Internet access

> ➤ Workgroup of 2–4 students

Activity Background

No matter how much time you spend planning and building a PC, the system won't work right unless the system components are compatible. You'll save yourself a lot of trouble by attempting to discover incompatibilities before you begin to build a system. In this lab you will figure out which components in your proposed system are incompatible and suggest compatible components so that the cost of building the system remains approximately the same.

14

Estimated completion time: **40 minutes**

ACTIVITY

1. Take your plan for your mid-range system and alter it by introducing component incompatibilities. Write this altered version of your plan on a separate piece of paper. (Or, if you have the time, develop a new plan that incorporates incompatible components.) Incompatibilities you might introduce are suggested below, but you can introduce a problem not listed here:

   - A processor not supported by the motherboard
   - An incompatible mix of SCSI and IDE devices
   - A type of memory not supported on the motherboard
   - Five IDE devices on a system
   - A video card that uses the wrong kind of AGP slot for the motherboard
   - Expansion cards included with a motherboard that already has built-in logic

2. Calculate the total cost of the components in the system and record it here:

   _____

3. Give the revised PC plan to another student in your group. Ask the other student to find the incompatible components and suggest replacement components while keeping the price approximately the same. Do the same with the plan that you receive, recording below the incompatibilities that you find, the original cost of the system, replacement components, and the final cost of the altered system.

   _____

   _____

   _____

   _____

   _____

   _____

4. With the entire group, discuss the incompatibilities you found in the plans and how you fixed them. Make note of any incompatibilities that were introduced but not found.

_____

_____

_____

_____

Review Questions

1. Did you or the other students in your group introduce incompatibilities not suggested in Step 1? If so, list them here:

_____

_____

_____

_____

2. Were all the incompatibilities introduced in the plans discovered? If not, which ones were not, and why do you think these might have been more difficult to find?

_____

_____

_____

_____

14

3. List the incompatibility problems you located in the other student's plan and explain how you solved them.

_____

_____

_____

_____

_____

4. Did the students in your group have different ways of solving the same incompatibility problems? Explain.

_____

_____

_____

_____

_____

5. For the plan that you reviewed and revised, what was the difference in the original cost and the cost after you incorporated your solutions?

_____

_____

LAB 14.5 EVALUATE AN UPGRADE

Objectives

The goal of this lab is to help you determine the ease and cost of upgrading a PC. After completing this lab, you will be able to:

➤ Determine whether a system needs to be upgraded

➤ Explain why a system needs to be upgraded

➤ List components necessary to upgrade a system

Materials Required

This lab will require the following:

➤ Lab computer

➤ Documentation for computer components, if available

➤ Internet access

Activity Background

An important factor to consider when purchasing or building a PC is how easy it will be to upgrade the system. Sometimes you might chose to upgrade an existing system rather than replacing it with an altogether new system. Factors that affect the ease of upgrading a system include the different processors supported by the motherboard, the size of the case, and the number and type of ports and expansion slots on the motherboard. In this lab, you will examine an existing system to determine whether you can make certain upgrades to it and then evaluate how practical those upgrades are.

Estimated completion time: **45 minutes**

ACTIVITY

Follow these steps to determine whether your system can be upgraded:

1. In Table 14-5, list the components currently installed on your system. Useful sources of information include Device Manager, the Control Panel, and the Properties windows for various drives and devices.

Table 14-5 Current system components

Device	Description
Motherboard (make and model)	
BIOS type	
Memory (type and size)	
Hard drive (type and size)	
Other drives installed (floppy, Zip, CD-ROM, etc.)	
Monitor (type and size)	
Printer	
Sound card	
Modem (or other Internet connection)	
NIC	
Other devices	
Operating system (including version number)	
Applications (including version number)	

14

2. Using the Internet and any available documentation for the computer, select three components to upgrade. Determine the following for each component and record the information in the space provided:

Component 1: _____

- Replacement component:

  _____

  _____

- Cost of the upgrade:

  _____

- Are there other components that must also be upgraded in order for this upgrade to work? If so, what are they?

  _____

  _____

Component 2: _____

- Replacement component:

  _____

  _____

- Cost of the upgrade:

  _____

- Are there other components that must also be upgraded in order for this upgrade to work? If so, what are they?

  _____

  _____

Component 3: _____

- Replacement component:

  _____

  _____

- Cost of the upgrade:

  _____

- Are there other components that must also be upgraded in order for this upgrade to work? If so, what are they?

_____

_____

3. Print a Web page showing the specifications and cost of each new component. What is the total cost of the upgrades?

_____

4. Suppose you had to sell the system in its current state (without the upgrades). What would be a reasonable price?

_____

5. In general, when upgrading an existing system, you should not allow the cost of the upgrade to exceed half the value of the existing system. Do you think your proposed upgrade would exceed that limit?

_____

6. Using *www.cnet.com* (or another site where you can compare several systems), locate a notebook with specifications that are similar to your lab PC. Compare the cost of upgrading the memory, the processor, and the CD-ROM drive on each. (Substitute another component to compare if your computer does not have a CD-ROM drive.) In Table 14-6, compare the cost of upgrading your lab PC to the cost of a similar upgrade for a notebook computer.

Table 14-6   PC upgrade versus notebook upgrade

Component	Cost of Upgrading on PC	Cost of Upgrading on notebook
Processor		
Memory		
CD-ROM drive		

14

Review Questions

1. What components did you choose to upgrade and why?

_____

_____

_____

2. Which would be cheapest to upgrade, your lab PC or a comparable notebook? Explain your answer.

_____

_____

_____

_____

3. What other resources, besides the ones you used in the lab, do you think might be helpful in planning an upgrade?

_____

_____

4. Among the components you selected, which upgrade was the most expensive?

_____

_____

5. If you were actually performing these upgrades, is there any component or any system that you would _not_ choose to upgrade? Explain your answer.

_____

_____

_____

_____

GLOSSARY

100BaseFX — A variation of 100BaseT that supports fiber optic cable.

100BaseT — An Ethernet standard that operates at 100 Mbps and uses twisted-pair cabling. Also called Fast Ethernet. Variations of 100BaseT are 100BaseTX and 100BaseFX.

10Base2 — An Ethernet standard that operates at 10 Mbps and uses small coaxial cable up to 200 meters long. Also called ThinNet.

10Base5 — An Ethernet standard that operates at 10 Mbps and uses thick coaxial cable up to 500 meters long. Also called ThickNet.

1394.3 — A new standard, developed by the 1394 Trade Association, that is designed for peer-to-peer data transmission and allows imaging devices to send images and photos directly to printers without involving a computer.

3-D RAM — Special video RAM designed to improve 3-D graphics simulation.

80 conductor IDE cable — An IDE cable that has 40 pins but uses 80 wires, 40 of which are ground wires designed to reduce crosstalk on the cable. The cable is used by ATA/66, ATA/100, and ATA/133 IDE drives.

Accelerated Graphics Port (AGP) — A slot on a motherboard for a video card that transfers video data from the CPU and runs at a frequency synchronized with the system bus.

active backplane — A type of backplane system in which there is some circuitry, including bus connectors, buffers, and driver circuits, on the backplane.

active matrix — A type of video display that amplifies the signal at every intersection in the grid of electrodes, which enhances the pixel quality over that of a dual-scan passive matrix display.

active partition — The primary partition on the hard drive that boots the OS. Windows NT/2000/XP calls the active partition the system partition.

active terminator — A type of terminator for single-ended SCSI cables that includes voltage regulators in addition to the simple resistors used with passive termination.

adapter address — *See* MAC address.

adapter card — A small circuit board inserted in an expansion slot and used to communicate between the system bus and a peripheral device. Also called an interface card.

address bus — Lines on the system bus used by the CPU to communicate memory addresses and I/O addresses to the memory controller and I/O devices.

Advanced Transfer Cache (ATC) — A type of L2 cache contained within the Pentium processor housing that is embedded on the same core processor die as the CPU itself.

alternating current (AC) — Current that cycles back and forth rather than traveling in only one direction. In the U.S., the AC voltage from a standard wall outlet is normally between 110 and 115 V AC. In Europe, the AC voltage from a standard wall outlet is 220 V AC.

ammeter — A meter that measures electrical current in amps.

ampere or amp (A) — A unit of measurement for electrical current. One volt across a resistance of one ohm will produce a flow of one amp.

amplifier repeater — A repeater that does not distinguish between noise and signal; it amplifies both.

ANSI (American National Standards Institute) — A nonprofit organization dedicated to creating trade and communications standards.

ASCII (American Standard Code for Information Interchange) — A popular standard for writing letters and other characters in binary code. Originally, ASCII characters were 7 bits, allowing 127 possible values. ASCII has been expanded to 8 bits, allowing 128 additional values.

ASPI (Advanced SCSI Programming Interface) — A popular device driver that enables operating systems to communicate with a SCSI host adapter. The "A" stood for Adaptec before that company licensed the technology to others.

asynchronous SRAM — Static RAM that does not work in step with the CPU clock and is, therefore, slower than synchronous SRAM.

AT — A form factor, generally no longer produced, in which the motherboard requires a full-size case. Because of their dimensions and configuration, AT systems are difficult to install, service, and upgrade. Also called full AT.

AT command set — A set of commands that a PC uses to control a modem and that a user can enter to troubleshoot the modem.

ATAPI (Advanced Technology Attachment Packet Interface) — An interface standard—part of the IDE/ATA standards—that allows tape drives, CD-ROM drives, and other drives to be treated like an IDE hard drive by the system.

attenuation — Signal degeneration over distance. The problem caused by attenuation is solved on a network by adding repeaters to the network.

ATX — The most common form factor for PC systems presently in use, originally introduced by Intel in 1995. ATX motherboards and cases make better use of space and resources than did the AT form factor.

audio/modem riser (AMR) — A specification for a small slot on a motherboard to accommodate an audio or modem riser card. A controller on the motherboard contains some of the logic for the audio or modem functionality.

autodetection — A feature on newer system BIOS and hard drives that automatically identifies and configures a new drive in the CMOS setup.

Autoexec.bat — A startup text file once used by DOS and now used by Windows 9x to provide backward compatibility. It tells the computer what commands or programs to execute automatically during boot and is used to create a 16-bit environment.

autorange meter — A multimeter that senses the quantity of input and sets the range accordingly.

Baby AT — An improved and more flexible version of the AT form factor. Baby AT was the industry standard from approximately 1993 to 1997 and can fit into some ATX cases.

back side bus — The bus between the CPU and the L2 cache inside the CPU housing.

backplane system — A form factor in which there is no true motherboard. Instead, motherboard components are included on an adapter card plugged into a slot on a board called the backplane.

backup — An extra copy of a file, used if the original file becomes damaged or destroyed.

bandwidth — In relation to analog communication, the range of frequencies that a communications channel or cable can carry. In general use, the term refers to the volume of data that can travel on a bus or over a cable stated in bits per second (bps), kilobits per second (Kbps), or megabits per second (Mbps). Also called data throughput or line speed.

bank — An area on the motherboard that contains slots for memory modules (typically labeled bank 0, 1, 2, and 3).

baud rate — A measure of line speed between two devices such as a computer and a printer or a modem. This speed is measured in the number of times a signal changes in one second. *See also* bps.

beam detect mirror — Detects the initial presence of a laser printer's laser beam by reflecting the beam to an optical fiber.

binary number system — The number system used by computers; it has only two numbers, 0 and 1, called binary digits, or bits.

binding — The process by which a protocol is associated with a network card or a modem card.

BIOS (basic input/output system) — Firmware that can control much of a computer's input/output functions, such as communication with the floppy drive and the monitor. Also called ROM BIOS.

bit (binary digit) — A 0 or 1 used by the binary number system.

bits per second (bps) — A measure of data transmission speed. For example, a common modem speed is 56,000 bps, or 56 Kbps.

block mode — A method of data transfer between hard drive and memory that allows multiple data transfers on a single software interrupt.

Bluetooth — A standard for wireless communication and data synchronization between devices, developed by a group of electronics manufacturers and overseen by the Bluetooth Special Interest Group.

BNC connector — A connector used with thin coaxial cable. Some BNC connectors are T-shaped and called T-connectors. One end of the T connects to the NIC, and the two other ends can connect to cables or end a bus formation with a terminator.

boot record — The first sector of a drive, which contains information about the drive. Also called boot sector.

boot sector — *See* boot record.

boot sector virus — An infectious program that can replace the boot program with a modified, infected version of the boot command utilities, often causing boot and data retrieval problems.

booting — The process a computer goes through when it is first turned on, preparing the computer to receive commands.

bootstrap loader — A small program that can be used to boot from a disk.

break code — A code produced when a key on a computer keyboard is released.

bridge — A device used to connect two or more network segments. It can make decisions about allowing a packet to pass based on the packet's destination MAC address.

broadband — A transmission technique that carries more than one type of transmission on the same medium, such as cable modem and DSL.

broadcast — Process by which a message is sent from a single host to all hosts on the network, without regard to the kind of data being sent or the destination of the data.

brouter — A device that functions as both a bridge and a router. A brouter acts as a router when handling packets using routable protocols such as TCP/IP and IPX/SPX. It acts as a bridge when handling packets using nonroutable protocols such as NetBEUI.

brownouts — Temporary reductions in voltage, which can damage electrical components.

burst EDO (BEDO) — A refined version of EDO memory that significantly improved access time

over EDO. BEDO was not widely used because Intel chose not to support it. BEDO memory is stored on 168-pin DIMM modules.

burst SRAM — Memory that is more expensive and slightly faster than pipelined burst SRAM. Data is sent in a two-step process; the data address is sent, and then the data is sent without interruption.

bus — The paths, or lines, on the motherboard on which data, instructions, and electrical power move from component to component.

bus mastering — A device other than the CPU controlling a bus on the motherboard in order to access memory or another device.

bus mouse — A mouse that plugs into a bus adapter card and has a round, 9-pin mini-DIN connector.

bus riser — *See* riser card.

bus speed — The speed, or frequency, at which the data on the motherboard is moving.

bus topology — A LAN architecture in which all the devices are connected to a bus, or one communication line. Bus topology does not have a central connection point.

byte — A collection of 8 bits equivalent to a single character. When referring to system memory, an additional error-checking bit might be added, making the total 9 bits.

cable modem — Uses cable TV lines for data transmission requiring a modem at each end. From the modem, a network cable connects to a NIC in the user's PC.

cache memory — A kind of fast RAM that is used to speed up memory access because it does not need to be continuously refreshed.

CAM (Common Access Method) — A standard adapter driver used by SCSI.

capacitor — An electronic device that can maintain an electrical charge for a period of time and is used to smooth out the flow of electrical current. Capacitors are often found in computer power supplies.

CardBus — The latest PCMCIA specification. It improves I/O speed, increases the bus width to 32 bits, and supports lower-voltage PC Cards, while maintaining backward compatibility with earlier standards.

cards — Adapter boards or interface cards placed into expansion slots to expand the functions of a computer, allowing it to communicate with external devices such as monitors or speakers.

carrier — A signal used to activate a phone line to confirm a continuous frequency; used to indicate that two computers are ready to receive or transmit data via modems.

CAS Latency (CL) — A feature of memory that reflects the number of clock cycles that pass while data is written to memory.

CAU (Controlled-Access Unit) — *See* MAU.

CCITT (Comité Consultatif International Télégraphique et Téléphonique) — An international organization that was responsible for developing standards for international communications. This organization has been incorporated into the ITU. *See also* ITU.

CD-R (CD-recordable) — A CD drive that can record or write data to a CD. The drive may or may not be multisession, but the data cannot be erased once it is written.

CD-RW (CD-rewritable) — A CD drive that can record or write data to a CD. The data can be erased and overwritten. The drive may or may not be multisession.

central processing unit (CPU) — Also called a microprocessor or processor. The heart and brain of the computer, which receives data input, processes information, and executes instructions.

chain — A group of clusters used to hold a single file.

checksum — A method of error checking transmitted data, whereby the digits are added up and their sum compared to an expected sum.

chip creep — A condition in which chips loosen because of thermal changes.

chip set — A group of chips on the motherboard that controls the timing and flow of data and instructions to and from the CPU.

CHS (cylinder, head, sector) mode — The traditional method by which BIOS reads from and writes to hard drives by addressing the correct cylinder, head, and sector. Also called normal mode.

circuit board — A computer component, such as the main motherboard or an adapter board, that has electronic circuits and chips.

clamping voltage — The maximum voltage allowed through a surge suppressor, such as 175 or 330 volts.

clock speed — The speed, or frequency, expressed in MHz, that controls activity on the motherboard and is generated by a crystal or oscillator located somewhere on the motherboard.

clone — A computer that is a no-name Intel- and Microsoft-compatible PC.

cluster — One or more sectors that constitute the smallest unit of space on a disk for storing data (also referred to as a file allocation unit). Files are written to a disk as groups of whole clusters.

cluster chain — A series of clusters used to hold a single file.

CMOS (complementary metal-oxide semiconductor) — One of two types of technologies used to manufacture microchips (the other type is TTL, or transistor-transistor logic chips). CMOS chips require less electricity, hold data longer after the electricity is turned off, are slower, and produce less heat than TTL chips. The configuration, or setup, chip is a CMOS chip.

CMOS configuration chip — A chip on the motherboard that contains a very small amount of memory, or RAM—enough to hold configuration, or setup, information about the computer.

CMOS setup — (1) The chip on the motherboard that holds configuration information about the system, such as date and time, and which CPU, hard drives, or floppy drives are installed. Also called CMOS or CMOS RAM. The chip is powered by a battery when the PC is turned off. (2) The program in system BIOS that can change the values in CMOS RAM.

CMOS setup chip — *See* CMOS configuration chip.

COAST (cache on a stick) — Memory modules that hold memory used as a memory cache. *See* cache memory.

coaxial cable — Networking cable used with 10-Mbps Ethernet ThinNet or ThickNet.

cold boot — *See* hard boot.

collision — Conflict that occurs when two computers send a signal on the same channel at the same time.

color depth — The number of possible colors used by a monitor. Determines the number of bits used to compose one pixel and affects the amount of data sent to the video card to build one screen.

combo card — An Ethernet card that contains more than one transceiver, each with a different port on the back of the card, in order to accommodate different cabling media.

communication and networking riser (CNR) — A specification for a small expansion slot on a motherboard that accommodates a small audio, modem, or network riser card.

compact case — A type of case used in low-end desktop systems. Compact cases, also called low-profile or slimline cases, follow the NLX, LPX, or Mini LPX form factor. They are likely to have fewer drive bays, but generally still provide for expansion.

constant angular velocity (CAV) — A technology used by hard drives and newer CD-ROM drives whereby the disk rotates at a constant speed.

constant linear velocity (CLV) — A CD-ROM format in which the spacing of data is consistent on the CD, but the speed of the disc varies depending on whether the data being read is near the center or the edge of the disc.

contention-based — A network system in which each computer on the system must compete for the opportunity to transmit a signal on the network.

continuity — A continuous, unbroken path for the flow of electricity. A continuity test can determine whether or not internal wiring is still intact, or whether a fuse is good or bad.

control blade — A laser printer component that prevents too much toner from sticking to the cylinder surface.

control bus — The lines on the system bus used to send control signals to manage communication on the motherboard.

CRC (cyclical redundancy check) — A process in which calculations are performed on bytes of data before and after they are transmitted to check for corruption during transmission.

credit card memory — A type of memory used on older notebooks that could upgrade existing memory by way of a specialized memory slot.

C-RIMM (Continuity RIMM) — A placeholder RIMM module that provides continuity so that every RIMM slot is filled.

cross-linked clusters — Errors caused when more than one file points to a cluster, and the files appear to share the same disk space, according to the file allocation table.

crossover cable — A cable used to connect two PCs into the simplest network possible. Also used to connect two hubs.

CSMA/CA (Carrier Sense Multiple Access with Collision Avoidance) — A method to control collisions on a network, whereby each computer signals its intent to send data before sending it. This method is used on wireless LANs.

CSMA/CD (Carrier Sense Multiple Access with Collision Detection) — A method that Ethernet networks use to monitor the network to determine if the line is free before sending a transmission.

data bus — The lines on the system bus that the CPU uses to send and receive data.

data cartridge — A type of tape medium typically used for backups. Full-sized data cartridges are 4 × 6 × ⅜ inches in size. A minicartridge is only 3 ¼ × 2 ½ × ⅜ inches in size.

datagram — *See* packet.

data line protector — A surge protector designed to work with the telephone line to a modem.

data path size — The number of lines on a bus that can hold data, for example, 8, 16, 32, and 64 lines, which can accommodate 8, 16, 32, and 64 bits at a time.

data throughput — *See* bandwidth.

DC controller — A card inside a notebook that converts voltage to CPU voltage. Some notebook manufacturers consider the card to be a FRU.

DCE (Data Communications Equipment) — The hardware, usually a dial-up modem, that provides the connection between a data terminal and a communications line.

de facto standard — A standard that does not have official backing but is considered a standard because of use and acceptance by the industry.

defragment — To "optimize" or rewrite a file to a disk in one contiguous chain of clusters, thus speeding up data retrieval.

demodulation — The process by which digital data that has been converted to analog data is converted back to digital data. *See* modulation.

device driver — A small program stored on the hard drive that tells the computer how to communicate with an input/output device such as a printer or modem.

diagnostic cards — Adapter cards designed to discover and report computer errors and conflicts at POST time (before the computer boots up), often by displaying a number on the card.

diagnostic software — Utility programs that help troubleshoot computer systems. Some DOS diagnostic utilities are CHKDSK and SCANDISK. PC-Technician is an example of a third-party diagnostic program.

differential — A signaling method for SCSI cables in which a signal is carried on two wires, each carrying voltage, and the signal is the difference between the two. Differential signaling provides for error checking and greater data integrity. Compare to single-ended.

digital diagnostic disk (DDD) — A floppy disk that has data written on it that is precisely aligned. Used to test the alignment of a floppy disk drive.

DIMM (dual inline memory module) — A miniature circuit board used in newer computers to hold memory. DIMMs can hold 16, 32, 64, 128, 256 or 512 MB or 1 GB of RAM on a single module.

diode — An electronic device that allows electricity to flow in only one direction. Used in a rectifier circuit.

DIP (dual inline package) switch — A switch on a circuit board or other device that can be set on or off to hold configuration or setup information.

direct current (DC) — Current that travels in only one direction (the type of electricity provided by batteries). Computer power supplies transform AC to low DC.

Direct Rambus DRAM — A memory technology by Rambus and Intel that uses a narrow, very fast

network-type system bus. Memory is stored on a RIMM module. Also called RDRAM or Direct RDRAM.

Direct RDRAM — *See* Direct Rambus DRAM.

discrete L2 cache — A type of L2 cache contained within the Pentium processor housing, but on a different die, with a cache bus between the processor and the cache.

disk mirroring — A strategy whereby the same data is written to two hard drives in a computer to safeguard against hard drive failure. Disk mirroring uses only a single controller for two drives.

disk striping — Treating multiple hard drives as a single volume. Data is written across the multiple drives in small segments, to increase performance and logical disk volume. When parity is used, disk striping also provides logical fault tolerance. RAID 5 is disk striping with parity information distributed over all drives in the array.

Display Power Management Signaling (DPMS) — Energy Star standard specifications that allow for the video card and monitor to go into sleep mode simultaneously. *See also* Energy Star systems.

DMA (direct memory access) channel — A number identifying a channel whereby the device can pass data to memory without involving the CPU. Think of a DMA channel as a shortcut for data moving to/from the device and memory.

docking station — A device that receives a notebook so that it can provide additional secondary storage and easily connect to peripheral devices.

dot pitch — The distance between the dots that the electronic beam hits on a monitor screen.

Double Data Rate SDRAM (DDR SDRAM) — A type of memory technology used on DIMMs that runs at twice the speed of the system clock.

doze time — The time before an Energy Star or "Green" system will reduce 80 percent of its activity.

drop height — The height from which a manufacturer states that its drive can be dropped without making the drive unusable.

DSL (Digital Subscriber Line) — A telephone line that carries digital data from end to end, and can be leased from the telephone company for individual use. DSL lines are rated at 5 Mbps, about 50 times faster than regular telephone lines.

DTE (Data Terminal Equipment) — Both the computer and a remote terminal or other computer to which it is attached.

dual porting — Allows the video chip set (input) and the RAM DAC (output) to access video memory at the same time. A special kind of video RAM is required.

dual-scan passive matrix — A type of video display that is less expensive than an active-matrix display and does not provide as high-quality an image. With dual-scan display, two columns of electrodes are activated at the same time.

dual-voltage CPU — A CPU that requires two different voltages, one for internal processing and the other for I/O processing.

duplexing — An improvement of disk mirroring in which each hard drive has its own adapter card.

DVD (digital video disc or digital versatile disk) — A faster, larger CD-ROM format that can read older CDs, store over 8 GB of data, and hold full-length motion picture videos.

dynamic RAM (DRAM) — The most common type of system memory, it requires refreshing every few milliseconds.

ECC (error-correcting code) — A chip set feature on a system board that checks the integrity of data stored on DIMMs or RIMMs and can correct single-bit errors in a byte. More advanced ECC schemas can detect, but not correct, double-bit errors in a byte.

ECHS (extended CHS) mode — *See* large mode.

ECP (Extended Capabilities Port) — A bidirectional parallel port mode that uses a DMA channel to speed up data flow.

EDO (extended data out) — A type of RAM that may be 10–20 percent faster than conventional RAM because it eliminates the delay before it issues the next memory address.

EEPROM (electrically erasable programmable ROM) — A type of chip in which higher voltage may be applied to one of the pins to erase its previous memory before a new instruction set is electronically written.

EISA (Extended ISA) bus — A 32-bit bus that can transfer 4 bytes at a time at a speed of about 20 MHz.

EMI (electromagnetic interference) — A magnetic field produced as a side effect from the flow of electricity. EMI can cause corrupted data in data lines that are not properly shielded.

Energy Star systems — "Green" systems that satisfy the EPA requirements to decrease the overall consumption of electricity. *See also* Green Standards.

enhanced BIOS — A system BIOS that has been written to accommodate large-capacity drives (over 504 MB, usually in the gigabyte range).

Enhanced IDE (EIDE) — A drive standard that allows systems to recognize drives larger than 504 MB and to handle up to four devices on the same controller.

EPIC (explicitly parallel instruction computing) — The CPU architecture used by the Intel Itanium that bundles programming instructions with instructions on how to use multiprocessing abilities to do two instructions in parallel.

EPP (Enhanced Parallel Port) — A parallel port that allows data to flow in both directions (bidirectional port) and is faster than original parallel ports on PCs that only allowed communication in one direction.

EPROM (erasable programmable ROM) — A type of chip with a special window that allows the current memory contents to be erased with special ultraviolet light so the chip can be reprogrammed. Many BIOS chips are EPROMs.

error correction — The ability of a modem to identify transmission errors and then automatically request another transmission.

ESD (electrostatic discharge) — Another name for static electricity, which can damage chips and destroy motherboards, even though it might not be felt or seen with the naked eye.

Ethernet — A LAN architecture that uses a bus or star topology, uses CSMA/CD when two computers are trying to gain access to the network at the same time, and is the most popular network architecture in use today.

expansion bus — A bus that does not run in sync with the system clock.

expansion card — A circuit board inserted into a slot on the motherboard to enhance the capability of the computer.

expansion slot — A narrow slot on the motherboard where an expansion card can be inserted. Expansion slots connect to a bus on the motherboard.

extended partition — The only partition on a hard drive that can contain more than one logical drive.

external bus — *See* system bus.

external cache — Static cache memory, stored on the motherboard or inside CPU housing, that is not part of the CPU (also called L2 or L3 cache).

faceplate — A metal plate that comes with the motherboard and fits over the ports to create a well-fitted enclosure around them.

Fast Ethernet — *See* 100BaseT.

FAT12 — The 12-bit wide, one-column file allocation table for a floppy disk, containing information about how each cluster or file allocation unit on the disk is currently used.

fault tolerance — The degree to which a system can tolerate failures. Adding redundant components, such as disk mirroring or disk duplexing, is a way to build in fault tolerance.

FDDI (Fiber Distributed Data Interface) — A ring-based network that does not require a centralized hub and can transfer data at a rate of 100 Mbps.

field replaceable unit (FRU) — A component in a computer or device that can be replaced with a new component without sending the computer or device back to the manufacturer. Examples: power supply, DIMM, motherboard, floppy disk drive.

file allocation table (FAT) — A table on a disk that tracks the clusters used to contain a file.

file allocation unit — *See* cluster.

FireWire — An expansion bus that can also be configured to work as a local bus. It is expected to replace the SCSI bus, providing an easy method to install and configure fast I/O devices. Also called IEEE 1394 and i.Link.

firmware — Software that is permanently stored in a chip.

flash memory — A type of RAM that can electronically hold memory even when the power is off.

flash ROM — ROM that can be reprogrammed or changed without replacing chips.

flat panel monitor — A desktop monitor that uses an LCD panel.

FlexATX — A version of the ATX form factor that allows for maximum flexibility in the size and shape of cases and motherboards. FlexATX is ideal for custom systems.

flow control — When using modems, a method of controlling the flow of data to adjust for problems with data transmission. Xon/Xoff is an example of a flow control protocol.

forced perfect terminator (FPT) — A type of SCSI active terminator that includes a mechanism to force signal termination to the correct voltage, eliminating most signal echoes and interference.

form factor — A set of specifications on the size, shape, and configuration of a computer hardware component such as a case, power supply, or motherboard.

formatting — Preparing a new floppy disk for use by placing tracks and sectors on its surface to store information (for example, FORMAT A:). Old disks can be reformatted, but all data will be lost.

FPM (fast page mode) — A memory mode used before the introduction of EDO memory. FPM improved on earlier memory types by sending the row address just once for many accesses to memory near that row.

fragmentation — On a hard drive, the distribution of data files such that they are stored in noncontiguous clusters.

fragmented file — A file that has been written to different portions of the disk so that it is not in contiguous clusters.

frame — The header and trailer information added to data to form a data packet to be sent over a network.

front side bus — The bus between the CPU and the memory outside the CPU housing. Also called the system bus.

full AT — *See* AT.

full-duplex — Communication that happens in two directions at the same time.

General Protection Fault (GPF) — A Windows error that occurs when a program attempts to access a memory address that is not available or is no longer assigned to it.

Gigabit Ethernet — The newest version of Ethernet. Gigabit Ethernet supports rates of data transfer up to 1 gigabit per second but is not yet widely used.

gigahertz (GHz) — One thousand MHz, or one billion cycles per second.

graphics accelerator — A type of video card that has an on-board processor that can increase speed and boost graphical and video performance.

Green Standards — A computer or device that conforms to these standards can go into sleep or doze mode when not in use, saving energy and helping the environment. Devices that carry the Green Star or Energy Star comply with these standards.

ground bracelet — A strap you wear around your wrist that is attached to the computer case, ground mat, or another ground so that ESD is discharged from your body before you touch sensitive components inside a computer. Also called static strap, ground strap, ESD bracelet.

guard tone — A tone that an answering modem sends when it first answers the phone, to tell the calling modem that a modem is on the other end of the line.

half-duplex — Communication between two devices in which transmission takes place in only one direction at a time.

half-life — The time it takes for a medium storing data to weaken to half of its strength. Magnetic media, including traditional hard drives and floppy disks, have a half-life of five to seven years.

handshaking — When two modems begin to communicate, the initial agreement made as to how to send and receive data.

hard boot — Restarting the computer by turning off the power or by pressing the Reset button. Also called cold boot.

hard copy — Output from a printer to paper.

hard drive — The main secondary storage device of a PC, a small case that contains magnetic coated platters that rotate at high speed.

hard drive controller — The firmware that controls access to a hard drive contained on a circuit board mounted on or inside the hard drive housing. Older hard drives used firmware on a controller card that connected to the drive by way of two cables, one for data and one for control.

hard drive standby time — The amount of time before a hard drive will shut down to conserve energy.

hard-disk loading — The illegal practice of installing unauthorized software on computers for sale. Hard-disk loading can be identified by the absence of original disks in the original system's shipment.

hardware — The physical components that constitute the computer system, such as the monitor, the keyboard, the motherboard, and the printer.

hardware interrupt — An event caused by a hardware device signaling the CPU that it requires service.

head — The top or bottom surface of one platter on a hard drive. Each platter has two heads.

heat sink — A piece of metal, with cooling fins, that can be attached to or mounted on an integrated chip (such as the CPU) to dissipate heat.

hertz (Hz) — Unit of measurement for frequency, calculated in terms of vibrations, or cycles per second. For example, for 16-bit stereo sound, a frequency of 44,000 Hz is used. *See also* megahertz.

hexadecimal notation — A numbering system that uses sixteen digits, the numerals 0–9 and the letters A–F. Hexadecimal notation is often used to display memory addresses.

hidden file — A file that is not displayed in a directory list. Whether to hide or display a file is one of the file's attributes kept by the OS.

high-level formatting — Formatting performed by means of the DOS or Windows Format program (for example, FORMAT C:/S creates the boot record, FAT, and root directory on drive C and makes the drive bootable). Also called OS formatting.

host — *See* node.

host adapter — The circuit board that controls a SCSI bus, supporting as many as seven or fifteen separate devices. The host adapter controls communication between the SCSI bus and the PC.

host bus — *See* memory bus or system bus.

hot-pluggable — *See* hot-swappable.

hot-swappable — A device that can be plugged into a computer while it is turned on. The computer senses the device and configures it without rebooting, or the device can be removed without an OS error. Also called hot-pluggable.

hub — A network device or box that provides a central location to connect cables.

HVD (High Voltage Differential) — A type of SCSI differential signaling requiring more expensive hardware to handle the higher voltage. HVD became obsolete with the introduction of SCSI-3.

i.Link — *See* FireWire.

I/O addresses — Numbers that are used by devices and the CPU to manage communication between them. Also called ports or port addresses.

I/O controller card — An older card that can contain serial, parallel, and game ports and floppy drive and IDE connectors.

IBM-compatible PC — A computer that uses an Intel (or compatible) processor and can run DOS and Windows.

IEEE (Institute of Electrical and Electronics Engineers) — A nonprofit organization that develops standards for the computer and electronics industries.

IEEE 1284 — A standard for parallel ports and cables developed by the Institute for Electrical and Electronics Engineers and supported by many hardware manufacturers.

IEEE 1394 — *See* FireWire.

IEEE 802.11b — An IEEE specification for wireless communication and data synchronization that competes with Bluetooth. Also known as Wi-Fi. Apple Computer's version of 802.11b is called AirPort.

in-band signaling — In modem communication, the name of the signaling used by software flow control, which pauses transmission by sending a special control character in the same channel (or band) that data is sent in.

instruction set — The set of instructions, on the CPU chip, that the computer can perform directly (such as ADD and MOVE).

Integrated Device Electronics or Integrated Drive Electronics (IDE) — A hard drive whose disk controller is integrated into the drive, eliminating the need for a controller cable and thus increasing speed, as well as reducing price.

intelligent UPS — A UPS connected to a computer by way of a serial cable so that software on the computer can monitor and control the UPS.

interlaced — A type of display in which the electronic beam of a monitor draws every other line with each pass, which lessens the overall effect of a lower refresh rate.

internal bus — The bus inside the CPU that is used for communication between the CPU's internal components.

internal cache — Memory cache that is faster than external cache, and is contained inside 80486 and Pentium chips (also referred to as primary, Level 1, or L1 cache).

interrupt handler — A program (either BIOS or a device driver) that is used by the CPU to process a hardware interrupt. Also called a request handler.

interrupt vector table — A table that stores the memory addresses assigned to interrupt handlers so the CPU can find one when needed. Also called a vector table.

IP address (Internet Protocol address) — A 32-bit address consisting of four numbers separated by periods, used to uniquely identify a device on a network that uses TCP/IP protocols. The first numbers identify the network; the last numbers identify the host, or the device. An example of an IP address is 206.96.103.114.

IPX/SPX (Internetwork Packet Exchange/ Sequenced Packet Exchange) — A networking protocol first used by Novell NetWare, which corresponds to the TCP/IP protocols.

IRQ (interrupt request) line — A line on a bus that is assigned to a device and is used to signal the CPU for servicing. These lines are assigned a reference number (for example, the normal IRQ for a printer is IRQ 7).

ISA (Industry Standard Architecture) slot — An older slot on the motherboard used for slower I/O devices, which can support an 8-bit or a 16-bit data path. ISA slots are mostly replaced by PCI slots.

ISA bus — An 8-bit industry standard architecture bus used on the original 8088 PC. Sixteen-bit ISA buses were designed for the 286 AT, and are still used in some Pentium motherboards for devices such as modems.

ISDN (Integrated Services Digital Network) — A digital telephone line that can carry data at about five times the speed of regular telephone lines. Two channels (telephone numbers) share a single pair of wires.

isochronous data transfer — A method used by IEEE 1394 to transfer data continuously without breaks.

ITU (International Telecommunications Union) — The international organization responsible for developing international standards of communication. Formerly CCITT.

JPEG (Joint Photographic Experts Group) — A graphical compression scheme that allows the user to control the amount of data averaged and sacrificed as file size is reduced. It is a common Internet file format. Most JPEG files have a .jpg extension.

jumper — Two wires that stick up side by side on the motherboard that are used to hold configuration information. The jumper is considered closed if a cover is over the wires, and open if the cover is missing.

keyboard — A common input device through which data and instructions may be typed into computer memory.

LAN (local area network) — A computer network that covers only a small area, usually within one building.

lands — Microscopic flat areas on the surface of a CD or DVD that separate pits. Lands and pits are used to represent data on the disk.

laptop computer — *See* notebook.

large mode — A mode of addressing information on hard drives that range from 504 MB to 8.4 GB, addressing information on a hard drive by translating cylinder, head, and sector information in order to break the 528-MB hard drive barrier. Another name for large mode. Also called ECHS mode.

large-capacity drive — A hard drive larger than 504 MB.

LBA (logical block addressing) mode — A mode of addressing information on hard drives in which the BIOS and operating system view the drive as one long linear list of LBAs or addressable sectors, permitting drives to be larger than 8.4 GB (LBA 0 is cylinder 0, head 0, and sector 1).

Level 1 (L1) cache — *See* internal cache.

Level 2 (L2) cache — *See* external cache.

Level 3 (L3) cache — *See* external cache.

line conditioner — A device that regulates, or conditions, power, providing continuous voltage during brownouts and spikes.

line speed — *See* bandwidth.

line-interactive UPS — A variation of a standby UPS that shortens switching time by always keeping the inverter that converts AC to DC working, so that there is no charge-up time for the inverter.

local bus — A bus that operates at a speed synchronized with the CPU frequency. The system bus is a local bus.

local I/O bus — A local bus that provides I/O devices with fast access to the CPU.

logical drive — A portion or all of a hard drive partition that is treated by the operating system as though it were a physical drive. Each logical drive is assigned a drive letter, such as drive C, and contains a file system. Also called a volume.

logical geometry — The number of heads, tracks, and sectors that the BIOS on the hard drive controller presents to the system BIOS and the OS. The logical geometry does not consist of the same values as the physical geometry, although calculations of drive capacity yield the same results.

lost allocation units — *See* lost clusters.

lost clusters — File fragments that, according to the file allocation table, contain data that does not belong to any file. The command CHKDSK/F can free these fragments. Also called lost allocation units.

low insertion force (LIF) socket — A socket that requires the installer to manually apply an even force over the microchip when inserting the chip into the socket.

low-level formatting — A process (usually performed at the factory) that electronically creates the hard drive tracks and sectors and tests for bad spots on the disk surface.

low-profile case — *See* compact case.

LPX — A form factor in which expansion cards are mounted on a riser card that plugs into a motherboard. The expansion cards in LPX systems are mounted parallel to the motherboard, rather than perpendicular to it as in AT and ATX systems.

LUN (Logical Unit Number) — A number assigned to a logical device (such as a tray in a CD changer) that is part of a physical SCSI device, which is assigned a SCSI ID.

LVD (Low Voltage Differential) — A type of differential signaling that uses lower voltage than does HVD, is less expensive, and can be compatible with single-ended signaling on the same SCSI bus.

MAC (Media Access Control) address — A 12-character value that uniquely identifies a NIC and is assigned by manufacturers. The address is often printed on the adapter. An example is 00 00 0C 08 2F 35. Also called adapter address or physical address.

main board — *See* motherboard.

make code — A code produced by pressing a key on a computer keyboard.

Master Boot Record (MBR) — The first sector on a hard drive, which contains the partition table and other information needed by BIOS to access the drive.

material safety data sheet (MSDS) — A document that explains how to properly handle substances such as chemical solvents; includes information such as physical data, toxicity, health effects, first aid, storage, disposal, and spill procedures.

MAU (Multistation Access Unit) — A centralized hub used in token ring networks to connect stations. Also called CAU or MSAU.

MDRAM (multibank DRAM) — A special kind of RAM used on video cards that is able to use a full 128-bit bus path without requiring the full 4 MB of RAM.

megahertz (MHz) — One million Hz, or one million cycles per second. *See also* hertz (Hz).

memory — Physical microchips that can hold data and programming, located on the motherboard or expansion cards.

memory address — A number assigned to each byte in memory. The CPU can use memory addresses to track where information is stored in RAM. Memory addresses are usually displayed as hexadecimal numbers in segment/offset form.

memory bus — *See also* system bus.

memory cache — A small amount of faster RAM that stores recently retrieved data, in anticipation of what the CPU will request next, thus speeding up access. *See also* system bus.

Micro Channel Architecture (MCA) bus — A proprietary IBM PS/2 bus, seldom seen today, with a width of 16 or 32 bits and multiple master control, which allowed for multitasking.

microATX — A recent version of the ATX form factor, addressing new technologies that have been developed since the original introduction of ATX.

microprocessor — *See* central processing unit (CPU).

Mini-ATX — A smaller ATX board that can be used with regular ATX cases and power supplies.

minicartridge — A tape drive cartridge that is only 3 ¼ × 2 ½ × ⅜ inches. It is small enough to allow two drives to fit into a standard 5½-inch drive bay of a PC case.

Mini-LPX — A smaller version of the LPX motherboard.

MMX (Multimedia Extensions) — Multimedia instructions built into Intel processors to add functionality such as better processing of multimedia, SIMD support, and increased cache.

modem — From MOdulate/DEModulate. A device that modulates digital data from a computer to an analog format that can be sent over telephone lines, then demodulates it back into digital form.

modem eliminator — *See* null modem cable.

modem riser card — A small modem card that uses an AMR or CNR slot. Part of the modem logic is contained in a controller on the motherboard.

modem speed — The speed at which a modem can transmit data along a phone line, measured in bits per second (bps). Also called line speed.

modulation — Converting binary or digital data into an analog signal that can be sent over standard telephone lines.

monitor — The most commonly used output device for displaying text and graphics on a computer.

motherboard — The main board in the computer, also called the system board. The CPU, ROM chips, SIMMs, DIMMs, RIMMs, and interface cards are plugged into the motherboard.

motherboard bus — *See* system bus.

motherboard mouse — *See* PS/2-compatible mouse.

mouse — A pointing and input device that allows the user to move a cursor around a screen and select programs with the click of a button.

MP3 — A method to compress audio files that uses MPEG level 3. It can reduce sound files as low as a 1:24 ratio without losing much sound quality.

MPEG (Moving Pictures Experts Group) — A processing-intensive standard for data compression for motion pictures that tracks movement from one frame to the next and only stores the data that has changed.

MSAU — *See* MAU.

multimedia — A type of computer presentation that combines text, graphics, animation, photos, sound, and/or full-motion video.

multimeter — A device used to measure the various components of an electrical circuit. The most common measurements are voltage, current, and resistance.

multiplier — The factor by which the bus speed or frequency is multiplied to get the CPU clock speed.

multiscan monitor — A monitor that can work within a range of frequencies and thus can work with different standards and video cards. It offers a variety of refresh rates.

multisession — A feature that allows data to be read from or written to a CD during more than one session. This is important if the disk was only partially filled during the first write.

narrow SCSI — One of the two main SCSI specifications. Narrow SCSI has an 8-bit data bus. The word "narrow" is not usually included in the names of narrow SCSI devices.

NetBEUI (NetBIOS Extended User Interface) — A fast, proprietary Microsoft networking protocol used only by Windows-based systems, and limited to LANs because it does not support routing.

network adapter — *See* network interface card.

network interface card (NIC) — The hardware device inside a PC that provides access to a network. Also called a network adapter.

NLX — A low-end form factor that is similar to LPX but provides greater support for current and emerging processor technologies. NLX was designed for flexibility and efficiency of space.

node — Any computer, workstation, or device on a network.

noise — An extraneous, unwanted signal, often over an analog phone line, that can cause communication interference or transmission errors. Possible sources are fluorescent lighting, radios, TVs, lightning, or bad wiring.

noninterlaced — A type of display in which the electronic beam of a monitor draws every line on the screen with each pass.

nonparity memory — Eight-bit memory without error checking. A SIMM part number with a 32 in it (4 $\times$ 8 bits) is nonparity.

nonvolatile — A kind of RAM that is stable and can hold data as long as electricity is powering the memory.

normal mode — *See* CHS mode.

North Bridge — That portion of the chip set hub that connects faster I/O buses (for example, AGP bus) to the system bus. Compare to South Bridge.

notebook — A personal computer designed for portability, using less power and taking up less space than a regular PC. Also called a laptop computer.

null modem cable — A cable that allows two data terminal equipment (DTE) devices to communicate in which the transmit and receive wires are cross-connected and no modems are necessary.

ohm (Ω) — The standard unit of measurement for electrical resistance. Resistors are rated in ohms.

on-board ports — Ports that are directly on the motherboard, such as a built-in keyboard port or on-board serial port.

operating system (OS) — Software that controls a computer. An OS controls how system resources are used and provides a user interface, a way of managing hardware and software, and ways to work with files.

operating system formatting — *See* high-level formatting.

out-of-band signaling — The type of signaling used by hardware flow control, which sends a message to pause transmission by using channels (or bands) not used for data.

overclocking — Running a motherboard at a frequency that is not recommended or guaranteed by CPU or chip set manufacturers.

P1 connector — Power connection on an ATX motherboard.

P8 connector — One of two power connectors on an AT motherboard.

P9 connector — One of two power connectors on an AT motherboard.

293packet — A data segment small enough to be transmitted on a network, including the data and the header and trailer used to identify the packet. Also called datagram.

parallel port — A female 25-pin port on a computer that can transmit data in parallel, 8 bits at a time, and is usually used with a printer. The names for parallel ports are LPT1 and LPT2.

parity — An error-checking scheme in which a ninth, or "parity," bit is added. The value of the parity bit is set to either 0 or 1 to provide an even number of ones for even parity and an odd number of ones for odd parity.

parity error — An error that occurs when the number of 1s in the byte is not in agreement with the expected number.

parity memory — Nine-bit memory in which the ninth bit is used for error checking. A SIMM part number with a 36 in it (4 $\times$ 9 bits) is parity. Older PCs almost always use parity chips.

partition — A division of a hard drive that can be used to hold logical drives.

partition table — A table at the beginning of the hard drive that contains information about each partition on the drive. The partition table is contained in the Master Boot Record.

passive backplane — A type of backplane system in which the backplane contains no circuitry at all. Passive backplanes locate all circuitry on a mothercard plugged into a backplane.

passive terminator — A type of terminator for single-ended SCSI cables. Simple resistors are used to provide termination of a signal. Passive termination is not reliable over long distances and should only be used with narrow SCSI.

patch cable — A network cable that is used to connect a PC to a hub.

PC Card — A credit-card-sized adapter card that can be slid into a slot in the side of many notebook computers and is used for connecting to modems, networks, and CD-ROM drives. Also called PCMCIA Card.

PC Card slot — An expansion slot on a notebook computer, into which a PC Card is inserted. Also called a PCMCIA Card slot.

PCI (Peripheral Component Interconnect) bus — A bus common on Pentium computers that runs at speeds of up to 33 MHz or 66 MHz, with a 32-bit-wide or 64-bit-wide data path. PCI-X, released in September 1999, enables PCI to run at 133 MHz. For some chip sets, it serves as the middle layer between the memory bus and expansion buses.

PCI bus IRQ steering — A feature that makes it possible for PCI devices to share an IRQ. System BIOS and the OS must both support this feature.

PCMCIA (Personal Computer Memory Card International Association) Card — *See* PC Card.

PCMCIA Card slot — *See* PC Card slot.

PDA (Personal Digital Assistant) — A small, handheld computer that has its own operating system and applications.

peripheral devices — Devices that communicate with the CPU but are not located directly on the motherboard, such as the monitor, floppy drive, printer, and mouse.

physical address — *See* MAC address.

physical geometry — The actual layout of heads, tracks, and sectors on a hard drive. Refer also to logical geometry.

pin array cartridge (PAC) — The cartridge that houses the Intel Itanium processor.

pin grid array (PGA) — A feature of a CPU socket whereby the pins are aligned in uniform rows around the socket.

Ping — A Windows and Unix command used to troubleshoot network connections. It verifies that the host can communicate with another host on the network.

pinout — A description of how each pin on a bus, connection, plug, slot, or socket is used.

pipelined burst SRAM — A less expensive SRAM that uses more clock cycles per transfer than nonpipelined burst but does not significantly slow down the process.

pits — Recessed areas on the surface of a CD or DVD, separating lands, or flat areas. Lands and pits are used to represent data on a disc.

pixel — A small spot on a fine horizontal scan line. Pixels are illuminated to create an image on the monitor.

Plug and Play (PnP) — A standard that makes installing hardware devices less complicated because the OS and startup BIOS automatically configure hardware devices at startup.

polling — When the CPU checks the status of connected devices to determine if they are ready to send or receive data.

port — A physical connector, usually at the back of a computer, that allows a cable from a peripheral device, such as a printer, mouse, or modem, to be attached.

port address — *See* I/O address.

port replicator — A device designed to connect to a notebook computer to provide additional ports.

port settings — The configuration parameters of communications devices such as COM1, COM2, or COM3, including IRQ settings.

port speed — The communication speed between a DTE (computer) and a DCE (modem). As a general rule, the port speed should be at least four times as fast as the modem speed.

power conditioner — A line conditioner that regulates, or conditions, power, providing continuous voltage during brownouts.

power on password — A password that a computer uses to control access during the boot process.

power supply — A box inside the computer case that supplies power to the motherboard and other installed devices. Power supplies provide 3.3, 5, and 12 volts DC.

power-on self test (POST) — A self-diagnostic program used to perform a simple test of the CPU, RAM, and various I/O devices. The POST is performed by startup BIOS when the computer is first turned on, and is stored in ROM-BIOS.

primary cache — *See* internal cache.

primary partition — A partition on a hard drive that can contain only a single logical drive.

primary storage — Temporary storage or memory on the motherboard, used by the CPU to process data and instructions.

printer — A peripheral output device that produces printed output to paper. Different types include dot matrix, ink-jet, and laser printers.

processor — *See* central processing unit (CPU).

processor speed — The speed, or frequency, at which the CPU operates. Usually expressed in MHz.

program — A set of step-by-step instructions to a computer. Some are burned directly into chips, while others are stored as program files. Programs are written in languages such as BASIC and C++.

protocol — A set of rules and standards that two entities use for communication.

PS/2-compatible mouse — A mouse that plugs into a round mouse PS/2 port on the motherboard. Sometimes called a motherboard mouse.

Quarter-Inch Committee or quarter-inch cartridge (QIC) — A standardized method used to write data to tape. These backup files have a .qic extension.

RAID (redundant array of independent disks) — Several methods of configuring multiple hard drives to store data to increase logical volume size, improve performance, and ensure that if one hard drive fails, the data is still available from another hard drive.

RAM drive — An area of memory that is treated as though it were a hard drive, but works much faster than a hard drive. The Windows 9x startup disk uses a RAM drive. Compare to virtual memory.

random access memory (RAM) — Temporary memory stored on chips, such as SIMMs, inside the computer. Information in RAM disappears when the computer's power is turned off.

RDRAM — *See* Direct Rambus DRAM.

read/write head — A sealed, magnetic coil device that moves across the surface of a disk either reading data from or writing data to the disk.

rectifier — An electrical device that converts AC to DC. A PC power supply contains a rectifier.

refresh — The process of periodically rewriting data, such as on dynamic RAM.

refresh rate — For monitors, the number of times in one second an electronic beam can fill the screen with lines from top to bottom. Also called vertical scan rate.

re-marked chips — Chips that have been used and returned to the factory, marked again, and resold. The surface of the chips may be dull or scratched.

repeater — A device that amplifies signals on a network so they can be transmitted further down the line.

request handler — *See* interrupt handler.

resistance — The degree to which a device opposes or resists the flow of electricity. As the electrical resistance increases, the current decreases. *See* ohm and resistor.

resistor — An electronic device that resists or opposes the flow of electricity. A resistor can be used to reduce the amount of electricity being supplied to an electronic component.

resolution — The number of pixels on a monitor screen that are addressable by software (example: 1024 × 768 pixels).

REt (Resolution Enhancement technology) — The term used by Hewlett-Packard to describe the way a laser printer varies the size of the dots used to create an image. This technology partly accounts for the sharp, clear image created by a laser printer.

RIMM — A type of memory module used on newer motherboards, produced by Rambus, Inc.

ring topology — A network topology in which the nodes in a network form a ring. Each node is connected only to two other nodes, and a centralized hub is not required.

RISC (Reduced Instruction Set Computing) chips — Chips that incorporate only the most frequently used instructions, so that the computer operates faster (for example, the PowerPC uses RISC chips).

riser card — A card that plugs into a motherboard and allows for expansion cards to be mounted parallel to the motherboard. Expansion cards are plugged into slots on the riser card.

RJ-11 — A phone line connection found on modems, telephones, and house phone outlets.

RJ-45 connector — A connector used with twisted-pair cable that connects the cable to the NIC.

ROM (read-only memory) — Chips that contain programming code and cannot be erased.

ROM BIOS — *See* BIOS.

routable protocol — A protocol that can be routed to interconnected networks on the basis of a network address. TCP/IP is a routable protocol, but NetBEUI is not.

router — A device that connects networks and makes decisions as to the best routes to use when forwarding packets.

sampling rate — The rate of samples taken of an analog signal over a period of time, usually expressed as samples per second, or hertz.

SCAM (SCSI Configuration AutoMatically) — A method of configuring SCSI device settings that follows the Plug and Play standard. SCAM makes installation of SCSI devices much easier, provided that the devices are SCAM-compliant.

scanning mirror — A component of a laser printer consisting of an octagonal mirror that can be directed in a sweeping motion to cover the entire length of a laser printer drum.

SCSI (Small Computer System Interface) — A fast interface between a host adapter and the CPU that can daisy chain as many as 7 or 15 devices on a single bus.

SCSI ID — A number from 0 to 15 assigned to each SCSI device attached to the daisy chain.

SDRAM II — *See* Double Data Rate SDRAM (DDR SDRAM).

secondary storage — Storage that is remote to the CPU and permanently holds data, even when the PC is turned off.

sector — On a disk surface, one segment of a track, which almost always contains 512 bytes of data.

sequential access — A method of data access used by tape drives, whereby data is written or read sequentially from the beginning to the end of the tape or until the desired data is found.

serial mouse — A mouse that uses a serial port and has a female 9-pin DB-9 connector.

serial port — Male 9-pin or 25-pin ports on the computer used for transmitting data serially, one bit at a time. They are called COM1, COM2, COM3, and COM4.

SGRAM (synchronous graphics RAM) — Memory designed especially for video card processing that can synchronize itself with the CPU bus clock.

shadow RAM or shadowing ROM — ROM programming code copied into RAM to speed up the system operation, because of the faster access speed of RAM.

shielded twisted-pair (STP) cable — A cable that is made of one or more twisted pairs of wires and is surrounded by a metal shield.

signal-regenerating repeater — A repeater that is able to distinguish between noise and signal. It reads the signal and retransmits it without the accompanying noise.

SIMD (single instruction, multiple data) — A process that allows the CPU to execute a single instruction simultaneously on multiple pieces of data, rather than by repetitive looping.

SIMM (single inline memory module) — A miniature circuit board used in a computer to hold RAM. SIMMs hold 8, 16, 32, or 64 MB on a single module.

single-ended (SE) — A type of SCSI signaling in which two wires are used to carry a signal, one of which carries the signal itself and the other is a ground for the signal.

single-voltage CPU — A CPU that requires one voltage for both internal and I/O operations.

slack — Wasted space on a hard drive caused by not using all available space at the end of clusters.

sleep mode — A mode used in many "Green" systems that allows them to be configured through CMOS to suspend the monitor or even the drive, if the keyboard and/or CPU have been inactive for a set number of minutes. *See also* Green Standards.

slimline case — *See* compact case.

SMAU (Smart Multistation Access Unit) — *See* MAU.

SO-DIMM (small outline DIMM) — A type of memory module used in notebook computers that uses DIMM technology and can have either 72 pins or 144 pins.

soft boot — To restart a PC, for example, by pressing three keys at the same time (Ctrl, Alt, and Del). Also called warm boot.

soft power — *See* soft switch.

soft switch — A feature on an ATX system that allows an OS to power down the system and allows for activity such as a keystroke or network activity to power up the system. Also called soft power.

software — Computer programs, or instructions to perform a specific task. Software may be BIOS, OSs, or applications software such as a word-processing or spreadsheet program.

software interrupt — An event caused when a program currently being executed by the CPU signals the CPU that it requires the use of a hardware device.

SO-RIMM (small outline RIMM) — A 160-pin memory module used in notebooks that uses Rambus technology.

South Bridge — That portion of the chip set hub that connects slower I/O buses (for example, ISA bus) to the system bus. Compare to North Bridge.

spacers – *See* standoffs.

SPI (SCSI Parallel Interface) — The part of the SCSI-3 standard that specifies how SCSI devices are connected.

spikes — Temporary surges in voltage, which can damage electrical components.

SSE (Streaming SIMD Extension) — A technology used for the Intel Pentium III and later CPUs designed to improve performance of multimedia software.

staggered pin grid array (SPGA) — A feature of a CPU socket whereby the pins are staggered over the socket in order to squeeze more pins into a small space.

standby time — The time before a "Green" system will reduce 92 percent of its activity. *See also* Green Standards.

standoffs — Round plastic or metal pegs that separate the motherboard from the case, so that components on the back of the motherboard do not touch the case.

star bus topology — A LAN that uses a logical bus design, but with all devices connected to a central hub, making a physical star.

star ring topology — A topology that is physically arranged in a star formation but is logically a ring because of the way information travels on it. Token ring is the primary example.

star topology — A LAN in which all the devices are connected to a central hub.

start bits — Bits that signal the approach of data.

startup BIOS — Part of system BIOS that is responsible for controlling the PC when it is first turned on. Startup BIOS gives control over to the OS once it is loaded.

startup password — *See* power on password.

stateless — A device or process that manages data or activity without regard to all the details of the data or activity.

static electricity — *See* ESD.

static RAM (SRAM) — RAM chips that retain information without the need for refreshing, as long as the computer's power is on. They are more expensive than traditional DRAM.

stop bits — Bits that are used to signal the end of a block of data.

streaming audio — Downloading audio data from the Internet in a continuous stream of data without first downloading an entire audio file.

surge suppressor or surge protector — A device or power strip designed to protect electronic equipment from power surges and spikes.

suspend time — The time before a "Green" system will reduce 99 percent of its activity. After this time, the system needs a warmup time so that the CPU, monitor, and hard drive can reach full activity.

swap file — A file on the hard drive that is used by the OS for virtual memory.

switch — A device used to segment a network. It can decide which network segment is to receive a packet, on the basis of the packet's destination MAC address.

synchronization — The process by which files and programs are transferred between PDAs and PCs.

synchronous DRAM (SDRAM) — A type of memory stored on DIMMs that runs in sync with the system clock, running at the same speed as the motherboard.

synchronous SRAM — SRAM that is faster and more expensive than asynchronous SRAM. It requires a clock signal to validate its control signals, enabling the cache to run in step with the CPU.

SyncLink DRAM (SLDRAM) — A type of DRAM developed by a consortium of 12 DRAM manufactures. It improved on regular SDRAM but is now obsolete.

system BIOS — BIOS located on the motherboard.

system board — *See* motherboard.

system bus — The bus between the CPU and memory on the motherboard. Also called memory bus, motherboard bus, host bus, external bus, or front side bus.

system clock — A line on a bus that is dedicated to timing the activities of components connected to it. The system clock provides a continuous pulse that other devices use to time themselves.

system resource — A channel, line, or address on the motherboard that can be used by the CPU or a device for communication. The four system resources are IRQ, I/O address, DMA channel, and memory address.

TAPI (Telephony Application Programming Interface) — A standard developed by Intel and Microsoft that can be used by 32-bit Windows 9x communications programs for communicating over phone lines.

TCP/IP (Transmission Control Protocol/Internet Protocol) — The suite of protocols that supports communication on the Internet. TCP is responsible for error checking, and IP is responsible for routing.

telephony — The technology of converting sound to signals that can travel over telephone lines.

terminating resistor — The resistor added at the end of a SCSI chain to dampen the voltage at the end of the chain.

termination — A process necessary to prevent an echo effect of power at the end of a SCSI chain, resulting in interference with the data transmission.

ThickNet — *See* 10Base5 Ethernet.

ThinNet — *See* 10Base2 Ethernet.

throughput performance — Also called data throughput. Throughput performance is a measure of the actual data transmitted by the bus, not including error-checking bits or redundant data.

token — A small packet used on token ring networks to send data from one station to the next.

tower case — The largest type of personal computer case. Tower cases stand vertically upright and can be up to two feet tall. They have more drive bays and are a good choice for computer users who will make significant upgrades.

trace — A wire on a circuit board that connects two components or devices.

tracks — The concentric circles into which the surface of a disk is divided.

training — *See* handshaking.

transceiver — The component on a NIC that is responsible for signal conversion. Combines the words transmitter and receiver.

transformer — A device that changes the ratio of current to voltage. A computer power supply is basically a transformer and a rectifier.

transistor — An electronic device that can regulate electricity and act as a logical gate or switch for an electrical signal.

translation — A technique used by system BIOS and hard drive controller BIOS to break the 504-MB hard drive barrier, whereby a different set of drive parameters are communicated to the OS and other software than that used by the hard drive controller BIOS.

TSR (terminate-and-stay-resident) — A program that is loaded into memory but is not immediately executed, such as a screen saver or a memory-resident antivirus program.

TTL (transistor-transistor logic) — One of two types of technologies used to manufacture microchips (the other type is CMOS). TTL chips require more electricity than CMOS chips and don't hold their data for as long. TTL technology is not as popular as CMOS.

turbo mode — A means of changing the external clock speed by pressing a button on the case of some older computers.

UART (universal asynchronous receiver-transmitter) chip — A chip that controls serial ports. It sets protocol and converts parallel data bits received from the system bus into serial bits.

unshielded twisted-pair (UTP) cable — A cable that is made of one or more twisted pairs of wires and is not surrounded by a metal shield.

UPS (uninterruptible power supply) — A device designed to provide a backup power supply during a power failure. Basically, a UPS is a battery backup system with an ultrafast sensing device.

USB (universal serial bus) port — A type of port designed to make installation and configuration of I/O devices easy, providing room for as many as 127 devices daisy-chained together.

USB host controller — Manages the USB bus. For the 400 series Intel chip set, the USB host controller is included in the PCI controller chip.

V.90 — A standard for data transmission over phone lines that can attain a speed of 56 Kbps. It replaces K56flex and x2 standards.

vector table — *See* interrupt vector table.

vertical scan rate — *See* refresh rate.

VESA (Video Electronics Standards Association) VL bus — An outdated local bus used on 80486 computers for connecting 32-bit adapters directly to the local processor bus.

video card — An interface card installed in the computer to control visual output on a monitor. Also called display adapter.

virtual memory — A method whereby the OS uses the hard drive as though it were RAM. Compare to RAM drive.

volatile — A kind of RAM that is temporary, cannot hold data very long, and must be frequently refreshed.

volt (V) — A measure of potential difference in an electrical circuit. A computer ATX power supply usually provides five separate voltages: +12V, −12V, +5V, −5V, and +3.3V.

voltage — Electrical differential that causes current to flow, measured in volts. *See* volt.

voltmeter — A device for measuring electrical AC or DC voltage.

volume — *See* logical drive.

VRAM (video RAM) — RAM on video cards that holds the data that is being passed from the computer to the monitor and can be accessed by two devices simultaneously. Higher resolutions often require more video memory.

wait state — A clock tick in which nothing happens, used to ensure that the microprocessor isn't getting ahead of slower components. A 0-wait state is preferable to a 1wait state. Too many wait states can slow a system down.

warm boot — *See* soft boot.

watt (W) — The unit used to measure power. A typical computer may use a power supply that provides 200W.

wattage — Electrical power measured in watts.

wide SCSI — One of the two main SCSI specifications. Wide SCSI has a 16-bit data bus.

wireless LAN (WLAN) — A type of LAN that does not use wires or cables to create connections, but instead transmits data over radio or infrared waves.

WRAM (window RAM) — Dual-ported video RAM that is faster and less expensive than VRAM. It has its own internal bus on the chip, with a data path that is 256 bits wide.

zero insertion force (ZIF) socket — A socket that uses a small lever to apply even force when you install the microchip into the socket.

zone bit recording — A method of storing data on a hard drive whereby the drive can have more sectors per track near the outside of the platter.